Return to Latvia

Marina Jarre

TRANSLATED FROM THE ITALIAN
BY ANN GOLDSTEIN

NEW VESSEL PRESS
NEW YORK

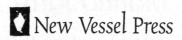

New Vessel Press

www.newvesselpress.com

First published in Italian in 2003 as *Ritorno in Lettonia*

Library of Congress Cataloging-in-Publication Data
Jarre, Marina
[Ritorno in Lettonia. English]
Return to Latvia/ Marina Jarre; translation by Ann Goldstein.
p. cm.
ISBN 978-1-954404-11-3

Library of Congress Control Number: 2022941361
I. Italy–Nonfiction

Psalm 56
Thou tellest my wanderings:
put thou my tears into thy bottle:
are they not in thy book?
King James Bible

Reunited at last in this dedication
are my father and mother,
who for some years loved each other in Riga,
where I was born.

1. Palestine

Three times now I've spent the month of July with friends, two couples, on the western coast of Sardinia, in a house fifty meters from the sea. The house was situated between two others, fairly distant, on a rise above a solitary beach, and was surrounded by thick, low mastic bushes bent by the wind. At the foot of the steps lay a carpet of pink saxifrage; around the corner to the southeast, which was more sheltered, grew a large purplish-red bougainvillea. A few days after our arrival, the flowers began to bloom furiously, to spread their petals; a jumble of new, runaway shoots emerged from the density. This was how the plant demonstrated its enjoyment of more regular watering.

I write *grew*, *lay*, *began*. I should, of course, replace those pasts with a present. The house is still there, the flowers bloom, the mistral slams it, and it meets the wind not unlike a solid ship against the storm. Yet if I think about the house, it appeared, rising up there on the hill, just as we got to it driving along the narrow sandy road. And so a few weeks later, when we left, it disappeared.

As twilight approached—a moment before the sun descended into the sea—I left the house and set out with my phone toward a hilly crest not far inland. You couldn't make calls from the house. I walked on the sand-and-gravel path in the rosy light as it faded to a luminescent pallor over the surrounding expanses, which here and there dipped down between rockier ridges.

On the way up, I placed my feet securely on the rocks, small thistles, and dry rockroses: the path itself guided me, leading me to the usual point where my call would be able to reach one of my people.

My people? Children, a grandchild, a friend. My people are few, increasingly confined to a small circle.

And increasingly vast and out of reach was the world around them, the crowd that lived, survived, died. Sometimes I felt that immense swarm of lives elude my grasp completely; readings, writings of all kinds and facts were no longer enough to perceive it, embrace it in thought and with the senses; groping around me I no longer touched a hand, no longer felt the warmth of other bodies, the breath of other mouths. This is old age, I said to myself, being absorbed in, limited to, one's own carcass.

As I walked along the known path, calmly placing my feet on the evening trail, the vise that locked me in myself loosened, relaxed into a void that wasn't anguished—whether because of the sense of well-being that came from daily swims, or the renewed pleasure of a long read (I was reading and rereading the rediscovered *Onegin*, during hours of repose on a bench, with the Russian dictionary beside me), or the cries exchanged by strangers in the neighboring house, hidden in an impenetrable thicket of small palms and eucalyptus.

In the meantime the sky was dimming, but had yielded a gray still pulsing with light, and here and there a paler rock preserved its outline in the spreading half-light.

I scanned the sky as it mutated from twilight opalescence to the clarity of evening. Sometimes we played a game among ourselves to see who would be the first to pick out Vesper the moment it appeared; but as soon as someone exclaimed, "There it is!" the star was already visible, its brilliance instantaneous.

I made calls while standing in the magic circle halfway up the hill. The voices that a few centimeters lower couldn't reach me now sounded close, familiar, as if in the next room, in fact as if originating within me. So unbounded was the space around me—the sea indistinguishable now from the shore, and, on the sea, the lost, distant, and intermittently flashing signal of the lighthouse to the right, and on the land the lost, random reflection of a light from a window of our house—and so infinite the orbit of the horizon that it seemed to me to truly evoke, with a gesture of domestic magic up there on the windy ledge, the voices of those dear to me.

Thus news and reassurance reached me, not many questions. I asked some, for form's sake. In fact I didn't want to know anything; I wanted to stay outside, I had finished. Oh yes, I had finished. I listened to those voices that required nothing more, requested nothing more; they sounded in my ear, detached from faces and presences, only because I listened to them, the voices of those dear to me in the evening.

If I went down in the dark, I didn't turn on the little

flashlight I carried in case I had to read a telephone number. I liked walking on the path in the darkness; I'd known it for centuries, there were no obstacles or unexpected obstructions. It was a secure path among rocks, rockroses, and dry thistles.

If I happened to go up at the end of the sunset, then when the phone calls were over I continued on in the last light and in a few steps reached the wild fig tree. Sheltered by the rounding at the top of the hill, it extended, low and sturdy, without fruit, and in the evening dampness its small hardy leaves gave off the last whiff of a bitter scent of sun.

Returning, I'd recall the serious, sweet child's voice of Giovanni, my youngest grandson, holding it in its small rainbow-colored shell. He happily gives me precise information, and if I get something wrong—bumbling grandma—he kindly, meticulously corrects me. He unconsciously measures my time, which is unlikely to extend into his adulthood.

One evening when I had just set out in the vast silence of the slope, the air above and behind me began to vibrate strangely with a regular, faint but energetic pulse. I turned and not far from the peak saw a flight of some twenty large birds, dark in the shadows. The flock was heading southwest with determination, wings beating in unison. Toward the island, I thought, that lay in that direction, whose shoreline could be glimpsed low on the horizon.

It was July, but the unexpected appearance and disappearance of the migrating flock seemed bizarrely autumnal.

Yet it didn't strike me as in the least unnatural, since the rapid rhythm of the tendons working in flight was audible and real as the big, dark birds passed swiftly, cleaving the air with a light rustling.

In an instant they were over the hill and out of sight. I was immediately sure that they carried a message, but I wasn't able to decipher it. Besides, I was in no hurry for predictions; I wait for such messages to reveal themselves on their own, for them to choose their moment.

I turned and continued my descent, and in the meantime my mind—prodded perhaps by my steps on the ancient path and, at the same time, by the wild odor of the barren fig or the swift rustling passage of the flock headed toward a resting place (along what route?)—began to scribble. To tell a story, I should say, first because this initial work is ragged and haphazard, but mostly because between telling a story and writing it an abyss opens before me: the language I write in and use daily. The language of my mother, which has perhaps become the language of my dreams (but do dreams really have grammar and syntax, or do they not speak within our souls while we sleep, with words, rather, that are all theirs and theirs alone?)—a language that's not immediate, that I have to grasp again every time, and control, to render the improper proper. A language that is never intimate. I use it as a tool even though, as we know, the craftsman is fond of his tool, cares for it, and puts it back after use.

So I, like a craftsman, am fond of it, take care of this language, and put it back. And I always have to take it out of the storage closet and polish it.

The girl is walking along the path, going to or coming from the well. She's barefoot or wearing sandals. I don't know how she's dressed. At first all I see of her is her smooth young brown legs. Her brown arms support the pitcher on her shoulder. She's carrying water for dinner, for the herb soup, for washing hands after work.

Nor do I know for now if she's a girl or a woman, perhaps a bride—I imagine her as young, anyway. Heading toward the small house where she lives, she's not thinking. She's satisfied with walking, feeling beneath her feet the imprint of age-old tracks left by her mother, her father, her grandparents, her great-grandparents. Her ancestors who came from Egypt.

My father's ancestors also came from Egypt thousands of years ago, crossing the Red Sea. Every time I remember that narrow passage of history from which they emerged to head toward the Promised Land, I'm gripped by a vertigo of disbelief and the miraculous. Their name has come down to me, and likewise their features—to my father, and thus to my sister and the child Irene, who died with him.

Are they the same as those of the girl who is walking quickly to get home? Surely she's not thinking of the ancestors who at the end of their long wandering gave her the safe, familiar path and the well with its clear water. She knows the stones along the way and the serpent's nest in the rock pile.

I can't decide whether to imagine her as a girl or a bride. Maybe she's engaged to the carpenter who lives not far from the well, and drawing water she exchanged a few words with him. Or he's already her husband, and for dinner and for him she carries the water in the pitcher on her shoulder. But maybe, as she hurries along the usual path, her slender legs bare under the short dress, she's laughing to herself at the words he said tonight for the first time. She was bending over to pull up the bucket.

What matters to her is the sensation of the breeze on her skin, the predictable reproach of her mother—or mother-in-law—because she's late. She gossiped with the other women about the future wedding of the beautiful Judith, about the black hen's dark eggs, about old Jacob's wife, who dreamed for three nights in a row that the well dried up and a palm with no dates grew out of it. She laughed and joked, and now she has to hurry.

The sun is setting behind her, and she follows her own shadow as it runs ahead of her. It's still hot, although the light breeze that marks the end of the day caresses her bare arms and legs. Happy the land that, unbeknownst to her, her ancestors gave her after long wandering, hot in summer, warm in spring and autumn, cold in winter, but only for a few weeks, it's said, up there in the city with the temple, seldom here on the plain amid the hills. One winter, her grandfather tells her, it snowed up there and even down here a few flakes fell on the low vines on whose bare reddish shoots the first leaves are about to sprout.

Miriam—her name is Miriam, like three other girls in the neighborhood, who are also hurrying home, big pitchers on their shoulders, anticipating the reproach of mother or mother-in-law—has been gossiping at the well with her friends about the beautiful Judith's wedding dress; they laughed at the fool who thinks he's marrying a virgin (he should ask Dan about it), talked about the strange dream of old Jacob's wife. Does it mean that their daughter will be barren? That something bad will happen in the village?

Already, from a distance, Miriam spies the courtyard, her mother in the doorway, but just as she speeds up along the path, with its stones, thistles, and rockroses, she stops. Behind her the wind has abruptly turned cold, and yet ahead of her the plowed fields are still illuminated by the sun. It's the start of autumn.

She doesn't have time to be surprised, because in that sudden intense cold behind her something falls from the sky, an immense hum becomes thunder, louder and louder, deafening—the pitcher slips from Miriam's grasp and shatters on the ground—and then, in this vast stormy rustling, there's a creaking at regular intervals, not very different, though sharper and more sonorous, from the sound of a rope that groans and squeaks as a bucket is raised. She doesn't try to understand, she doesn't dare to turn around, she's frightened, she's never heard a sound like that.

No, she's not even frightened; the trembling and the agitation that invade her, the sweat that runs down her face and armpits have nothing in common with any fear that belongs to her girl's world—this trembling, this agitation she's never felt, they immobilize her, she can barely make out the wooden gate of her courtyard at the end of the path with its stones, dry rockroses, and thistles. And meanwhile, in the noise that has become a storm roaring behind her, the rope-like creak has gone silent. But the cold wind continues to blow, as if an enormous fan were turning at her back.

She says later that a voice spoke to her, but she doesn't know how to describe what it said, all she understood was a name, "Maria, Maria," Maria, and in the name were other words she couldn't understand. She was trembling, and it seemed to her that the whirlwind behind her never ceased. Her mother had seen her running down the path and repeats that she didn't stop, that, yes, she dropped the pitcher, because she stumbled, not because she suddenly came to a halt.

"It will happen, it will happen," said Miriam, but she couldn't explain what would happen, because in the event announced by the words contained within the name Maria—which were impenetrable, and not spoken in her language—events and misfortunes and fortunes not only extended back to the narrow passage where the ancestors had emerged from the Red Sea to enter history but continued, all mixed together and scattered and reunited by the wind: events and misfortunes and fortunes, onward, onward, forever and ever into the future.

The archangel (Michael, Gabriel, or Emanuel?), accustomed to roaming through galaxies in great arcs of flight and sheltering stars and planets under his outstretched wings, plunged from eternal space into the narrow enclosure of earthly time and braked—this had happened on other occasions (in truth those, too, belong to the circumscription of earthly time)—with some effort. And as if in the passage from the heavenly realms to the atmosphere he had reached a certain age, his tendons creaked and groaned, as if they were, indeed, old by now. Besides, he somewhat resented being disturbed—he was listening to Sonatina K. 1200—by the order, naturally unexpressed, to go down to Nazareth and look for Miriam, the one with the pitcher on her shoulder.

That in Nazareth there were four Miriams—and which one was married and which a girl and which a widow and which a child—didn't matter, the archangel would descend (or descended?) on the right one.

He would in fact rely on angelic chance, which has nothing fated about it but flutters around to take us by surprise, just like a butterfly net.

What else can be told that goes beyond the mysterious fear of the event? A fear that only Miriam felt, anyway. The others commented, judged, quibbled.

A Melchite monk spent his life in a cell in Syria calculating how wide and full and immense the pitcher that Miriam dropped must have been; its fragments have become relics, and lie venerated in countless Christian churches. Calculating and recalculating, he found that the pitcher could have contained St. Peter's and everything in it. Which, if you think about it, was another miracle.

"We didn't understand," said the grandfather. "It must have been a ukase from the tsar. So we bury the chest in the garden, we lock the door and hide in the attic."

"And I," said the grandmother, "I haven't finished packing the bags. I don't know what to take."

"If I see him near you tomorrow, I'll smash his head," said her brother Elias. "I've never liked that Joseph."

"Excuses," said the husband, Joseph. "You're always at the well! What are you doing there?"

"Let's go to Rabbi Garfunkel," said the other brother. "It's already three Saturdays since Miriam's been going back and forth between the well and the house. Let's get advice from him."

"The other girls go there, too," said the aunt. "You can't stay home all day."

"He'll be a beautiful baby," said the mother, who until then had been silent. "He'll be born in spring, and that will bring him good fortune."

"Before we leave," said the father, "I'll prune again, so when we return the wine will be livelier."

"If we return," said the grandfather.

Meanwhile the snake, which had gone into hiding at the sudden approach of freezing weather, stuck its head out from under a rock and enjoyed the day's last rays of sun. The archangel stretched its wings which had grown stiff during the enforced pause in that thick air, creaked, groaned, grated (a particular sound made by archangels' wings), unfolded his feathers, and rose in flight toward Sonatina K. 1200. We can't follow him: we're puzzled and prostrated and, to be candid, we're a little afraid.

And Miriam? Miriam let the others comment, suspect, rack their brains, and she shut herself in her room, bewildered. She didn't ask questions or give herself answers; she sank into her empty childlike mind and got lost in apprehension. But she was absolutely certain of that name, the name she had heard, clear, commanding, and inevitable. She uttered it with feverish lips, and it was his.

Sometimes I wonder if I'll be telling stories until I die, how and when and why I'll have to stop. What will I do then, when I'm limited to staying alive? I try to imagine an existence in which nothing more happens, which I have to fill with small daily routines. I'll have to strain for modesty, humility, patience—abstractions I can't imagine becoming concrete. I am not, it should be said, modest or humble or patient.

Will I reach the point of describing myself as a centenarian typing away on the keys of this old Olivetti?

Will I be able to describe the minute acts that keep me alive day after day, the unexpected, toothless giggles amid the few sentences picked up by indulgent listeners? In truth, the story a centenarian tells has no importance; he is his own story, and his tremulous gestures don't matter: for good or ill, they merely affirm "I am here."

The memories we hear evoked by one who is very old are not hazy or indistinct; rather, they are thin and bony, reduced to the particular, random. They emerge from a jabbering interior that is not at all historical—and therefore neither is ours, we who are listening or asking—but is fiercely his; we won't get even a hint of suffering, joy, indignation from him, from what has survived. He will speak of the time he saw the president go by in a car—he was a small child—and that other time, when his friend Pinin died next to him. He was a small boy.

As my son Pietro and I drove toward Tallinn—we had arrived in Latvia three days earlier—we traveled for hours on a road that ran straight between tall, thick black forests of firs, until we lost track of time.

We encountered almost no vehicles and, except on the first stretch, passed through no city or village. Nothing changed at the border (except a fine for speeding, pocketed, I suppose, by two Estonian policemen who looked like bandits), and only when we were approaching Tallinn did we emerge onto the plain. The sea was supposedly on our left, yet we couldn't see it amid the tree trunks.

I didn't know the country, I'd never been there, nothing had ever happened there that concerned me, I had no obligation to remember or commemorate, and I felt calm. Exactly like a centenarian, I was bound to the present moment, in which neither images nor sounds could provoke or test me. With my mind free on our day of rest, I would have given in to an idle touristic curiosity if the straight road through the tall black forests hadn't taken on, as the hours passed, an unreal immutability—were we moving forward or going back? Beyond the dark trunks there was no village, there were no cows, meadows, boats on the sea. There was only the road.

At one point—I don't know when, it seems to me we were still in Livonia—we saw high in the sky a small flock of birds. They were flying from the northeast to the southwest.

"Look," I said to Pietro, "it's a migrating flock, they're leaving, they're fleeing winter."

It was the end of September.

"What do you mean?" he said. "To me they look like any birds flying for the fun of it."

"It's a migration," I said. "Look how they're flying in formation, in a triangle, headed by their leader."

"Birds," he contradicted me, "head south to spend the winter. Those are going west."

"Southwest," I said. "There must be islands in the Baltic, near Scandinavia, where the winter's less cold."

He was silent, and after a moment he said, "It's true, last year in Sweden I saw islands covered with birds."

2. Stones and Ritual Tears

The moment the plane, departing from Turin, began to taxi, I turned—I was sitting next to the window—covered my face with my hand, and started to cry. Pietro noticed and joked:

"Mamma," he said, "we're going to Frankfurt, you still have time before you start crying."

But I wasn't going to Frankfurt, I was going to Riga, where I was born and where my father died. The hum of the engines cast me back to childhood, to my weeping when my sister Sisi and I had left Latvia, sixty-four years earlier. A farmer from the estate took us in a farm cart—I've already written about it—to the train, which would carry us to Italy from the little station in the woods. Our departure was kept secret from our father, and we left on a secondary rail line. Mamma was taking us to her mother's house in Torre Pellice, in Piedmont, out of fear that the judge in their divorce case would decide to award him custody of us.

Sitting next to my sister I had burst into silent tears. I have a precise memory of how surprised I was by that sudden emotion. Was I crying because I wouldn't see the sweet little ducklings grow up, which had tagged along behind the cart for a stretch, swaying and chirping? I wouldn't dare call those tears an omen, although my weeping as an old woman, into the palm of my hand, makes them such. The adult I would turn out to be had a premonition of the tragedy to come.

Right after the war I had twice tried, somewhat indecisively, to get a visa for Latvia, since we'd had no further news. The Soviet authorities never granted me one, and in the meantime I had obtained Italian citizenship. The presumed death of my father had established itself in my life with slow persuasion, not with the shock of a sudden blow. When, after a good sixteen years, the certainty of it reached us thanks to a letter from a distant cousin in Switzerland, who had escaped the extermination as the Aryan wife of a Jew, I felt I no longer had a reason to go looking for traces that by now had surely vanished. My father's entire family had been killed, along with him and the six-year-old child, Irene, he'd had with a German lover.

Time passed—I worked, got married, had children, then grandchildren, I wrote, I got old—and the fragments of that long-ago era, unconnected to one another, inalterable small pictures, were fixed in the form in which I'd preserved and presented them in my autobiographical book, *Distant Fathers*. In that portrayal, I hadn't thought to verify them in an objective way—I had mistaken (for example) dates and some circumstances—but had collected and transmitted them to the page just as I had found them in my memory, now the only place where the events had occurred. Riga no longer existed outside of me. There was no longer a country I could recognize.

My return loomed before me like an insurmountable wall, on the other side not even the graves.

(But, aside from this, I was afraid of returning and wouldn't admit it even to myself.)

I hadn't talked about what had happened in Latvia except, and rarely, to my husband. In the car with him behind the hearse that was carrying my mother's coffin to cremation, I had said with sudden tears, here, too, provoked by an unexpected emotion, "My poor father." My sister, who was sitting in the van with the coffin, had arrived with two bouquets of flowers, one white and the other red—I don't remember what kind of flowers, it was early October—and, feeling herself a child again, regretted that the red wasn't the red of the Latvian flag. I had long since lost—and with reason—any Baltic patriotism, but naturally I didn't say anything to her. Besides, I never talked about our father, and still less of his death, even with her. We never recalled him with the name of Father. Once, returning from London, where she had met some old friends of our mother, Sisi had reported to me, as if amazed and almost gratified, "You know, Aunt Jo said 'he' was really brilliant and witty."

"My dear, your father treated your mother badly, but he was a charming man."

To those who asked whether, if I ever returned to Latvia, I would be able to find some relative or acquaintance, maybe a classmate, I answered no, and usually I didn't explain further. From the question itself and from the puzzled embarrassment in response to my no, so brusque and absolute, I judged that it would have been impossible for me to give a reason for my denial, to describe, to tell. I felt a distance I wouldn't have known how to bridge, a distance not only between the events of that time and the inquiries of those who asked the question but between me and them.

Talking on the phone with a very dear friend after I returned, I confided that I had found the places of their deaths, and she asked me if the names were there. "Names . . . names," I was confused, "but if there were *****!" I said the number. There was a stunned silence on the phone.

The figure had slipped out in spite of myself: I was ashamed to cite numbers and promised myself that I would never again give in.

But mainly I felt a befuddled embarrassment at the thought that someone might suspect me of pretending a suffering that at the time I hadn't felt.

The slaughter had touched me, unaware, and I carried the weight of an inappropriate mourning, in which serious personal experiences were so tightly interwoven with the atrocity of history that I couldn't present myself in a clear and unambiguous way. It seemed to me that I had no right to mourn.

"The first stakes for the barbed wire fence were planted on Maskavas Iela"—*Iela* is Latvian for street—"at the corner of Lacplesa." To prevent people from throwing packages of food and other aid over it, the fence was doubled.

I hadn't heard the sound of the hammers driving in the stakes around the Riga ghetto, situated by the Germans in the "Moscow" suburb, which had been emptied of its residents. It was October of 1941, I was starting high school in Torre Pellice, where I had been living for six years, with Sisi, in our maternal grandmother's house. Mostly I was thinking about meeting the boy I was in love with as soon as possible; in a drawer somewhere lay the strange letter from our father that had arrived at the end of July, begging us insistently to help him get out of Riga. He didn't explain why; he declared that he was sick, and as usual he didn't mention little Irene—we knew that the child's German mother had returned to her own country in 1939, leaving the child with him—and as usual he reproached (at least it seems to me) our mother.

The letter was very long, covering two entire large sheets of yellowish paper. (Was there, I wonder, some clearer hint in that incomprehensible scribbling?) In the central fold of one page was an unevenly underlined sentence, whose fatefulness I didn't understand: "because remember that you, too, are Jewish." I can still see it distinctly, word for word.

Some months before, unknown to us, the extremely slow divorce proceedings had ended. The folder with the documents and the final judgment reached us in the spring of 1942; the judgment bore the stamp—the eagle above the swastika—of the Foreign Office of the Reichskommissariat Ostland.

Date: February 19, 1942; signed "Weidecker." Our father had been dead for three months.

So I was ashamed of my lack of awareness, even if it was blameless, but the horror of the facts disturbed and restrained me even more, creating a chasm between me and any questioner. It seemed to me that I couldn't introduce these facts into the conversation, that their iniquity would in itself extinguish any sympathy. Or, even worse, doing this might cause the tedium that comes from hearing a presumably well-known event evoked too often.

Exactly: an event described, not a reality lived.

There is in fact a treacherousness in repetition, a treacherousness that, just like the magnitude of the numbers, contributes to rendering events abstract, making them the subject of discussions and dissertations, giving them at most a pedagogic character, taking away their flesh and blood and screams and blood and death rattles and blood. Once our mind accepts them, once the first jolt of dismay and horror has passed, they acquire an aspect I would call consolatory. We transform ourselves into readers or spectators; we reassure ourselves—"It couldn't happen to me"—and we don't want to reread the same page, witness the same scene.

Between the event itself and we who read, listen to, watch, the survivors go around, compelled to keep the experience alive. We are assured that that will serve to avoid such barbarities in the future. And they narrate and remind and hope, and we along with them, that the torture of remembering is useful and necessary, but their narrative is addressed to the countless who had to succumb, not to us who listen and watch. Their remembering, which is tenuous, erratic, and repetitious, struggles painfully to summon the countless from the grave of anonymity.

Easier to count and give names to the few who bear witness.

To Yitzhak Bloch, for example. He was ten when the shots missed him, hiding in a bush in a village near Kaunas. It was late June 1941, and as he ran he heard the voice of his mother for the last time: "Run, Yitzhak, run!"

To Śëma Spungin. He was twelve when, in July of 1941, the Germans arrived in Daugavpils. After enduring beatings, interrogations, arrests, and escapes, he managed, with false documents he got by chance, to find work in a village. One night, he cried out in Yiddish in his sleep. The Latvian farmer he was working for became suspicious, but he convinced the man he'd cried out in German. From then on he couldn't truly sleep.

To Mrs. Fischgott, whose first name we don't know, and who wandered across the steppe looking for her son. The German Army reached Crimea on October 31, 1941. Her false Karaite document was missing the registration stamp from the German authority, and no *starosta*, or elder, wanted to welcome her into his village. Here and there peasants gave her food. She sustained herself on frozen corn, and as she walked, she shouted the name of her son. Shouting was a kind of relief. Finally the *starosta* of Kražnyi Pajar offered her shelter. When she was freed by the Red Army, in 1943, she learned that her son, a second lieutenant, was fighting on the southern front.

To Hanna Katz. During the shooting she fell into the pit alive. At dawn she managed to drag herself out; naked, she took a shirt from the pile of clothes nearby and put it on. Lithuania, October 24, 1941.

To Frieda Fried. On Monday, December 8, 1941, in Rumbula, Riga, she fell to the ground, struck in the head by the butt of a revolver, but she remained alive under the shoes that were piled on top of her. At night, to avoid being discovered as she fled, creeping over the snow, she wrapped herself in a sheet found in the heap of infant clothes.

The same irrational, miserly fate that helped Hanna and Frieda did not allow Isaak Rosenberg to see the day of liberation. His Russian wife had hidden him in a hollow under the stove. There, in Monastyr, Smolensk, he lived shut up for twenty-six months; at night he came out and could barely stand up. Not even his two children knew their father was concealed in that hiding place; the mother had assured the Germans they were children from an earlier marriage. During the fighting, when the Soviets got close to the village, the inhabitants hid in the woods. When the fighting was over and the Germans retreated, the wife hurried to the house. From a distance, she could already see the smoke of the fire that had burned and destroyed it: Isaak was dead, suffocated in his hiding place.

Russian friends, the Kilenkos, were able to save the fisherman Josif Weingartner's youngest child, keeping him with them as their own. Josif climbed out of the ditch, wounded but alive. In the darkness he tried to find his wife's body among the others. He lifted up heads and, his fingers smeared ever more thickly with blood, probed the features, until he touched her face, dead. Kerch, 1941.

The Lithuanian priest Paukštis filled out a hundred and

twenty baptismal certificates for a hundred and twenty Jewish children. Blessed be his memory. And blessed the memory of Janis Lipke, a dockworker at the port of Riga, who in the three years of the German occupation—Riga was liberated in October of 1944—with the help of relatives and friends from his village, saved forty-two Jews, getting them out of the ghetto and hiding them wherever possible.

And so some were saved. With a pocketknife Manja cut the canvas cover over the truck and jumped out. Evsej Efimovich Gopstein, hidden by a Russian woman, a friend, for twenty-eight months, could witness, as the sole survivor of Simferopol, the arrival of the Soviets. Cinka was found by Captain Krapivin in a hole in the forest near the village of Golas, in Byelorussia. A skeleton, her hair long, hands and feet wounded, she had survived her family; occasional companions hiding, like her, in the forest but discovered and killed; and her childhood.

"No one will ever be able to tell what happened," the Germans said to the eighty prisoners—seventy-six Jews, three Russian prisoners of war, a young Pole who had helped the Jewish girl Liecka—assembled, chains on their ankles, in Ponary, Lithuania, to cremate the corpses pulled out of the immense pits.

Ponary, an enchanting vacation spot on the hilly shores of the Neris near Vilnius. Kaiserwald, west of Riga, on the sandy plain between the red Daugava and the beautiful Art Nouveau villas. Concentration camp of Ponary, concentration camp of Kaiserwald (Mežaparks).

The stacks of pinewood, more than three meters high, sprinkled with gasoline—it took three days and three nights for a pile to be consumed—burned corpses for five months. In the summer of '44 the job still wasn't finished.

The bones were ground up, the ashes sieved for some last possible gold or silver loot, the rest thrown back into the pits, whose surface was then leveled.

"No one will believe you," the Germans said. They burned and recorded, burned and recorded. They burned in Ponary, they burned in Rovno, they burned in the woods of Biķernieki and Rumbula, in the ancient Jewish cemetery of the Moscow suburb of Riga, they burned in Bialystok, they burned in Treblinka—for eight months they burned in Treblinka, in special ovens—they burned in Sobibor. They burned in Klooga, in Estonia, but couldn't finish the job; the Soviet Army descended swiftly and found, next to three carbonized piles, one on the point of being ignited.

"Even if some of you happen to survive and report, no one will ever believe what you say," said the Germans, who carefully counted the corpses they dug up.

But at the end of the day the men returned to their underground cell also compared the figures. They compared and noted them in their memory.

Some they had found clothed—men had covered their eyes with their caps, women with their hands—others naked; some killed with a shot to the head or the neck, others machine-gunned. And, they recounted, you could see children with their tongues sticking out of their mouths. They didn't waste bullets on children; they threw them into the pits alive.

Of the eighty at Ponary who fled through a tunnel dug out of the underground cell where they were locked up, thirteen escaped.

The youngest grandson of Furma Riva Burstein, whom she had hidden in a basket, escaped—and luckily he can't remember. The other two, when they were carried off, cried, "Grandma, I'm scared."

But we don't know if the boy—or girl—a few weeks old who was found on the ground, wrapped in rags, by Max Kaufmann and his comrades survived. It was Sunday, November 30, 1941, in the afternoon. They had been ordered to clear the area around the entrance to the Riga ghetto, under the surveillance of Latvian guards. Objects were scattered everywhere: torn knapsacks, open suitcases, purses, gloves, galoshes, crushed baby carriages, coats, shoes, a baby bottle with the oatmeal mush frozen. The cold was intense, but the child was lying calmly in his rags, eyes wide. One of the guards took him and carried him off. Mad, miserly fate perhaps had given him a straight nose and blond hair. Or maybe not.

Max Kaufmann and his comrades were not allowed to go into the ghetto. There was a great silence on the streets that could be discerned from a distance—Ludzas, Sadovnika, Daugavpils, Jekabpils, Katolu, Kalna—and on the snow hoofprints and horse manure. Under their soles from time to time a creaking, the copper casings of the bullets. When at night some managed to enter—the day before, the able-bodied men had been separated from their families and assembled in a temporary lodging on Vijanu Iela, also in the Moscow suburb, which would later become the "small" ghetto—only pools of blood and bloodstains on the snow revealed that there had been "an action." The guards at the gates avoided their gaze and pretended not to see those who, despite the ban, ran through the streets—Sadovnika, Ludzas, Jekabpils, Daugavpils, Katolu, Kalna—to search, to ask. The streets were empty, the doors broken down. The residents remaining in some of the houses had crawled out during the night.

Meanwhile, in the "small" ghetto it was learned that in the course of the day men had been taken from the work teams to remove the corpses from the streets, from the houses, from the hospital, from the old people's home, to bring them from the "big" ghetto to the old Jewish cemetery, now in disuse, in the Moscow suburb. For the most part, it was said, these were old people, sick people, and some unlucky souls who had run into the random gunshot of a drunken cop. Many, but not children—children, no. Children, along with the women and reasonably healthy old men, had been lined up in columns—you've seen the columns, right?—and sent off on Maskavas for the transfer to Salaspils, to Jumpravmuiža, according to the communiqué of Saturday the 29th. The "big" ghetto was overcrowded; the majority of the population had to be housed elsewhere. You saw them in the morning, pulling sleds and pushing carriages loaded with baggage, holding children by the hand

and in their arms. In fact, very few children's corpses were brought to the old cemetery (mercy, mercy on them)—not yours, not mine, not ours—killed by chance, by a terrible fate. The bodies piled up during the day along the cemetery wall were almost all adults, and, meanwhile, it was a struggle to dig the graves in the frozen ground. Certainly, there had been "an action," a pogrom, but the others, the others were transferred. You saw a big blue city bus coming and going; those who couldn't walk were forced to get on it, and were brought to Rumbula, the station on Maskavas, a few kilometers from the city, where the railroad switch was.

"But, but . . ." someone murmured and was quickly silenced, "but what was Cukurs[1] doing there early in the morning? We were waiting on Maskavas for them to escort us to the job, standing next to one of the columns of people who were leaving. He arrived in a car, in his leather jacket, the big Nagant gun beside him; when he got out of the car, he walked among his German comrades in the brown uniforms—weren't there too many for a transfer?—and went to give orders to his men in the Latvian guard. And not only the foot police, police on horseback also escorted the evacuees. A big, too big a show of forces for a move!"

Another contradicted him: "At the head of the first group was Dr. Eliašov in person, really him, in his elegant black fur coat, the blue-and-white Jewish Council band

1 Herberts Cukurs (1900–65) was a famous Latvian pilot and a commander of one of the squads involved in the mass murder of Latvian Jews during the Second World War.

with the star of David around his arm. He was smiling, he was calm."

In the following days those in the ghetto waited in vain for word from those who had been transferred. They seemed to have abruptly disappeared. From Aryan Latvian acquaintances came uncertain but terrible news—leaked through the guards? They talked about enormous pits dug by Soviet prisoners on the edge of the forest opposite the Rumbula station, next to the Quadrat factory. And they talked about mass shootings. Some Jews who worked at Gestapo headquarters saw piles of clothes arrive with the star of David sewn onto the left side at chest level and on the back, as people in the Riga ghetto wore, and Latvian passports. The documents weren't left in their hands, but a glance had been enough to recognize Jewish surnames.

But, people murmured, it's not possible, it's not credible, they'll send word. They are *****, they are many, they are too many! Half the entire population of the ghetto. They were evacuated, they're at Salaspils, they're in Jumpravmuiža, they were sent to Dwinsk.

A card arrived from someone, from Dwinsk. Of course, they're in Dwinsk.

Eight days after the first transfer a second took place, not as large, calmer; one could believe that many had adapted to their uncertain fate. The few left in the "small" ghetto were still waiting for news.

Until a woman came to take refuge in the "small" ghetto. She had lived in makeshift shelters, never more than one night in the same place. Two weeks earlier, she said, at night, she had climbed out of a pit in Rumbula. Another woman was hidden by a shepherd.

I read the history of the extermination of the Jews in the Baltic countries, Byelorussia, Ukraine, Crimea, and Poland, for the first time a few years after I received confirmation of my father's death. I was looking for information and testimonies for a book I was writing that eventually had the title *Un leggero accento straniero* [A Slight Foreign Accent]. I had called it *Monumento al parallelo* [Monument to the Parallel].

I was interested mainly in the proceedings of the Nuremburg trials, in the witnesses regarding the Einsatzgruppen that had been active in those countries, in the collections of documents. There was the Eichmann trial in Jerusalem. My book was to be about the executioners: they alone, one of my protagonists declared, could be investigated. The victims couldn't be represented, because to invent their stories would be to take away their lives a second time. The victims are sacred, untouchable.

"For them let us cover our faces and weep," the book's dedication urged.

Lost in the crowd of the countless was my father, whom I didn't dare to mention openly while my mother was still alive. I didn't ask myself—nor did I ask her—if such wary discretion had truly been demanded.

Even now, decades after that long-ago book, published for the first time in 1968, I recoil from the idea that it's permissible to portray, in a work of fiction, victims of the Shoah. It's still a struggle for me to decide to see a film on the subject. Another of my protagonists—thirty years later—states again:

"Only the witnesses can tell of this horror. And we, and I, can't write about it because this thing, this thing can't be invented. So no novels, no films, no commemorations, nothing at all. Only they, only those who survived have the right to bear witness. If they can. This thing can't be narrated, it can't tolerate literary expression; the extermination can't be told, words refuse, words become livid, words seek refuge in silence. To tell is to betray."

So I regularly returned to celebrate the funeral rites for my father and his family in my books, entrusting the task of evocation to the pure and simple chronicle of the testimony of others.

I had consigned him, alive, to a few pages of my autobiography, as I almost reluctantly found him in now-faded childhood memories. Besides, the total elimination of the imprints that the dead leave behind in objects, wills, images, tombs, the uncertainty about how, exactly, he died and the fate of my other relatives (how to reconstruct an individual fate in a mass killing?), the dispersal of goods that no one could reclaim (a mass theft is necessarily unpunished)—all that led me to carry their story and their cenotaph hidden in myself, in a resigned, protracted, undirected grief. I recalled, always, and I wrote to commemorate. To the child Irene, whom I never knew, I dedicated my first book. I placed Jewish memory stones on the insurmountable wall.

What name to give such an insubstantial but persistent bond if not ritual obligation? I wasn't at all trying to reattach my tortured paternal roots; I was intending to remedy a completely inner, confused, and incurable past, not plumb its depths. If I wrote my thesis on the *Adversus Judaeos* of Tertullian, what drove me more than a sense of belonging to the race of my beloved grandfather Maurice was my usual critical fixation on historical Christianity, my polemical wish to destroy the filthy anti-Jewish inanities of the Fathers of the Church. I didn't succeed in the end, because of the purely philological intentions of Don Pellegrino, my professor of ancient Christian literature, who later became a cardinal; instead, yawning, I had to compare the text with the *Adversus Marcionem*, which, to tell the truth, was just as ugly.

Also, in the face of the very few physical items—documents, letters—I found myself paralyzed; it disturbed me even to touch them, much less decide to read them, evidence of a personal experience unrecoverable in its obscure incompleteness.

It was such a long time afterward, however, that the cousin who had given us the definite news had mistaken the date of the mass shooting by a month; she had put it at the end of October. I re-established with precision the day (or night) shortly before leaving for Latvia. Though not yet the places.

In the envelope that contained the certificates and proceedings of the divorce, my mother had written on a card in her clear handwriting: "*Il* Gersoni, died in the Riga massacres, October–November 1941." The cold, bureaucratic article, *Il*, or *the*, that preceded the name—why, when he was redeemed by his terrible death, hadn't she granted him the name Samuel, Samuel Gersoni?—wounded me. As for the exact date, I didn't care.

In fact, when I found the cousin's letter among my mother's papers after her death, I hadn't read it attentively. It was written on transparent paper in Gothic script, difficult, I said to myself, to decipher.

At some point over the years (although, as I've written, I can't say exactly when) I had destroyed that last request for help from my father (I didn't know it was the last), and had destroyed the pictures of him.

I remember his features very clearly in one of those photographs—and I remember them also in reality—and even his face as a young man, the eyes black and shining, the curls on his forehead, the cream-colored photograph on thick paper. Surely I've thrown away other letters. In my autobiography I had "adjusted" something in one of those letters—that last one, of course! At the top of one of his large yellowish sheets was a list of lovers attributed by him to his wife; this list I placed in the proceedings of the trial. Not unlike the cold article that preceded the surname of her ex-husband on my mother's note, it proved yet again their mutual hatred, the vengeful fury in his intention to defame her in front of us, his daughters, and perhaps justify his own conduct before her bitter and contemptuous silence. At every point of the trial he demanded her presence, but neither one ever appeared in person; they accused and vilified each other through their lawyers.

One day in Torre Pellice in late September of 1999, after I returned from Latvia, I knelt in the attic amid dusty old suitcases and black bags full of papers, photos, and books—my maternal family saved everything; I even found manuscripts of my uncle's, already crumbling—and dug through everything, trying to find some minimal remains that might have to do with him, my father. I was really looking for the lost letter, and I knew, as I searched, that I wouldn't find it, but, who knows, maybe a scrap had escaped destruction, a torn photo. I looked at the negatives against the light and examined the figures, but nothing of him. Bits of my childhood, yes, but of him, of him or my grandparents in Riga, nothing.

In those same weeks I reopened the packets of letters that Mamma had saved, unfolded and reread them almost randomly. We had written to her regularly, first in Riga, where she stayed until 1940, teaching at the university, and later in Bulgaria, where she was the director of an Italian cultural institute. But I didn't find her letters to us in that period. Had I destroyed those, too?

Finally, as I continued to cry real, not ritual, tears, tears of fresh mourning, I deciphered for the first time the letter from the cousin, who, with a few strokes, restored my father to me in his final suffering.

The cenotaph, as is fitting for a cenotaph, had remained empty until the moment the plane leaving Turin began to taxi, and my father in truth had remained buried within our silence, within my fears.

3. Empty Roads

When we set out for home we certainly don't expect that we won't find it, or that we'll find it changed, that we'll have to make comparisons between the home that stands before us as we put the key in the lock and the one we left a short while before. There is no interval in between, not so much because the absence was brief as because inside ourselves we have remained fixed in our daily habits.

The weight of the years that had elapsed between my departure—the two of us sitting next to each other on the farm cart taking us to the little station in the woods—and my return to Riga in September of 1999 didn't fall on me until later, when I was back in Turin. Pietro and I traveled through the city and the countryside, and meanwhile time slowed down until it was suspended, in an apparently indefinite pause. I wandered with him from place to place in a state of mind that was for the most part, I think, serene gratitude, so readily did the memories I preserved adapt to memory rediscovered. Nothing surprised me, I didn't make comparisons, it didn't occur to me to say, "Look at that square, that house, that street, they're just the same!" Or, "How they've changed!"

I didn't perceive the distance that spanned the course of an entire life between my departure as a child and my return as an old woman, because an inner gaze must have accompanied the worn steps leading to the doorway of Andreja Pumpura Iela 2, our last address in Riga, as, year after year, they eroded. I had continued to go out every morning with my schoolbag, my little sister beside me, as I had that day when, without our father knowing, we went to join Mamma. A morning in December, I think, like other mornings. Never to return.

Getting off the plane at the small airport that was obviously new to me, I immediately smelled in the clear air the sharp, intense scent of the surrounding forests, of resin and sun.

It was a sunny day, the clouds were light and swift, driven by high winds from the sea. I waited in the service area for Pietro, who was dealing with the car rental. A happy mild relief took hold of me and stayed with me for the first hours. I wasn't at all moved; I had climbed over the wall without realizing it—to my great relief—had exchanged my lire for *lati*, and at passport control the short, blond, tidy Latvian, barely older than my grandson Giacomo, had handed mine back with an unexpected cheerful and conspiratorial little smile.

On the drive toward the city I pointed out the route to Pietro—traffic signals in Latvia are truly scarce—and immediately realized where we would be once we crossed the Daugava, my Düna, although we had only a small map from the Michelin Guide.

How many places there were, in fact, where I had never been as a child in my narrow, protected, privileged world!

Never, of course, in the Moscow suburb, one of the most wretched in the city, where those who were not granted permission by the senate to live in Riga resided in olden times: poor Russians and, mainly, Jews. I had never entered one of the many small wooden houses on the vast outskirts of the city. The little dachas in the forest along the sea were also made of wood, and we had spent a summer or two in one of them.

When I saw the summer cottage belonging to my adopted aunt and uncle von Braunschweig, Erna and Frommi, in a photo I'd found in the attic in Torre Pellice, I felt again on my skin the breath of cold wind that reminds me of those summers. In the photo we're very tan, in bathing suits, along with them and a pale-skinned child who—I suddenly remember—was named Ruth and had a big pink nose. The sand blew into the garden of their villa, which faced the beach. I wonder if the house, which they were especially proud of, is still there, and who is in it. They didn't have children. I never thought of them again, though they were so attached to us.

From the airport we took a nice wide street between brown wooden houses and brown woods with yellowing leaves; I had probably never passed by there, but they were familiar to me, like an image from a recurring dream.

In us dwells, perhaps, an incorporeal memory of the soul, not conscious, unconnected to events, and submerged in a broad, boundless impression not of figures or forms, sounds or touch, but of atmosphere, which hovers around us children and goes beyond the house, the carriage, the first uncertain steps. That was how the city came toward me.

We arrived at midday, and left the hotel between four and five in the afternoon. On the map in the telephone book I found in the room—more detailed than the Michelin—I had soon oriented myself and had realized that Andreja Pumpura Iela was five minutes away. We turned onto the wide avenue, so wide even then that the New Year's market was held there, and, naturally, towering over it was the enormous neoclassical building, which I didn't know was neoclassical, and at the corner of the first cross street on the right was the yellow building, my last house in Riga. The inner doorway was shut with a lock as decrepit as the worn steps. A shabby electrical wire was connected to a bare bulb hanging outside next to the entrance. But that building with its big windows—we lived on the first floor—still had a spare, linear elegance of structure.

"I'm about to cry again," I said to Pietro (it seemed to me that I had to apologize for the many tears I would shed), but I didn't cry at all. Nor did I cry later, as the days passed, except for the next day on Maskavas, in Rumbula.

I walked back and forth, observing. The street was very quiet; there were shadows, tall trees. It seemed to me I had seen these grow, too. Behind me Pietro was taking pictures, and his picture-taking invariably brought me back to tranquility, to a feeling that I was visiting, as an adult. He was the reality that kept me suspended in the right balance between past and present. And, besides, I wasn't looking for people, only places. No one could have recognized me and I couldn't have recognized anyone. The streets were empty.

We continued along the route I took to school. I seem to remember that at the beginning of the second year I had received permission to go by myself sometimes, with my sister. Before turning after a brief stretch onto the broad Elisabethstrasse, now called, similarly, Elizabetes Iela, I looked around for the villa that I remembered as the Soviet Embassy, on whose sidewalk we were forbidden to walk. Now we saw a beautiful Art Nouveau villa, just repainted a cream color; from the balcony an American flag waved, also very new.

The Michelin Guide says that on Elizabetes are some of the most famous Jugendstil houses in Riga; the city boasts more than six hundred, according to the guide.

We admired them greatly, the magnificent houses in the most beautiful Jugendstil of the north. Leaning on Pietro's arm, I walked and contemplated.

The one that Mikhail Osipovich Eisenstein, the film director's father, built had just been restored and repainted, and many others had been similarly refurbished. Although I paid no attention to these splendid dwellings, I was proud of them and felt them, very tall beside me, on the walk to school. The thought that Pietro could derive some touristic pleasure from them—he photographed everything diligently—cheered me. I hadn't realized that they were Jugendstil, passing by with my schoolbag: the sumptuous houses on the right, on the left the parks—trees, trees, trees—matched my memory.

As for Mikhail Osipovich Eisenstein, a cousin of my grandfather had married an Eisenstein, I don't know which one, but—I recall—he took legitimate pride in it for the family. I learn from the guide that the "architect" was the city engineer.

We turn onto Auseklas Iela; I've heard the sound of the name but didn't remember it. Shadows, trees, and suddenly there's the Vorburg, the huge gray residential complex made up of a series of uninterrupted blocks around a courtyard dense with rather wild trees and shrubs, a long narrow square between two big entrances. On the first or second floor on the left is the apartment of my early childhood, looking toward the Düna. Probably the second floor, because I could see the river from high up and thought I was right on the shore. In fact, a street runs between the shore, which is protected by a fence, and the Vorburg.

The river is certainly one of my earliest memories. It's present in my daily life like a person, and even if I'm not at the window—to see it I climb up on something and am spellbound watching it—there it is, beyond the windows, gray, flowing without pause, the houses on the opposite shore lost in fog; I live over a river, rather, I'm on a ship and I go and go. "*Es zieht mich immer fort.*" (It's always pulling me away.) A flood of nostalgia drags me along, aboard the ship.

In the same courtyard, also in a building on the left, was my school. My mother had lived on the right—the guest of German friends for a while after her separation from my father—so it was easy to go to her that December morning.

I don't talk about it with Pietro. I'm thrust outward into a complete absence of thought, but every so often a latent weariness overwhelms me. It's not only the sleepless night on the eve of my departure; it's the anguish that was unnoticed behind the wall, now finding its resolution, so simple, so obvious, even banal. I wanted to return, but now enough, I've had enough, I'm unable to do any more.

Pietro insists that we look more carefully for my Lutherschule, since it's right here. But I refuse, I can't. Just a little while ago I refused to ring the doorbell at the entrance of Andreja Pumpura Iela 2. I can't; thanks to him I managed to get here, I can't do any more. Besides, the fact that I don't speak Latvian makes me uneasy, and that ignorance of mine isn't the ignorance of an ordinary tourist. I was born Latvian, but I don't know how to speak, I don't know how to express myself in Latvian. I'm a defective tourist and a defective Latvian.

At the hotel, we registered under Pietro's last name, which is, after all, mine by marriage; however, it's not on my passport. Here is my last name that looks Italian but that in Riga everyone knows, or knew, is Jewish. Who knows why, but being incognito calms me.

At the reception desk they didn't even ask for my documents.

At night we walk toward the old city along Brivibas Bulvaris—*brīvība* means "freedom"; it's one of the few Latvian terms I know—a grand avenue with an immense though squat fenced-off monument. The three stars held up by the large woman are intended to represent the three Latvian provinces: Livonia, Courland, Latgale. I continue to consult the guide. I inform myself. Courland? Yes, Courland.

We're in the midst of a crowd of mostly young people headed to the old city; Pietro observes, laughing under his breath, that he had heard about the fantastic girls of Riga. I look more closely, yes, there's an incredible number of tall, delicate blondes; they have none of the angularity or excess of the Scandinavians, and they wear a kind of T-shirt—you can't really call it a minidress—that covers their bottoms to just below the buttocks. I assure Pietro they're not Latvians, they're Russians—half the city is Russian. We meet more and more of them. So they're Latvians, too.

As a child—I think later—I lived on a German island, essentially not unlike people who live in a colony in a conquered country; but I wasn't a daughter of the conquerors. Besides, we were many: on this side, very close by, the Estonians; on that side, very close by, the Lithuanians; across the sea, when it froze, the Finns could be reached on sleds.

Our pediatrician was German; our driver Polish; the cook Latvian; the sleigh drivers Russian; the man who beat the carpets Latvian; my teacher German; Mamma's lawyer Latvian. I was born in a German clinic. Mamma is Italian, but I wasn't able to speak even with the Italians. How many foreigners we were, sitting under the lamp in the never-ending winter, welcomed in our beautiful city, which thus belonged to no one.

We sit down in a small restaurant tucked into a corner of the cathedral square. I don't understand a word of the menu in Latvian; luckily I find a familiar Russian soup and I choose an unfamiliar Baltic fish. Was *sole* written on the menu? But where do these savages come from, these Balts, fishing in the sea later called Baltic? For the Germans it was the Ostsee. Points of view.

Pietro orders in English; he'll always do the talking with the Latvian Latvians. I'll talk to the German and Russian Latvians.

I eat the delicious fish—a real northern sole—the salad of mixed greens is very good, and the custard at the end of the meal is also very good. The flavors are new; eating, I will seldom have flashes of childhood recognition as I did once in Italy when, after sixty years, I tasted Swedish herring with dill, the German dill of my childhood.

Tall blond girls continue to pass by. What legs, my goodness, what legs! There are also a lot of drunken youths, and one confronts us as we're returning to the hotel, asking for money in broken Italian. He doesn't insist, but quickly resigns himself to our refusal.

During dinner I looked at the brick cathedral on the other side of the square, which descends below street level at the back. It's growing dark as evening falls; I feel no curiosity to enter, I remember it as dim and frightening. Am I there to see the tombs of the knights of the Black Head, the visors of their helmets covering the faces of those who'd gone on the crusade? I don't say anything to Pietro, who, besides, is on his phone. He talks on the phone while he walks, speaking in English, rapidly as usual. I feel guilty; he's given me five days of his dizzying work life.

At night, reading the guide, I note that it doesn't mention knights' tombs in the cathedral, only aristocratic wooden shields. Also, they don't have black heads, but are knights of the Order of the Sword. I must have invented the detail of the visor, or it's from somewhere else. The members of the Black Head, also German, aren't even knights; maybe it's a confraternity of wealthy merchants, beer drinkers, who had that famous building on the square; it was bombed by the Germans, now they're reconstructing it.

Ah, memory... or would it have been Leni, my beloved governess, the daughter of a Prussian general, who told me about the crusader knights?

The crowd has thinned out a bit, but there are still a lot of people on the street, even though it's a weekday. A thin, pale, blond girl, in a light-colored dress, holding a flower on a long stem, begs in Russian. She glides swiftly among the knots of people almost without stopping: "Пожалуйста, пожалуйста"—"*Pozhalujsta*, please." An old woman walks a little dog, a jazz orchestra plays at the corner of Raina Bulvaris, and groups of youths crowd around holding bottles of beer. I'm in Riga, I'm an Italian tourist.

I don't think about anything while I peer at the names on the street corners, looking for the street where my grandparents' house was: Kirchenstrasse 13. I'm surprised by the sight of a bag of garbage in a courtyard between two houses destroyed in the war. The old city appears scrupulously clean everywhere; indeed, we'll find the whole country clean.

We return to the hotel. I notice the pale girl holding the pale long-stemmed flower again, slipping amid the groups; she barely stops to murmur her prayer, takes a coin from this one or that, holding out her free hand, then immediately withdraws it. Small diaphanous ghost of the empty streets, with her unknown flower.

I've seen the same shy gesture made by a Roma girl I encountered on a bus in Turin. I'm sitting in the back and a young Roma with two little girls approaches. I move to the corner and one of the children sits next to me. I keep my purse locked and glance at the child. She raises her face toward me and we look at each other; under the gray dirt her cheeks are delicate, slightly rosy over the cheekbones. She has large gentle brown eyes and long gilded eyelashes with darker tips. I smile at her, and she, staring at me, holds out her little hand to beg. I shake my head, and she quickly withdraws her hand and smiles at me in turn, a barely allusive half-smile of complicity.

As I'm falling asleep, exhausted, on the first night in Riga, amid the confused impressions I suddenly have a lucid thought, again internal, addressed to my inner self, again held in the vise of my personal story. I see the girl holding the flower amid the crowds of passersby, recognizable, distinguishable, and real, even in her instantaneous appearance in the swarm of strangers. Tomorrow, I think, we'll look for Rumbula, but we won't find the place. I can't go beyond this flicker of a thought and I fall asleep.

It happens, it happens more and more often, that at night I amuse myself by grouping together encounters that at first glance seem random but, on second thought, appear instead to anticipate or warn. Tracing the moods of the day, I give them different meanings: they preach, they try to keep me from self-pity, they want to remind me of names or people. More rarely a coincidence of unexpected affections cheers me, and often I end up persuading myself—resigned and a little gloomy, it should be said—that the same fate unites us, us humans, a fate within which my particular experience is lost rather than asserted. And it doesn't matter whether I know the people I run into or not. In truth, they're all created by me, as I move along empty streets.

The bus offers the best opportunities. I'm surrounded by people who chat and converse, and it doesn't matter that they're not actually talking to me; on the contrary, eyes resting on a magazine, I read and with a furtive ear listen. These days I take advantage of cellphones to spy on fragments of others' lives. The possibilities have multiplied. These, too, are encounters.

The girl who moves from a greeting intended to be indifferent to an offer of having a sandwich together, if not at my house at yours, or we can get a pizza, ah, if you're busy we can meet for a moment at the café, no, this evening I'm free, you can't, then let's do tomorrow. No, tomorrow you can't, let's do the day after, a couple of sandwiches at the café and I have to study, you know, psychology.

Or the Chinese cook who stinks of frying and complains, in a language that mixes English with Piedmontese, to the Black man in torn work jeans who stinks of sweat: the boss doesn't pay overtime.

Or the big Albanian kids, broken shoes on the seats opposite, who—I imagine—boast loudly in their incomprehensible language about not having paid for the ticket, and proclaim, shouting aggressively, that soon they'll get money for better shoes, cars, weapons.

I have the usual curiosity about foreign languages—basically I'd like to know them all—and try to catch even a single word that might lead me to grasp the subject of the talking, shouting, murmuring.

There aren't many people on the tram one day in mid-morning, and behind me I hear the rustling sound of a woman's voice. She's speaking in a hurry, without punctuation; she doesn't raise or lower her tone. I can't distinguish the language; it has Latin cadences, but here and there I pick up a Slavic term. The voice is reading, mechanical, polite, and indifferent to the text. Reaching my stop, I see the young blond woman behind me, who has stood up; she holds a child by the hand and sticks a plain printed notebook in her purse. On the cover is a black-and-white drawing of a small fairy in a peaked cap. I ask her what language she was reading to the child, and she answers readily, in excellent Italian, "Romanian, it's a little like your language."

"There are some Slavic words," I say. That seems to annoy her, she's surprised.

"No!"

And she gets off in front of me. Without intending to I must have stuck my nose into some complicated Balkan resentment.

I like to go to sleep listening to the radio—not music, which keeps me awake, but voices talking about philosophy, astronomy, art, reading prose. Not poetry, poetry also keeps me awake. Just on the point of falling asleep I reach out my hand to turn off the radio, but sometimes I doze on the thin stream of voices. I wouldn't be able to do that if I were watching something: the image absorbs me, grabs me, I can't get free of it.

I hold inside myself the sound of countless voices, voices of those who've been dead now for many years. The voice of Franki, who was my professor and friend, and who died a good forty-five years ago; the voice of Adolfo, whom I was so in love with; the voice of my uncle, whom I didn't love at all; my mother's; my maternal grandmother's; Gianni's—but I lived with him for forty years—my sister's. I can't bring back my father's voice.

And yet I hear the voice of the kind Pugliese porter in our building in Piazza Solferino. He lived on the floor below and you entered his small apartment from the gallery that ran the length of the building and faced the courtyard; in Turin such a building is called a *casa di ringhiera*, a "railing" house. He usually kept the kitchen door open, except in the middle of winter; it was the entrance, and from morning to evening the fragrance of coffee wafted out. I saw coming and going along the gallery not only him, his wife, and their adolescent son, who still lived with them, but all his family—married children, in-laws, sisters, grandchildren, brothers. One evening he hurried to meet his son, who had just become a father, and tenderly kissed the tiny bald head of the newborn in his arms. How warm and enveloping the southern speech that rises toward my balcony, benevolent, carrying an ancient wisdom, a little conspiratorial. I'm sitting at the round table in the dining area off the kitchen. I don't understand a word of what they're saying on the balcony below. I'm correcting homework. My turtle is sleeping with its head on my shoe.

Sometimes I seem to dream of voices in a great indistinct murmur: those dead I wrote about just now are talking together, in words that have a fragmented and inarticulate sound, that belong not to a language but to memory, and reveal nothing that I don't already know; but they occupy my sleep, murmuring and calling. Waking, I emerge from a tiny place overflowing with noises, whispers, cries—yes, also cries—into a silent room that is mine. Outside, barely the warble of a bird.

One morning, on Pumpura Iela, my father is sitting in his pajamas in a corner of the living room and reading his Russian newspapers. I try to get his attention, I take the page away from his face, he defends himself, holds the newspaper still, says something, says to leave him in peace. He's annoyed, complaining, and I—maybe Sisi is with me, too—continue: he doesn't get angry, but he grumbles, he pays no attention to me (I don't recall that he ever scolded me) and fends me off with his hand as one does a kitten. And meanwhile he's promising me something.

Of his voice I retain only an echo. I no longer know what name he used when he told me to leave him in peace to read his newspapers. What name he called me—if he called me anything—when he ran after me in the alley that leads from the narrow street where my grandparents' house is in Torre

Pellice to the main street, to pick me up in his arms and kiss me, weeping. The last time we saw each other.

I was eleven. In my autobiography it was twelve.

In a book of mine I found in the attic in Torre Pellice I read in the dedication from Tante Erna the name Minni, which I didn't remember. In the letters my sister wrote to Mamma in German, in our early days in Torre Pellice, I sometimes find it as Mini. But mine of the same period are signed Michi.

Very few sounds of the city, its streets empty, remain in my memory, as if it had been gradually depopulated by an evil magic. No hum of traffic, or tapping of rain on windows, no rustling of trees. Only the jingling of the sledges on the morning of the first snow, the din of the icebreaker when we're crossing the river and, letter by letter, I read the commercial signs on the buildings on the opposite bank. And, finally, the thunder of the thaw at night on the river. Spring arrives.

When I write that I can easily remember singing hymns at school in the morning before classes started, I don't hear the sound of our chorus. I don't know what the memory of hearing is, what corner of the soul it hides in, and what forced it to such a point and rendered it silent every time I try to get it to give me back the living city of my childhood. The alien city where my father was killed.

4. Gersoni, Gersony, Герсонъ

The second evacuation began on Monday, December 8, 1941 (the eighteenth day of the month of Kislev). The same procedure was followed as in the first one, only it was somewhat calmer and there were fewer victims. Once again the blue buses drove back and forth, and the columns of people marched in the same direction. A German marched at the head of each column, but otherwise these processions of misery were surrounded by Latvians on foot and on horseback. If anyone fell behind while marching, he was beaten with truncheons and shot. These beasts had evidently still not been sated by the blood that had flowed the previous week.

On these days, too, I went to work at the Kommandantur with my son.

At the work station I organized an expedition to find out in which direction the columns of people were marching. Together with the driver Becker from the headquarters, whom I paid well for this, I put together a work group to gather wood. In a truck we drove through Salaspils toward Ogre. As we approached the Quadrat factory we encountered the first evacuees. We slowed down. They were walking quite calmly, and hardly a sound was heard. The first person in the procession we met was Mrs. Pola Schmulian (wife of the wholesale lumber dealer and sister of Mrs. Baruchsohn). Her head was deeply bowed and she seemed to be in despair. I also saw other acquaintances of mine among the people marching: the Latvians would occasionally beat one or another of them with their truncheons.

From afar I also saw two other columns, which were drawing closer to the Rumbula railway station. There they halted. In this way, the organizers wanted to create the impression that from there they would be transported to points farther on. But in reality they were herded in groups into the forest and slaughtered.

On the way I counted six murdered people who were lying with their faces in the snow.

The murderers showed their "compassion" for the bitterly weeping small children by stopping some of the sledges, emptying them, and roughly throwing the children into them. I can still hear their thin, weeping little voices today! We drove on.

At the edge of the road, hidden by a small wood, stood two trucks and between sixty and eighty soldiers. They were soldiers of the German Wehrmacht. Only a short distance past the wood we saw machine guns set close together in the snow. As far as I could judge, they reached from Rumbula to the banks of the Daugava River, about three kilometers away.

When I saw this, I instantly realized that a great catastrophe would occur here.

However, our driver, Becker, explained as a professional military man that these were merely preventive measures to keep people from escaping. But I held on to my suspicion, which was later confirmed.

Everything I had seen proved beyond a doubt that the German Wehrmacht was deeply involved in these mass murders.

We drove on, in order to examine the whole route. Next to the church in Salaspils stood a large camp, but it was for Russian prisoners of war. They told us they knew nothing at all about the Jews.

On the way back we chose another route. When we returned with all of this news to our comrades at the field headquarters, they were of course overcome by dread.[2]

This account is by Max Kaufmann, in *Die Vernichtung der Juden Lettlands* (*The Destruction of the Jews of Latvia*), written in German and published in Munich in 1947. Having endured the Riga ghetto and the concentration camps of Kaiserwald, Stuffhof, Buchenwald, and Sachsenhausen, he was one of around a thousand Latvian Jews who survived,

2 English translation (unattributed) from the website of the Museum of Family History. Museumoffamilyhistory.com/cl-pt1.htm

and were liberated in Germany. I have a photocopy; the book was lent to me, more than twenty years ago now, by my friends Eva and Bruno, who received it directly from the author, in the United States. I didn't ask myself at the time why they had gone in search of such a specific text. In Italy people barely know where Latvia is, and even Italian Jews are generally ignorant of the total numbers and the dates of the extermination of the Jews in the countries of the East. For us Italians the Shoah begins with Auschwitz.

I didn't read the entire book. I leafed through it looking at the chapter titles and I stopped really reading at the point where the excerpt above ends; I didn't even notice that the dates mentioned by the author didn't correspond to the ones I got from my Swiss cousin. If my husband hadn't bothered to photocopy it, I would have given the book back without noticing anything. Besides, the names of the places mentioned weren't familiar to me; I didn't know where in Riga they might be and didn't care about them.

The author also listed the surnames he was able to remember, and in the long list I found the name Gerson and that of "Doctor Tall," named elsewhere as "Thal." Talrose was the name of my cousin Saul, a young doctor; it should be said, however, that Tall is also a Latvian Jewish surname.

Once I had returned from Latvia and read the whole book, I reconstructed the probable reason for Eva and Bruno's interest in what happened there. As early as December of 1941 the Germans had begun to transport Viennese and German Jews to the Riga ghetto, where they occupied the houses left empty by the "evacuees." Were Eva's parents, or one of her relatives, among the Jews deported from Berlin to that final destination? We never talked about it.

In the summer of 1998 my son Pietro had to go to Riga for a work meeting. He mentioned it to me in the spring and asked if I wanted to go with him. I said yes right away, with great trepidation. I immediately understood that I couldn't say no, but at the same time, in the enormous inner turmoil that overwhelmed me when I said yes, I ardently hoped that nothing would come of it.

But I went to the police station to renew my passport. I hadn't used it for years and when it was handed back to me I had the usual sensation of gratitude mixed with a clean conscience; I felt I was "in order," as always when, without difficulties, the document was returned to me renewed, or when, no different from any ordinary traveler, I managed to cross some border.

During a trip to Egypt I was stopped on arrival in the airport's large, tall atrium by a booming voice that called me by name: Gersoni Marina. While my group—it was a group trip—proceeded, two Egyptian officials accompanied me and our guide to an office. Behind the reasonable thought that I immediately tried to formulate—they're just checking—panic invaded me: they had noticed my surname. Israel was in a period of heightened isolation among the Arab countries, all of which were hostile.

Among our suitcases only mine had been lost (it was later recovered), but that instant terror showed me yet again that no, I wasn't at all in order, I didn't have a clean conscience.

Thus I saw myself in my surname in a conflicted but conscious way. In Torre Pellice people had immediately deformed it by changing the initial hard *G* into a soft Italian *G*, and I had struggled for a while in a vain attempt to keep it as it was. I had resigned myself, but from then on I always felt a slight annoyance—and I still do—at the mangled pronunciation. For a long time, more out of acquired habit than as a residue of ancestral prudence, I abandoned it almost entirely. I realized that in this disloyalty there was, again, a disloyalty toward my father. I remember that I also asked my mother if we could adopt her surname, Coïsson, which was awkward in Italian but well-known in the Waldensian valleys. (She had refused, horrified, she so law-abiding.) I think I asked in an attempt to flatter her.

When I was young, married women were called by their husband's surname at work, so as a teacher I was Jarre, which in Italy is even more difficult than Gersoni; Gersoni could at least seemingly sound Italian, even though I often had to repeat it when I introduced myself.

My first writings bore both my surnames, unmarried and married. I don't remember when, once I'd become a writer, I lost mine, or why. Besides, Jarre goes well with Marina. And so for a long time I was just Marina Jarre, and only as a widow did I begin again to use my mangled Gersoni, at first slightly embarrassed, then more and more willingly. In fact, it grew on me, even with its imprecise *G*, like the scaly shell of an old turtle. The age-old carapace of the Gersonis.

Reading the Bible I had happened on the Gershonites, first in Numbers, and later, farther back, in the beginning, Gershon, who was Moses's first son, born to his Midianite wife. Of this incredible antiquity—and of the meaning of the name, which contained in itself a mark of future exile, the Hebrew root *ger*, foreigner—I could even have been proud, if I hadn't had to explain my "nobility" every time to good-natured but indifferent idolaters. Not to mention that the *Encyclopedia Judaica* declares that the etymology of the name, frequent among the Levites, is unknown.

In the United States my sister had a curious experience. She was invited to dinner by Orthodox Jews who were outraged that a Gersoni—really, a Gersoni!—could have married a goy. Sisi had appeared surprised and amused by the particular importance they gave our surname—how did they pronounce it? She was ignorant of the fact that, in the end, even Moses had married a Gentile, although from a tribe, the Midianites, considered more or less cousins of the Jews; were they a little less fussy in those days about which girls they chose?

I can only wonder if my father's mixed marriage had incensed people in Riga. At Eva and Bruno's I had once encountered, briefly, the wife of a dear Hungarian friend of theirs—they had all four met in 1939 on the ship that was carrying them to safety from Europe to the Americas—who, by singular coincidence, was a Grete Weinberg from Riga, a first cousin of my father's, younger than him. In the grip of my usual paralysis, crouching behind my wall, I didn't ask her anything, nor did it seem to me that I had anything to ask. She herself mentioned the cousin, said he was a "somewhat bizarre" type, and recalled having met him one winter, when he had told her that he was about to marry a *kleine Italienerin*, a little Italian.

My father was very tall and my mother of average height, but maybe in that *kleine* there was the tenderness of a love affair at its beginning.

After that first travel plan didn't work out, Pietro didn't return to the subject until the following spring, warning me like someone continuing a conversation.

"So in September we're going to Riga."

I asked if he had work to do in Latvia; he said, "In Latvia no, probably in Sweden." Maybe from there we could take a ferry across the Baltic Sea, or he could leave me in Riga and come and get me afterward. There was a possibility that he would have to go to Tallinn.

So finally I would have to return. I didn't ask myself when and why the idea had occurred to Pietro; it seemed to me that I had never talked to my children about the events of my childhood and the death of my father—maybe some chance mention—though it could also be that they had read about them in my autobiography. I never know, in fact, if they read my books; I suppose so, but I don't dare ask. When I'm writing, I allude only in passing to what I'm doing, and once the book is finished I present it to them, not unlike an illegitimate little brother, with a certain embarrassment.

Yet I feel bound to my children by a kind of umbilical cord through which runs an unspoken mutual knowledge, not to be communicated in words. If—afraid of being misunderstood or, even worse, forced to justify myself—I have to explain or even defend myself out of fear that this subterranean current will be cut off, I'm lost, like someone who is missing a vital element.

So I didn't ask myself how Pietro had reached the decision to take me to Riga on a journey that turned out to be not for work but devoted solely to me.

Nor did I ask myself why it had occurred to him, as we returned to Riga on the same road taken by Max Kaufmann in search of the columns of evacuees, to measure the kilometers that separated Rumbula from the city; it was six kilometers, he said to me later, without my having asked. To reach the Moscow suburb, around two more. Thus they had walked eight kilometers along Maskavas, which so naturally runs in a straight line from the ancient neighborhood on the outskirts—Forstate—to the woods around Rumbula.

It was still raining as we returned in silence along the wide gray road between trees that were starting to turn yellow, broad-leaved trees and pines, certainly not the same ones as then. I formed disconnected thoughts that I immediately dispelled. I didn't speak, I sniffled, I dried my tears. I said to myself: I don't know, I mustn't, I'll never know.

I'll never know if this is the road that he, too, walked; I'll never know about the child, if it happened here or before, in the ghetto. I thought and dispelled those thoughts as soon as I envisioned figures or situations.

"You will not form any image."

Snow, freezing cold. Maybe he was ill, he was old, he felt old—he was only fifty-five, I tell myself—he had the child with him. The blue bus came and went, carried those who couldn't make the walk. I mustn't. I will never know if it was during the night or in the morning or if it had already happened in the ghetto the night before.

And in our silence, while I was blowing my nose and drying my tears, those thoughts that I didn't dare think were rushing toward my son, perhaps through the umbilical cord.

Before we left Turin I wasn't sure of actually finding the place on the outskirts of Riga from which we were now returning to the city. I intended, if without conviction, to look for it, but, as I've said, I had no idea where it might be, nor did I believe that I would be able to pick out such a small place on a map. On the map of Latvia, bought in Turin, I had found only Salaspils and had understood that Rumbula must be outside the city, on the road that led there. It didn't occur to me until later to get a map of Riga. I knew that a grassy green carpet had been spread over the old Jewish cemetery in the Moscow suburb—it had become a public park—and that, in general, a mantle of deliberate oblivion covered every trace of those slaughters and depredations in which some of the population had taken part fifty years ago.

From the earliest days of the German occupation, there had been executions, and pits had been dug in the great forests east of Riga, especially in the forest of Biķernieki. Was Rumbula situated here, on the edge?

To tell the truth, after our journey had been decided, in the spring of '99, I hadn't bothered to read in more depth. I was gathering my strength for the now inevitable leap over the wall: later I would see, later everything would emerge by itself. And so it was, in effect. Yet the fate that led us to the places of my childhood had a hidden aspect and a firm grip that pushed me, reluctantly, onward.

I had written to some friends that I was getting ready to return to Latvia to say a prayer in the place where the grave of my father should have been. That desire was, however, more a literary artifice than an inner necessity. Hadn't I for my whole life carried in my heart the grave of my father, whose remains, along with those of the uncountable others, had been burned in the immense pyres that were meant to eliminate any trace of the slaughters? Biķernieki and Rumbula were merely names to me, and, I presumed, I would never get there.

I tried instead to live day by day until the inevitable morning of departure. Abandoning every defense, however precarious, I would have to leave home to confront myself in a confused past beyond the barrier of the pages of my autobiography.

Had I had a premonition of this new trip when I ended the book with the words "perpetually revise"?

Meanwhile, I was writing a story that I was enjoying, and I avoided any reflections on the future journey. I put it off, I put it off. Before me were the July days that I would spend with friends for the third time in my beloved retreat in Sardinia. In the half-light after dinner I would go down to the sea that came swishing toward me on the beach with its oblivious nocturnal waves.

One evening my grandson Giacomo comes by to see me; he tells me, in conversation, "Can you believe that last night I thought I saw you on television? They announce a Marina Gersoni and instead there's some unknown character with beautiful eyes."

He didn't say anything else, but it occurred to me that that "unknown character" was not unknown to me. By a curious coincidence she had not only my last name but also my first name. She was a journalist the age of my children; she had been among the contributors to the now long-defunct newspaper *Indipendente*, and that's where I'd noticed her name for the first time. She must now be a contributor to the *Giornale*, because I had been asked if I wrote for that daily. I had never looked into the homonymy; besides, it was obvious that there were still some Gersonis in the world if not in Latvia.

I recalled that my sister at twenty had run into a Kurt Deutsch whose mother was a Gersoni. In the attic in Torre Pellice I had also found a photo of the young man, with the dedication: "To my cousins Sisi and Marina." I had seen him only once or twice, and I hadn't been interested in his ancestry, which, it appeared to me, had nothing to do with Latvia. His relatives had met in Vienna around 1920. Another story. Other wanderings.

When Giacomo left that afternoon, I went to the door with him, returned to the living room, and here, driven by a completely unusual impulse—was the fate with the hidden aspect already driving me forward?—I picked up the phone to ask Information for the number of Marina Gersoni in Milan. I had chosen Milan purely by intuition, given that my homonym wrote for the *Giornale*. I get the number immediately, put down the telephone, take a walk around the room—I hate calling people I don't know and have a hard time doing it—pick up the phone again (it is now seven-thirty), and dial the number. A young, thin, shy voice answers, with a distant sweetness. I say, "I'm Marina Jarre."

At the other end the voice becomes animated.

"I know very well who you are," it says.

"You know," I say, "I wanted to ask you where your surname comes from."

"From," the young voice hesitates, ". . . from Riga."

"My grandfather," I say, "was actually from Libau."

So I had been told. The voice gets excited.

"We're also from Libau!"

She pronounces Libau in the Italian way, with the accent on the last syllable.

We start talking randomly, we're both moved. Among the first names we exchange, I find no known Gersoni, but I discover that Kurt Deutsch is a cousin of her father's. She doesn't know any more than I do about Libau directly; her grandfather Harry was born in Romania. Yet the coincidence is strange; how many Gersonis could there have been in Libau? I cling to our surnames, and the young voice tells me about an article by Isabella Bossi Fedrigotti, who, twelve years ago, reviewed my book *Distant Fathers*. The phrase "magical Latvia" appears in the article's title; I understand that information about Latvia was filtered through more generations to reach the Marina of Milan, and it remained magical for her—a little like my sister's homeland. It's not the one I know. Yet how many Gersonis could there have been in Libau? I still didn't know that, like Riga, the city had prohibited Jews from entering and living there until around the mid-nineteenth century, and that, surely, increased the possibility that it was the same family group.

I don't remember the reason—it seems to me that she was very busy at work—but one Saturday I decided to go to Milan. I would meet another of her relatives; Kurt Deutsch had been admitted to the city's Jewish rest home to convalesce. Maybe he would have more precise information about the family in Libau. In reality it was unlikely—why, in fact, not tell us when Sisi had been friendly with him? But at the moment I didn't think about it; I wanted it at all costs—I suddenly wanted some definite forebears. Actually, no, I wanted some relatives, some living Gersonis.

Waiting for me at the station in Milan is a beautiful girl with blue-green eyes, tall, elegant, with no trace of my dark Gersonis. At her house, looking through the family album, I discover in the face of her sister Amarilli a clear resemblance to my sister Sisi; they are, to tell the truth, the features of Miriam hunted down by the archangel, that is what unites them. The only certain thing is that her ancestors and mine crossed the Red Sea together in the Exodus. How many Miriams must there have been since then?

I also discover that Marina pronounces the hard *G*, preserved by her family with stubborn pride, along with the pride of being Gersonis, and when her father, Guido, calls me months later, I am filled with emotion hearing him say Gersoni on the phone. Yet in their wandering the final *i* has become a *y*. By whom and on what occasion was it transformed? From *i* into *y* or from *y* into *i*? Was it my grandfather Mosè or her grandfather Harry? My grandfather Mosè, who called himself Maurice, or her grandfather Harry, who was certainly born with a different name. Since the end of the preceding century, maybe in the innocent—but they were hardly innocent—worldly attempt to make themselves more accepted, many Jews chose an English name more "elegant" than Herschel or Schlomo. The distant cousin my sister met in the United States was called Percy, the husband of the Swiss cousin Felix, and so on. Only in the next generation did they get to real "Gentile" names. My father was called Sammy.

In Marina's family—she, too, comes from a mixed marriage: her mother is a graceful blue-eyed Lombard—as in mine, the ancestral past is enveloped in heroic legend.

While my grandfather dealt in furs in Siberia to make money and marry his beautiful girl from a good family—

he was poor and, although intelligent, nearly illiterate, said my mother—Marina's great-grandfather, or a brother of his, had actually tried to assassinate the tsar and because of that they'd had to flee to Romania, taking a substantial fortune with them. They were grain merchants.

Marina has on her shelves, in a large, luminous room overflowing with books, a book on the revolutionary Gershuni.

Was he the assassin ancestor? I express some doubts, although I don't know anything. But it seems to me that Gershuni—which, like Gershwin or Gershenzon or Gershonovitz, kept its original *sh* sound—is a variant more common in Russia than in Latvia. As far as I know, the only Latvian Gersoni revolutionary was my hare-brained Papi, who used to tell me about his flight across the Düna with the Reds, who had defended the city in vain when it was attacked by Latvians from the civilian militia and German gangs. He fled in a boat on the river while the bullets whizzed past him. It was 1919. Taking refuge in Soviet Russia, he had worked as a sports instructor to return as soon as possible to, I suppose, a more comfortable life in Riga. The residue of his revolutionary activity, I recall, was a bitter distrust of any nationalist or dictator; he grumbled, without my understanding either the terms or the motives, about Ulmanis, the dictatorial president of the Latvian republic, Mussolini, and the Zionists.

Regarding the Gersony who attempted to assassinate the tsar, I discovered later, in the fall, that at the time of the last (successful) attempt on the life of Alexander II, Marina's great-grandfather Isidoro was ten years old and the Gershuni who was secretly still in Russia at the start of the century was the same age. But precisely as a result of the tsar's assassination, oppressive measures against the Jews were revived, including threats of restricting their assets. Around three hundred thousand emigrated from Russia, among them probably great-grandfather Isidoro—there's more than one Isidoro among the Jews of the time, in the usual attempt to transform the too biblical name Yitzhak—but not my grandfather, who had set up a leather factory in Riga and had married his girl with the chestnut-blond curls, which were passed down from her through me to Pietro and my grandson Daniele.

With Marina and her mother I go to see Kurt. Sitting in a chair, well groomed, an eighty-year-old very similar to the youth of fifty years ago, he doesn't look me in the eye and evades every question—obviously he doesn't recognize me, he saw me maybe a couple of times. At the end, suddenly scrutinizing my face, he murmurs, "Desenzano." Where grandfather Harry had a villa and my sister visited.

But what made me feel most closely related to Marina during our meeting in Milan was the scrap of paper on which she had written the names of her forebears, in a genealogical chart whose head was her ancestor Joseph—pronounced in the English way, but in Courland maybe Jassip or Jazeph—a scrap very like those I write on taking notes while I'm reading, on the first bit of paper that comes to hand. Scraps of paper that seem to be in disarray, random, easy to lose, but which I never lose as I wander from Palestine to the Rhineland, from there to Poland, and flee to Romania, finding them at the right moment. To write, I a book, she an article.

Every so often in the months that preceded my return to Riga I applied myself to deciphering the puzzle of the final *y* of Gersony. In Latvian the *y* doesn't exist and in Russian it has the *u* sound. And is there a *y* in Hebrew? I don't think so.

As for my simple *i*, the people at the center for documentation at the Jewish Museum in Riga doubted that the ending was original. It was an "Italianization," they stated. I protested that my grandfather Mosè had never set foot in Italy and that on my parents' marriage license he was "the witness Gersoni."

The woman who oversaw the rooms in the museum of the Riga ghetto had transcribed the name Gerson in Russian for me: Герсонъ. She knew it well, it was the surname of her mother, who was from Tuckum; in Russian the hard sign at the end could be confused with the *i* of the plural. She had said, lost in thought, "Either it's a mistake in transcription or a name that indicates a family, 'the Gersoni family,' that is a husband, wife, and children, or two brothers with their families."

She had never heard it, either. And yet in the Libau telephone book of 1930 there were still two Gersonis (no Gersony), but in Riga today even the Jews are surprised by my surname; to such a degree had the Gersonis disappeared from the land.

5. Jesus's Pillow

Returning from Rumbula—it was around one o'clock—we stopped at the edge of the city in a small restaurant full of young people eating salads and drinking beer. It was the lunch break, and the small tables were crowded with office workers, students, and laborers, talking and joking; in the din of chatter and laughter I was incapable of uttering a word. Pietro as usual did the ordering, salad and beer for both of us, and for me a dessert as well. He managed to get someone to open a small bathroom, with a floor of worn linoleum, a chipped toilet, a tiny old sink with mismatched taps. The whole place and the fixtures were extremely clean.

I was exhausted, but before returning to the hotel to rest for a while we again passed along Skolas Iela, next to the hotel, where at number 6—I had noted it—the Jewish Museum was situated. I wanted to find out the opening hours. Turning back I read—actually I had already read it—the name of the street on the corner where our hotel was located. It was wide and had a bygone elegance like the others in that neighborhood: Baznicas Iela. *Baznīcas* resembles *basilica*, I thought.

An hour later, on the way to the Jewish community, I looked again at the street name Baznicas and translated it into German for myself: mightn't it be *Kirche*? But we were headed to the museum. It was one of the confused goals that gradually appeared in my mind; Pietro, tireless, forced me to pursue them as soon as I hesitantly mentioned them. At my side, he was not unlike a nurse helping a gravely ill patient. He waited for me even in front of the elevator in the hotel, not wrongly suspecting that, incapable of ringing a doorbell, I wouldn't even be able to press the right buttons.

In the morning he brought me down to breakfast and, taking advantage of my good mood, brought on by the black bread with butter and jam—oh delicious taste of childhood!—made me talk about possible plans for the day. Only the really long—for him, who drove for seven hours—trip to Tallinn was his idea. For the rest he led me in the wanderings that almost by chance—a chance, however, that afterward seemed to me preordained—I chose.

The address of the Jewish Museum was one of two I had written down before leaving (I had also taken the map of the ghetto from Kaufmann's book); I had found it in the book *Baltische Reise* [Baltic Journey], by Verena Dohrn. The second was that of the house where my father had lived in Majori, on the sea, outside Riga. I had got the information from the proceedings of the trial; he had lived there, supported by his parents, with the German Ilse and their child, Irene. I thought it was his last home.

I didn't go there then; as I've said, I gave myself up to the day, one goal was the same as another, the places came to me, it wasn't I who went to them.

In the broad, light-filled entrance hall of the sumptuous

mansion, where painters were working everywhere, a young Russian woman with a round face framed by the window of a wooden porter's booth answered every question with frightened whines and, shaking her head, continued to point to the magnificent staircase that led to the upper floor. She said, "*Musej, musej*," pushing us away with her gesture. It wasn't my Russian that intimidated her (she wasn't even listening), it was having to give information she evidently didn't possess. So we went up, and on the first floor, to the left, entered the rooms of the museum of the ghetto. While Pietro stopped in front of photographs and charts, I hurried to the last room, where books were arrayed, harmlessly, on the shelves. I passed quickly through the other rooms, merely glancing at the dark photographs. I was again unnerved, no, I didn't want to see the alleys of muddy, trampled snow between the wretched shacks; none of the dark bundled figures moving around there could be my father, my handsome father.

Looking sideways I glimpsed a photograph of an enormous open pit, three meters deep, overflowing with extremely thin, naked white bodies. On the edge, Germans in uniform. One of them had taken a picture. The label, merely glanced at, mentioned German Jews, shot in the forest of Biķernieki in 1943.

My handsome father.

In the entrance hall a woman with dark eyes, her sad face marked by suffering and cares, was sitting beside a small table. I spoke to her in German, and she answered me, immediately, in fluent German. I don't remember exactly what I said, but certainly that I was from Riga and my name was Gersoni. She was amazed; she told me about her mother, a Gerson from Tuckum, and transcribed her name in Russian. Of what had become of her mother she didn't say, nor did it occur to me to ask.

I had seen on the shelves some books that interested me, especially one, from the nineteenth century, on the history of the Jews in Latvia by Rabbi Wunderbar. I would have liked to have a copy. I followed the trail of my conjectures about Gersoni/y. The woman pointed out the director's temporary office, on the second floor (they were restoring the entire building); he could give me an answer about that. We found him with no trouble.

Sitting at a desk covered with orderly papers, the man, whose name I forgot to ask, welcomed me very courteously. Having learned my age he congratulated me on my appearance and said he was my contemporary. It was he who claimed that the *i* of Gersoni was Italian. In a jumble of questions and explanations, I spoke, in German, a little about everything. Never about November 30, 1941.

At a certain point he said, "You see, we're speaking German; for us from Courland it's our language."

Thus I learned for the first time that we Gersoni were from Courland, with or without the *i*. We were Curonians. I told him about my Talrose cousins, and he said, "Ah yes, very well-off people." He didn't say if he knew when and how they had died. I named my school and, smiling, he recalled that it had been his sister's school as well. He didn't say if she had survived. Our discussion was accompanied by an implicit understanding, as strong as a close bond of kinship. He asked about Pietro, if he was a grandson; I told him about my four children and he said the Lord had blessed me.

I mentioned the Latvians, their "indifference," I said cautiously. And he, cautiously, told me about his schoolmates "of the time" who had moved up the ladder. They, like him, were sixteen in 1941.

He didn't say anything else, but shrugged his shoulders in a gesture of resignation. I don't think that with that age-old gesture he was alluding to those classmates. He translated into Latvian the name Bienenhof, the area on the opposite shore of the Düna: Bišumuiza. I remembered my grandfather's factory there, on an island. I was elated by the ease of finally speaking with someone, of speaking German, even if it was sometimes incorrect. Meanwhile Pietro, standing behind me, waited content and patient until we had finished.

As for Rabbi Wunderbar's book, the director whose name I forgot to ask—might he have been the historical Margers Vestermanis, cited in *Baltische Reise*, who was among the Jews spared by the Germans and assigned to perform various jobs?—gave me the address of the Latvian National Library, where I would find it, and where, perhaps, a copy could be made.

Leaving, I felt I was departing a place that I had known before and that had welcomed me back. We set out on Elizabetes toward the hotel to get the car and, at the corner of Baznicas Iela, I stopped and looked down the street. To the left, a few blocks away, was the large black building where my grandparents had lived. At 13 Kirchenstrasse. Just as I remembered it: the low, grim entrance, the black stone arch. I had looked for it in vain in the old city, where my memory had placed it, on a dark narrow street among dark houses, also on the left, also at number 13! I think it was the house where my parents lived when they were just married. On their marriage certificate, found in the attic in Torre Pellice, yellowed and dried out by time, and later deciphered with the help of a small German-Latvian dictionary, my father was said to be divorced, occupation merchant, resident of Baznicas Iela 13. My mother, single, *lektrise* at the university, of the Calvinist faith, he Mosaic. As for nationality, she Italian, he žids, Jewish, according to the tsarist definition that was still in use, evidently, in the free Latvian republic in December of 1924.

After Pietro photographed the house—I had had a grandfather I loved and who loved me—we went to get the car, which we had had to park in the hotel garage. It was strictly forbidden to leave it on the street, as we had done when we arrived. A Latvian had stopped to explain to us eloquently in his language that it wasn't possible. The eloquence, not the speech, had persuaded us.

Now that my grandparents' house had appeared to me so simply at 13 Baznicas Iela, the next goal seemed to me not only unattainable but almost pointless. I had deciphered on the map in the phone book a likely Jewish cemetery, the new cemetery—maybe my grandparents, who had died, as far as I knew, in 1940, were buried there. Šmerlis the place was called, in the northern part of the city; Pietro, naturally, intended to get there.

First, in any case, he pushed me relentlessly to visit the nearby National Library, where I didn't get past the entrance. But he didn't insist, he let me do as I pleased; he asked the smiling receptionist—everyone smiled at him—for the email address of the library, and she wrote it for him on a scrap of paper that I brought back to Italy. That first scrap of paper was the inception of this book.

In retrospect, I would have done better to force myself to ask immediately for a copy of the book that Rabbi Wunderbar had published in Mitau, the capital of Courland, in 1853. It was a book I longed to see, but every time I took a step I had to stop and catch my breath.

In fact, as soon as I returned to Turin, the book and Latvia all seemed to plunge, alas, into a black hole in which they got lost. I started out by applying to the National Library in Turin to get a photocopy of the text from a Jewish cultural center in Frankfurt. I had chosen the address myself from a list in German that one of the assistants for borrowing from abroad had brought me as a rare and incomprehensible find. After two months, the National Library let me know, in answer to my requests, that, according to the German center in question, the book couldn't be photocopied. Among other things, the same assistant for borrowing from abroad had advised against asking for photocopies from "those" countries, meaning Russia and its neighbors: it would cost a fortune. The email address was useless, she told me.

After a few attempts that went nowhere, one Sunday morning I managed to enter the Jewish Library of Turin. It hadn't been easy to get in between the many Jewish holidays, the ritual cleanings, the tacit, not ritual but convenient, Christian vacation days. Once I had found a sign announcing that the library was closed; another time a young male voice, with a strongly marked *r*—I don't know whether it was a Piedmontese or Jewish accent—had answered the intercom. The library was closed, he had told me, without giving further explanations or hope for a future opening.

When I finally entered the building annexed to the synagogue, I wandered around and arrived at some offices, not yet the library, which I got to, oh miracle, the next Sunday. I already knew the spacious room in the sub-basement under the beautiful brick vault; I had been there many times and had consulted books there. Also, all our children had gone to the Jewish school, my daughter only for middle school, the boys for nursery and elementary school as well. My husband had at first disapproved of the choice of a private school, but later, realizing the influence of the Roman Catholic Church in public primary school, had agreed with me. We weren't the only ones; other non-Jewish parents of unbaptized children like ours had made the same decision.

So we planted trees in Israel, and our children celebrated Sukkot and Purim. Andrea, the youngest, learned Hebrew and some prayers; today he remembers only the numbers up to twenty and the start of a prayer whose meaning he no longer knows. The rabbi almost never called on him during

Hebrew class, and he came home furious because he would have been able to answer much better than Jonathan, the son of the rabbi himself, but he was "the son of no one" and so wasn't highly regarded.

The school was secular in its own way (thirty years have passed, and I don't know the current situation): the religious teaching, which wasn't obligatory, was the natural core around which the courses unfolded, but there was no religious interference in the content, nothing polemical or provocative.

In elementary school Pietro and Andrea had two teachers who were extraordinary in different ways. Andrea learned to type and to play chess; in second grade, he solved all the math problems up to the fifth-grade level and mastered the binary system. The teacher, Luciana, had her students print a little newspaper; they not only put in their "thoughts" but learned that "we can make newspapers ourselves, and we shouldn't take as gospel truth what we read in them." One day Andrea asked me how the roller was made with which I printed my books. Pietro—even in the uninterrupted din of a class of around fifteen students asking questions, answering, and arguing, with each other and with the teacher, Virginia—learned to read and calculate, history and geography, but also, and especially, to speak to anyone with self-assurance, if somewhat quickly, I suppose to be heard over the noise.

When Luciana, after two years of scoldings and unusual surveillance by the head of the elementary school—"that fascist," said my children—asked for a transfer, the teacher who took her place found Andrea's class (it was third grade) sitting on the floor in a silent sit-in.

At the center of this tiny multicultural world created by students and teachers was the principal of the middle school, Amalia Artom. "The principal said so, too," my children said to assert that a matter really was like that and couldn't be discussed further. If the mathematics teacher was absent from a class, the principal came to fill in. "It's about time!" said my children.

I liked to stop and chat with her. She was tiny, always in a black smock, with dark eyes in a face resembling that of the woman in the museum of the Riga ghetto, marked by suffering and cares yet without that hint of patience and weariness that sweetened the features of the latter. The principal was in fact a rebel. We never spoke about her dead, but about the school, her family, my children. I had once gone to ask about my daughter, more gifted than studious, and she, in a rush of enthusiasm, said, "What a lovely creature, what a lovely creature." She told me once that her husband, who was beloved and esteemed, was a monarchist, and when the royal march was played on the radio he would stand; the two sons, out of respect for their father, also rose, but not her—she was from a socialist family. On a single occasion she alluded to their fate, recalling how devoted her husband was in caring for the children: "Before every outing he checked the brakes on their bicycles. And yet . . . " Here she stopped.

Her brilliant younger son, Ennio, at twenty had stumbled while on a mountain path and plunged to his death. The older son, Emanuele, seized as a partisan by the fascists, had been tortured and killed in Via Asti. The school where she was the principal was named for him.

One of the women caring for her when she was dying said to me, with amazement not free of reproach, "She didn't want to die." I don't know what God she believed in, but certainly she believed firmly in life and in the clear, precise duties of the day.

In my soul that over time became more and more of a harlequin, I didn't feel that frequenting the Jewish world put me in an ambiguous situation. In my mind, I realized that the choice of that school was also a ritual stone; the customs appeared to me a little exotic, but they were almost all happy and festive, and I liked them. Besides, I was grateful for the generous welcome given to my children.

I was speaking of my harlequin soul. What to do about it? From my parents I inherited a reserve regarding any definite, unambiguous religious position: both had had a somehow distant (though it's hard to say if it was conscious) attitude toward the faith of their ancestors. My father was certainly an absolute nonbeliever and in my mother's case the Waldensian "homeland" got on her nerves; she disapproved of "that unbearable chauvinism" in her own father, and sniffed, in her habitual gesture of criticism. With her we never talked about religious matters. As for my Papi, I suppose mainly to irritate his wife, he liked to remind her that we, the two daughters, were Jews. He said it ironically—and here I seem to hear an echo of his voice—reminding her that we had inherited from him an unfortunate if noble problem that she would in no way be able to remedy.

I don't know if he drew on this declaration of our irremediable surname for strength. In fact, we Jews lacked a Jewish mother. The ones over there wouldn't want me. Our mother was not informed of this, and yet, though it was not intentional, she had "remedied" the innate misfortune.

My famous Gersoni, in any case, inspired no impulse of joyous recognition when I managed to penetrate the offices of the Jewish community of Turin. They were very polite, they took note of my rather bizarre request—a book published in Mitau in 1853; Mitau, but where is it?—which I wrote in a message for the director of the library, absent that day, and they advised me to return after Passover. I followed that advice and this time reached the library; here a woman, also very kind, recognized me under the name Jarre and asked about my sister-in-law Paola, her classmate. She wasn't the director, but the director's daughter might be around that day, coming to consult books for her thesis. The daughter had a cousin in Germany; maybe through him my Rabbi Wunderbar could be sought in some library. But . . . but . . . I stammered, wasn't it easier to get it with an official request from one Jewish library to another? Well no, they had no relations with any Jewish library in Germany, assuming there was one. In Turin, besides, the library assistants were volunteers.

The black hole widened, became deeper every day. Had I ever been in Latvia? And did Latvia exist?

Waiting for the girl, I leafed through a volume of the *Encyclopedia Judaica* and found a Gersoni with the *i*, a scholar in Vilnius in the second half of the nineteenth century. When I looked up I saw coming toward me through the big room Daria from my book *Leggero accento straniero* [A Slight Foreign Accent], emerging from its pages:

"She was tall and refined and easy in all her movements, whether she was simply folding her hands in her lap or walking down the street or climbing, as now, the stairs . . . She had high cheekbones, the cheeks growing abruptly thinner near the small round chin, brown eyes with full lids . . . The nose sharp and delicate like a section of almond cut above her beautiful mouth."

This Daria's hair wasn't smooth but fell in small, thick golden-brown curls around her beautiful face.

We talked—the cousin was no longer in Germany, her mother was away—but I didn't pay much attention to what she said. I looked at her and wondered: How was it possible that I had imagined her twenty years before she was born? My wonder was such that I was completely diverted from my research; we talked, we found that we both objected to the fact that in Italy attention was given so exclusively to the subject of Auschwitz that the totality of the Shoah was relegated to the background. I no longer remember the subject of this girl Daniela's thesis, but I know that it seemed interesting. All this was the surface: in my depths I was immersed in my past, in what had led me, between 1960 and 1965, to write the book from whose pages my Daria had miraculously stepped, alive.

And I thought: Ritual stones, what else ties me to them, to this room? Certainly not the line marked with an uncertain hand—the last cry for help—under my father's "Remember that you, too, are Jewish." He's not enough to make me Jewish, even if, nonbeliever though he was, he was killed as a Jew. My grandfather Maurice, who loved me, is not enough.

I'm doubly orphaned, of my father and of that monstrous number that doesn't belong to the world of humans, that has spread beyond history, crossed its borders, and there's no point trying to confine it within names, dates, places.

Which makes even me anonymous.

My Roman Catholic sister-in-law, who lived in this neighborhood, is a closer relative of her schoolmates and neighbors, sharing roots and common experiences, than I am, in my multicolored rags.

Sometimes momentary flashes that don't seem to refer to anything I've actually experienced are kindled in my memory. They go back, I say to myself, to my earlier lives.

> And so, up there, in that house, I seem to see a small window that casts a reddish light in the night. I can't see the outline of the house, only the reflection of a lamp placed in the room.
>
> I'm a Palestinian shepherd near Jerusalem, whether Jew or Gentile I have no idea. It's the days before Passover, I've guided my sheep to the sheepfold, and now, at sunset, I'm sitting behind a blackberry hedge. I'm looking up at a small window in a building that's

not very tall, but I'm in a valley and so the window at the top of the slope appears far above me.

They've told me that the rabbi of Nazareth is there with his companions. They're all men. They're having dinner, and in the room you can see the light of the lamp flicker. It's the evening breeze or the shadow of a passing figure, just glimpsed.

So there is the rabbi of Nazareth, the one who arrived a few days ago, and a lot of people went to see him and said he was riding an ass, and someone threw wildflowers at him. Some say that he performs miracles, heals wounds. But some say that his companions grumble about the Romans and their taxes, and that too many are listening to them. There are always people who listen to those who grumble about the Romans. One mustn't be caught by the soldiers or even the priests, who don't want trouble. But he, they say, speaks even against the priests. There are some who have touched his garment and felt cleansed of all suffering, but there are some who say he has a mean, unsmiling face, and they don't understand him when he speaks. Some swear he's Elijah who has returned, but others that he can give orders to evil spirits who obey him because he's their master. He's followed by good-for-nothings and beggars and some prostitutes, who, of course, seek clients everywhere, even among the beggars.

I stare at the unsteady reddish light flickering in the room up there open to the evening breeze and realize I'm curious; I'd like to know what that rabbi is like. I also feel some fear. I wasn't there when he entered the city on the ass; I was still in the fields with my flocks. I'd like to run away, but I can't stop looking. What are they doing up there, while they're having supper and one of the men at the table maybe shifts the lamp so the light falls more brightly on the rabbi of Nazareth, who is speaking?

One of my characters, Francesca, in *Un altro pezzo di mondo* [Another Piece of the World], after hearing the Gospel of Mark read several times, becomes convinced that Jesus truly existed and that that is what counts above any later argument about doctrine.

I, too, reread Mark every so often. In fact I read the whole book in one sitting, mingling with the small crowd that is following Jesus from village to village, anxious to touch him or fearful of having to stare him in the face. I can't stare him in the face.

Mark is an anguished, dark gospel; from the start it foretells through signs the death of the bridegroom, who for a brief moment will give us the privilege of his presence.

It is illuminated with a dazzling yet terrible light only in the vision on the mountaintop, when Jesus, talking to Elijah and Moses, is transfigured. He never seems to be still except when we see him sleeping on a pillow in the stern of the boat on the lake—the Sea of Galilee—which is turning stormy. Otherwise, driven by a prophetic and conscious melancholy, he wanders through Palestine and beyond, along with disciples who don't understand him but can't help following. He has to teach them like children, using stories, and is constantly reminding them not to talk about the miracles he's performing. Peter sometimes takes him aside, even rebukes him, and only Peter himself can remember this. Later he describes these incidents to the man who will write the Gospel.

I'm sitting in the church, like the shepherd who watched the light move in the window. I believe in him, the rabbi of Nazareth, so deeply that I'm afraid of him. Maybe I went as far as Golgotha, but I kept my distance, hidden in the crowd; I glimpsed the three crosses and heard a cry pierce the darkening air, but I couldn't understand the words.

So I'm sitting in church, it's a Waldensian church, I'm a proto-Christian, and I'm listening to the pastor read the Credo. Returning to the original version, he now reads, "I believe in the Catholic Church," and I perceive my *barbetti*, the Waldensians, shudder in silence; the word is still hostile. Besides, I, too, shudder, having inherited a little of my grandfather's chauvinism. I realize that I am in fact a proto-Christian (and, what's more, scarcely that), but I feel at ease; I could, so to speak, unwind completely, expose myself, and, perhaps, my *barbetti* would accept me, heterodox as I am. I could confess to them that I don't believe in a unique revelation, that I don't believe the Messiah of the Jews will ever come, and, as for the young Joshua, I dare to approach him only when I see him sleeping, exhausted from his frantic run, driven by divine command. Could I tell them? Could I?

6. Objects

The map in the telephone book said, "*Jaun ebreju kapi.*" The word *jaun*, I learned, goes back to the obvious Indo-European root of *young*, and in Latvian also means "new." The *u* must be the ending of the genitive plural, and *kapi* can be understood from the crosses on the map; it's "cemetery." Thus: "the new cemetery of the Jews." North of Riga, in Šmerlis, just past the thin dark line indicating a railway.

We have no trouble getting there, and Pietro parks near the entrance, a broad gateway in a crumbling wall. On the other side black treetops rise against the cloudy sky. The place is isolated, there are no houses around. When we enter, we're alone. To the left, a long pale-gray single-story building, covered with pink flowering vines. The wooden door is ajar, a window has café curtains. A short distance ahead are three stele. We'll look at them more closely when we leave. There's a profound silence in the twilight air darkened by the tall, damp black trees that arch over the whole cemetery. The same dampness spreads everywhere.

I said to Pietro that the graves of my grandparents must be there—but where? It doesn't even occur to me to look for the custodian in the long flaking building—another bell to ring. I will find out later, months later, that there are no records before 1951. I no longer recall from whom, but surely from my mother, I learned that my grandparents died in 1940. My father had time to inherit the leather factory and sell it to his own very wealthy nephew Benno, to perhaps pay some debts, and squander the rest. Or he needed it to take care of himself. In the last letter he said he was ill; he had had an operation for a melanoma in 1934.

No one had been buried in the old Jewish cemetery in the Moscow suburb, south of the city, for many years before the war. Because—probably by chance—it was included within the ghetto set up by the Germans, it was put to use again, and those murdered in the ghetto on Sunday, November 30, 1941, were transported there. Once it was in use, pits were dug continually.

For three nights in a row in the spring of '42 the Germans blew up graves in order to get more space deep down. The survivors in the "small" ghetto, awakened by the reverberations of the detonations, listened in the dark to the explosions that were exhuming their past—since 1725 the community had rented the land outside the city walls from the senators—and in the end destroyed it.

Entering the cemetery of Šmerlis, Pietro and I separated; he went to the right, I to the left. It must have been the late hour, the drizzly day, the dark shadow of the big trees, but the "young" Jewish cemetery had a very old and eroded aspect. Few of the tombs had visible writing in Hebrew, most were covered by brambles and ivy; some, encircled by a low hedge, had a bench. On many I read the epitaphs of

Jews who had arrived from the Soviet Union after the war. I saw an upright stone that bore, in Latin letters, on one side the names of a couple who had died in the seventies, on the other a short surname—Gez, Bok, I don't recall—crudely carved in small, crooked letters in the stone and next to it an impossible date: XII 1941. How could a body have been brought here from the ghetto or from the forest? And, if the death was secret, how could the body have been buried without anyone noticing? Who would have dared to give a Jew burial? And yet the writing incised by an inexpert hand revealed an anomalous event. A votive inscription, a gesture of remembrance?

When we met again at the entrance, Pietro said he had seen some dates from '41, from the spring, of course; none from '40.

I didn't particularly regret not finding my grandparents' grave. In truth, walking along the dirt paths covered with rotting autumn leaves under bare branches that seemed sodden with repressed tears, I had thought about them in a vague way, absorbed in a mourning not very different from the formless grief I'd devoted over the years to unknown people like these, hidden by brambles and ivy.

More than anything, oppressed by the neglect of the place, I had wondered why in the world I was walking aimlessly like that among the graves, randomly reading names and names, only names.

The neglect of this "new Jewish cemetery," under the ancient trees with the bent, tearful tops, was very different from the brazen, deliberate abandonment of the Waldensian cemetery in Torre Pellice, where during my adolescence my grandmother, heedless of my fear, sometimes brought me to walk. In cheerful and somewhat gossipy chatter she described the lives of those who were buried here and there. The ostentatious negligence would be the usual useless lesson for the *catholiques*. In a warning from the Waldensian synod in the eighteenth century we read, "For heaven's sake there's no need to overdo it, with the cows grazing right on the graves." Then, the cemeteries of the *barbetti* didn't have fences, thanks to one of the many persecutions of the papists. I suppose that today people in the valleys have given up trying to convert them; maybe, besides the flowers, there might even be a photograph on some of the Waldensian graves.

Here in Riga, among the overgrown hedges, very few benches offered a resting place for a reassuring conversation with the deceased. The dead of 1941 hadn't been buried there, and, besides, how many of their relatives had been left to weep for them?

But finally in 1996 someone had come into free Latvia, and had had the three stele installed at the entrance, each of which bore a date: December 6, 7, 11, 1941.

The inscriptions were in Latvian, the term *National Socialism* could be distinguished in a different form depending on the case; I reconstructed the number *tukstos*, a thousand. Pietro photographed all three stones and, having noted on one the name Gerson, but not as a surname, turned around and also photographed the wording on the back:

"On 7/12/1941 around a thousand Jews"—*jüdische Menschen* in German; *Menschen,* human beings—"were deported from Cologne to the Riga ghetto. They lived all together until 1943. Among them were Gerson Ungar and Martha and Heinrich Stern. Mass graves remember them."

And below, listed: Köln, Siegburg, Bornheim, Rosbach, Rheidt, Euskirchen.

On another stele: Bielefeld, Münster, Osnabrück.

On top were the memory stones.

I don't know where the custom of leaving stones or pebbles on Jewish tombs comes from, but I imagine from a remote era, when the Jews, wandering in the desert on the way to the Promised Land, covered with stones the sandy graves of those who died along the way.

A small stone, the humblest symbol, which in itself has no value, since affection has value only as long as it remains among the living. Theirs is the task of perpetuating that affection.

That alone is the link I can imagine between the deliberate neglect of cemeteries by my Waldensian fathers—they, too, handed down to their children the task of enduring—and the funerary restraint of my Jewish fathers.

As for what is every so often called "the Waldensian ghetto," I find the expression unsuitable. It bears no resemblance to the ghetto in which the descendants of Gershon lived for centuries.

Although my maternal forebears were shut up like plague victims in their valleys, they were free to wander on the peaks, to hunt chamois, to let their voices echo to the skies, to hand down from father to son a piece of land and a roof. If they were then driven from that piece of land and from under that roof—my Waldensian fathers and my Jewish fathers had the same ancient enemy, yes, and, at least in part, the same "book" they remained faithful to—the survivors of the slaughters returned stubbornly to take them back. Forbidden to use weapons, they fabricated a great billhook that at the right moment, instead of cleaning out weeds and brush, smashed heads. When the time came for weapons, someone more obstinate and bolder devised a harquebus, whose barrel was long enough, when supported on a wall, to hit ignorant papists, busy at the market in the village below.

In calamitous times, let's face it, the object they held most dear was the harquebus.

My Waldensian fathers were so settled in the fields of their valleys that they claimed to have received the good news directly from the apostles, one of whom had chanced to come up there and warm his feet at a hearth in Angrogna.

Even when the Catholic Marchese Rorengo—who wasn't wrong this time?—fought on the street with the shepherd Gilles, shouting that the claim was impossible, and angrily threw his plumed hat on the ground, those shepherds stuck with their convictions.

By tradition rather than by nature, they themselves, with strong, capable hands, fashioned objects for work in the vineyards and on the farms, for harvesting grapes, figs, chestnuts, for transporting milk, hay, rye, wood. At home the women wove hemp and wool, and maybe one of them, with the proceeds from the eggs, managed to buy at the market a bright-colored head scarf, which, however, was criticized in church the next Sunday.

My Waldensian fathers didn't find the joy in the not immediately useful objects that my mother, although she was their daughter, found to the highest degree: a hat, an ancient cup, a small church on the banks of the Arno. Joy, in fact, not only in the possession of these objects but also in the contemplation of them. Since she had had to abandon in her husband's house, when she left him, her own very beautiful Russian silver, she had bought it back piece by piece and carried it with her when she fled Latvia on a false Italian passport before the arrival of the Soviets in 1940. From her it was passed on to my sister, and from her to my children. As for what remained in Riga, my father, I assume, spent it, along with the diamond ring that in their last furious fight she—so she told me—threw in his face.

My father lived day by day, enjoying like a gypsy what the day itself offered, heedless of preserving and caring for anything. He liked to give grandiose presents—and, certainly, the ring, which could have been used to pay for our studies until we got our university degrees, was undeniably magnificent—I've already written about the enormous white felt rabbits he brought us after discovering us in our hiding place at Waltershof. Some months had passed since that December morning when we left home to join Mamma.

Likewise, I've written about the immense doll—just one, bought by chance and given by chance—that I couldn't play with. In his last visit to Torre Pellice he gave the two of us a camera, to each of us a pen, and to me a large watch that was incongruously heavy on my child's wrist.

Saying "I've written" and writing now, I'm aware of a distance different from the one that separated my writing from myself in *Distant Fathers*. Then I intended to portray very small, fragmented events as my child's gaze had observed them. Now, returning from Riga, having breached the wall that separated me so long from the child I was, I have to reflect as an old woman on what happened.

Just the other day, almost a year after the journey to Latvia, I suddenly thought that some of our nice games or elegant clothes might have been handed down to little Irene, although she was only two when, because of a bankruptcy, our father sold the furnishings of the place where we had lived with him.

Who knows, I thought, maybe Irene had even played with my porcelain dolls' tea set, which I missed so much that I lost any real interest in objects. That interest is reawakened only in sporadic and thus uncontrollable jolts, and, since I am no longer the mistress of a house, is in general nearly spent; I've returned now to the useful objects of my maternal grandparents.

I wouldn't know whether this intense longing contained an inadmissible regret for the life I'd left behind. When we joined Mamma that December morning, carrying with us only our schoolbags, she made us put on new winter shoes, suitable for our destination in the countryside. Afterward everything was, necessarily, new.

Only recently did it occur to me, in my fantasies, that Irene's mother, living at Majori with my father and their daughter, had herself thought of saving our things or our clothes. Not him, I don't think it's possible. And while I imagined the child Irene playing with my porcelain dolls' cups, I was suddenly pervaded by the sensation that she was in the room beside me, that I was hugging her, and that touching her, I recognized her. My heart gave her the name that I had already given her in writing or speech. My little sister with the face of Sisi, now also dead. Mysterious mediation of objects, which sometimes seem to shed a material force of their own, transmitting the living warmth of a hand from us to others, from others to us.

My little sister, who looked so much like her father—our father—that her mother hadn't had the courage to take her to Germany when, in 1939, obeying Hitler's summons, she left Latvia with the other Baltic Germans. Among them were more than a few Nazis, and many knew who the illegitimate father of the child was. They could have informed on her; *Rassenschande* ("race defilement") would have been the charge.

Schwester Ilse (she was a nurse whom my father had met in the clinic where he'd had his surgery), according to what I learned from one of my mother's "German" letters, had married in Germany after the war. Scattered in what they called their "exile," the Baltic Germans passed around any news that had to do with their community.

After our return to the hotel from Šmerlis, and before going out again to dinner, I look from the window of my room, on the sixth floor, onto the street that—I realize—is Baznicas Iela. And I see, exactly at the point where the street is hidden by other buildings on the right, the long, straight, black edge of the corner of number 13, where my grandparents' apartment was. It's a dark strip, an object, not a house, the only object, I tell myself, that I've found in Riga.

But I didn't come, I repeat to myself, in search of people or things; I came with no agenda, awaiting day by day what fate offered me along the thread of the few places I was able to retrace. Without intentions, flushed out of my interior hiding place by my son's decision.

When, in Turin, I awaken in my silent room, emerging from the noise of the dreamed voices of my dead, I realize that in fact I am retreating further and further toward an inner refuge that, during the return to Latvia, disappeared, annulled by the effort made to face reality. And yet—I consider—I had to be very practical; I raised children, I cooked, I pruned plants, I ironed shirts, an incredible number of shirts. I held objects and used them. Would I still have been able to do all this without the consolation of my fantasies?

Fate had forced my Jewish fathers into narrow spaces; there are cities in Europe where the ghetto was only one street. Ebreju Iela it's called in Riga, for example: the street in the Moscow suburb where the hovels of those who until the mid-nineteenth century couldn't go into the city, except with a temporary authorization from the senate, were situated. Within the walls lived a mere fourteen wealthy families of *Schutzjuden*, privileged people who had permanent permission. The original name of the street that led to the old cemetery has been only recently restored; under the Soviet occupation there were officially no Jews and officially no massacres of Jews.

We didn't walk around the Moscow suburb; we passed through it in the car several times, and Pietro recognized one of the places he'd seen in a photograph in the museum, probably a corner in the "small" ghetto. I wasn't interested in visiting those places. I still had no idea where my father had spent the last days of his life—the "big" Jewish ghetto in Riga lasted thirty-seven days—nor did I think I ever would know.

My grandparents—and even my great-grandparents—didn't live segregated lives. I knew the address of their first house, next to the factory. Pietro and I looked for it on an island that, in my memory, you reached by a wooden bridge: I remember the dull thud under the tires as we drove across it. Anyway, I discovered that not only the island was called Bišumuiza but the entire neighborhood along the shore. All we found there was a mass of ruins, no wooden bridge over a canal or branch of the river. And according to the phone book, printed in three languages—Latvian, Russian, English—there were no leather factories in the city.

From the other bank, I saw at the edge of the old city along the river an immense building that disfigured the view amid the steeples of the old churches. The usual Soviet monstrosity, not unlike the enormous Orthodox church built at the highest point in medieval Tallinn in the late nineteenth century, also a symbol of the Russian empire's arrogance.

"Someone should take up a collection in Europe to knock it down," I had said to Pietro.

Countless times my ancestors, on some narrow Jewish street, lost objects that for centuries must have been merely useful, but, as soon as the news spread that there would be a pogrom, it was pointless to hide even these objects. The *pogromšiki*, informed by their people in the police or the administrative offices, prepared bags, baskets, knives in order to carry them off. And the inhabitants of the wretched huts, mutilated, cut to pieces, and burned in the fury of the voracious, drunken multitude, became objects themselves, not useful, however, and not usable. The sacred scrolls were torn, reduced to ashes, trampled in the mud. Not all of them; it's likely that there was always someone who managed to save a part, to re-establish the rites, if only in a wooden hut under a straw roof and paying the duty levied on wax candles.

My father was nineteen when, in the turbulent year 1905—it was October—there was again a pogrom in tsarist Riga. Followers of an ultra-nationalist Russian group prophetically called the Black Hundreds, along with a rabble from the slums armed with clubs and axes, left the Orthodox church of the neighborhood carrying portraits of the tsar and poured into Ebreju Iela, the poor against those who were a little less poor. Shooting, the Cossacks dispersed the Latvian workers and the Jews who rushed to their defense.

At that point, however, the Jews had been out of the ghetto for more than fifty years; they had reached the point where they could eat food that was not the daily half kilo of bread, salted herring, and four onions; they finally possessed furniture, synagogues, ritual baths, and objects they could love and even accumulate.

And yet instilled in them by now was the instinct to reduce the object in order to more easily hide it, the instinct even to make it abstract. They calculated and calculated, this one owes me so much and that other even more; what was owed was concealed in their head, if it hadn't already become money, sewn into the hem of a ragged garment that wouldn't tempt anyone. An appearance that was only imagined, the image before the money itself, the sole guarantee of escape.

But how to endure the walls, the gray muddy street, the gates, the sudden insult, the fear for the children that kept you awake, listening in the darkness to the approach of drunken voices and the tramping of many feet? Only by imagining in the heavens not the Messiah—the Anointed of the Lord, He who waits in Jerusalem, the city invoked every year at Passover—but yourself flying away from the ghetto, over the walls and roofs of the hovels. In light and colored flight toward a finally secure refuge. Again, the fantasy of flight was, like a real object, only in the mind: the business deal that gave you enough money to embark on the ship, the lucky encounter with the stupid cop or the stupid peasant, the message from that uncle in the Americas who hadn't been heard from since his departure.

Therefore—and my understanding comes so late—my father had sent the letter of July 1941 to his daughters in Italy. In the Baltic country a beautiful warm, sunny July preceded a frigid autumn and winter. As early as October it snowed on the last leaves.

The night of Monday, June 30, had been silent in Riga, and in the early hours the lumbering rumble of the Soviet tanks that had remained to protect the retreat could be heard as they left the city. From behind half-closed windows Soviet soldiers on the run could be glimpsed in the gray of the summer night, rushing through the streets and occasionally looking up, fearful of a shot from a roof or an attic.

In the preceding days the city had been bombed and shelled by the Germans, and the highest steeple, with the weathercock, had fallen off the Petrikirche, while the bridges over the Düna had been blown up by the Soviets. The morning of June 29th two exceptionally long trains had left the central station in Riga, one filled with wounded soldiers, the other overflowing with refugees. The families and employees of the Russian occupiers had already been evacuated.

On June 27th, in a message that turned out to be the final one, the commanding officer, General Savronov, had communicated by radio that a group of Latvians had been shot, among them the son of ex-president Ulmanis's right-hand man, an unknown Russian, and a Jew. Guilty of collusion with the enemy. Identified and killed according to the same ruthless, haphazard criteria that had dictated the lists of Latvians—men, women, children—deported in trucks and cattle cars as "capitalists" two weeks earlier. Of the fifteen thousand expelled to Siberia, five thousand were Jews; for more than a few of these, deportation was relatively good luck.

On Tuesday, July 1st, the German troops, orderly and elegant, entered a jubilant Riga, decked with Latvian flags; from the windows, open wide to the sun, came the notes of the national anthem, which the radio was playing for the first time in a year. *Dievs sveti Latviju*, God save Latvia, sang the crowd dressed in their Sunday best, with no suspicion that from that day on the anthem would be banned.

SS-Brigadeführer Walter Stahlecker, commander of the SD (*Sicherheitsdienst*), the intelligence agency (literally, "security service") of Einsatzgruppe A, had just been installed at police headquarters when the Latvian fascists of the Pērkonkrusts ("thunder cross," the swastika) and the paramilitaries of the Aizsargi ("protectors"—of the country, obviously) came out of their hiding places, where they had been lying in wait during the Soviet occupation. They distributed weapons and armbands with the Latvian colors—garnet red and white—to volunteers, students, whatever lowlifes showed up (they themselves were only a few hundred), and they got to work. The century was suddenly turned upside down: the Jews lost face, name, career, profession, kin—they were no longer anything but Jews. The commanding officer, a general in the Wehrmacht, signed the first anti-Jewish edict: the requirement to wear the yellow star; gradually others came, bans on walking on sidewalks, lining up in front of shops, using public transportation.

My father, evidently, couldn't flee; perhaps he had no money, and he had his daughter with him. Besides, in the general uncertainty, the majority of Jews had remained. The river of refugees arriving on foot, in horse-drawn carts, on bicycles had not succeeded in passing all the checkpoints along the Soviet border. At more than one place they had been turned back.

When, on July 2nd, use of the telephone was suspended, news was transmitted of suffering upon suffering, and all testimony shattered into harrowing personal experiences. Impossible to understand or predict from what direction the danger would arrive. Besides, no one—not even the Latvians—knew what was being decided high up. The Germans, as usual, maintained absolute secrecy, so much so that no written order or report of any meeting has come down to us. The fact that Stahlecker had established himself at police headquarters leaked out only gradually. Events occurred as if hurled onto the heads of the doomed by the lightning bolt of an unknown and inscrutable god.

"We were afraid to raise our heads, to open our eyes, to breathe," Ida Bocian testifies on December 15, 1969, in the trial of Erhart Grauel, at the court in Hannover.

I don't know what my father could find out; I don't even know how long he stayed outside Riga or if he returned to find shelter with a relative. Certainly, he was informed immediately that on July 4th the big synagogue on Gogol Iela had been set on fire, and also that young Latvians in civilian clothes, with the red-and-white armbands, obeying undisclosed orders, entered homes, guns leveled, and dragged Jews to police headquarters, at first seizing them randomly, often on the street, and later making arrests—of men, for the most part—according to a plan, and also according to information given by those who wanted a house, a shop, revenge.

The Latvians knew them all, their Jews, knew them individually, knew their houses, their shops, their businesses, their factories, hospitals, schools, community centers, synagogues, cemetery.

I don't know if my father listened to the radio or read the papers that, in German, Latvian, Russian (the last published by the resurgent Blacks, of the Black Hundreds), called for hunting Jews, first merely hinting, then louder and louder. But certainly one of those flyers, which attributed responsibility for the many executions carried out by the Soviets on the eve of their departure to the Jews—Bolsheviks all!—had fallen into his hands or he saw it pasted to a wall. The Germans immediately made this into widespread propaganda, with photographs and documents showing the decaying corpses exhumed by relatives and the police.

In the meantime officers of the Wehrmacht, the SD, and the Gestapo furnished the apartments; informers had indicated the wealthiest houses, where they would find furniture, carpets, fittings. A Jewish work force, provided it was strong or expert, came from all over, gratis. In the complete vacuum of local power, the Germans were the masters; sometimes the intervention of a simple German soldier was enough to orient a situation toward life or death.

The number of the incarcerated grew daily. The Zentralka, the central prison, was soon overflowing. Mocked, beaten, tortured, and then killed. Thrown off the trams, expelled from the hospitals, driven out, if recognized, from the lines in front of the grocery stores. The few survivors, in their depositions at the trials and in their memories, appear to have been more stunned by the unexpected rancor of their fellow citizens than by the treatment inflicted by the German occupiers.

I don't know if something, anything, happened to my father. Although aged and perhaps bent and in bad shape, he was very recognizable in his resemblance to a great Oriental prince.

The cousin writes, "If the Latvians hadn't offered their services as executioners, the situation wouldn't have become so terrible."

The first perpetrators were, in fact, Latvian fascists and troublemakers, but without a doubt there were, here and there, episodes of hostility in which ordinary citizens took part. And it's understandable how at first such episodes astonished the victims almost more than the anti-Jewish measures imposed by the Germans. In the testimony of the survivors, the Latvians are cited more frequently than the Germans. Were they not their neighbors, the dairymaid who provided their milk every morning, the porter who handed them the mail, the classmate? They couldn't tell if the men who broke down the door in the night to carry someone off were from the Pērkonkrusts or the Aizsargi or the Latvian SD—for the survivors, they were Latvians period.

It's reasonable to assume that all these interventions, subtly incited, would have served, on the one hand, as a pretense to indicate that there was a vast, spontaneous anti-Jewish insurgency (which there wasn't), and, on the other, would have provoked possible episodes of intolerance among the population; how many saw the synagogues burning on July 4th and basically weren't more than a little surprised!

There was in general a widespread passivity, even among the Jews, who felt caught in a trap; they expected harassment, destruction, and, alas, killings, but they certainly weren't able to imagine the scale of the tragedy that followed.

The Latvians said later that what would happen so soon couldn't have been predicted. Yet they seem to have been sufficiently resigned to accept the increasing wave of persecutions, which became harsher and more systematic by the day.

The naval officer Reinhard Wiener, stationed in Libau (Liepaja), testified, also at the trial of Grauel, that he had counted two hundred spectators at an execution of Jews on July 21st. He secretly filmed it, making a short documentary.

Certainly more than one inhabitant of Riga saw the Aizsargi, led by the lawyer Viktors Arājs, leaving for the countryside in a couple of blue city buses; they were responsible for the majority of killings outside the city. The executions usually took place after the inhabitants of the towns and villages were forced to shut themselves up in their houses. From the nearby forests the sound of the shots reached them. Not all of Latvia was densely populated by Jews; where there were only a few families, the local police assembled them and transferred them to a single center, to simplify the slaughter. In some places the police themselves took part.

Wolfgang Janiko, who served on the General Staff of the 281st division in Rositten (Rezkike), testified that he was present at a mass execution of Jews. The slaughter went on for several days, and after a soldier was discovered taking photographs, the German troops were forbidden to be present at the site. Thus, news of the provincial massacres couldn't reach the capital right away. And yet at the end of August the extermination in the countryside was nearly complete.

In the city, meanwhile, there was starting to be talk of mass graves in the forest of Biķernieki. News spread of the first suicides. So my father, who, unlike many, saw what was ahead, wrote to his daughters. Since he wasn't allowed to send mail abroad—martial law was in force in Latvia—he probably found a German soldier who was going on leave, the cousin suggests, to whom, speaking his perfect German, he could entrust the letter. She herself had been unable to communicate with her relatives in Switzerland, who for years believed she was dead.

In early August, Stahlecker, while he methodically continued the cataloguing of the Jews, judged that the time was right to start a more coordinated and incisive action in Riga. The Latvians, he complained, were too slow at killing: only three hundred a day in Rositten. Also, they drank and, afterward, talked. Wouldn't it be better to eliminate them as well, in the end?

Immediately, at the start of the German occupation, by order of the commander-in-chief of the Wehrmacht, my Jewish father was required to wear the yellow star; someone sewed it onto little Irene's shirt. The same order prohibited my Jewish father from walking on the sidewalk; he had to walk in the adjoining ditch, and he was forbidden to enter parks and public baths and was assigned a ration that was half the already meager amount provided for Aryan Latvians. Since a Jew had to be recognizable from behind, too, my Jewish father had a second star pinned to the middle of his back, and one was also attached to Irene's tiny back. She was six, and would not get to be seven.

In his mind, nonetheless, the extreme fantasy of salvation whirled, the same that had made his forebears, who were also mine, flee the ghetto. He had someone outside the walls, free. His daughters—I was sixteen, my sister fifteen—would help him. He would warn them of the danger—not in a clear way, no, the letter had to pass more than one censor, but underlining only the fateful words that would summon them to solidarity. For him there was a chink in the walls that would be a way out.

Maybe it seemed impossible to him that we had not caught even a whiff of the terrible tragedy that had befallen the Jews of the East, but could he really imagine that we, very young, poor, half Jewish, could get help for him through

Europe overwhelmed by the war? For a long time I couldn't believe that he had really deluded himself with that hope. But I was reasoning like someone who had never lost her own face and her own name—I reasoned, in short, and was unable to understand the stunned delirium of absolute impotence in which he clung to the ancestral dream.

How many times, if I think about it, had he pondered in his savage mind the good deal that seldom worked out for him, the vendetta that turned against him, the betrayal that, after it was carried out, left him alone. The women he had loved passionately and who had passionately loved him had finally abandoned him. Wrapped up in his eccentric calculations, how many times had he been strangled by those same calculations!

Nothing gives me the sensation of that precarious and intense vitality of his, of his indomitable desire to live and enjoy, as much as klezmer music. It consumes and torments with an unrestrained, impetuous joy in the present day, a joy that won't reach tomorrow because it doesn't know what the next day holds. Or intuits it and fends it off by singing. It's music that doesn't belong to my childhood world; to that, instead, belong the lieder of Schubert and the chorales of Luther. Yiddish, which I can barely decipher, sounds horrible and alien to my German ears; my grandparents spoke German to each other, very occasionally resorting to some Yiddish term so that we wouldn't understand.

Nevertheless, from those notes, at once wild and sad, and from those mangled words, my father's message, at the time not understood, reaches me, repeats itself, and floods me with grief.

At the airport, leaving Riga, I stopped suddenly in front of a shop window displaying some amber jewelry. At home I had a long, splendid amber necklace that my husband had brought me from Russia, and in summer I often wear a choker made of the amber beads remaining from a large necklace my mother gave me, most of which, through my neglect, was lost. I like necklaces; they're among the little jewelry I wear.

Walking through Riga we had seen in the jewelry stores of the old city amber necklaces of every type, every gradation: transparent, luminous, like the splinters of amber that on summer evenings at sunset Sisi and I collected on the beach amid the black debris that came from the sea. Those were yellow amber, the amber of my mother's necklace; she herself had taught me that it was "antique," and more precious. I had looked at them all through the distant eye with which, before Christmas, I consider the oppressive quantity of gifts destined for the greedy consumption of the celebration. Getting older, I indulge in small senile avarices despite widespread waste: as if we were living in the time of my grandparents' youth, I gladly turn off the lights going from one room to another, I seldom use the electric heater, I save any leftovers, I try never to throw away bread—good Lord!—and I don't take a taxi unless I'm really forced to. I've always been miserly about paper (I couldn't live without it) and I try to keep my grandchildren from wasting it.

Yet if a fit of acquisitiveness seizes me—and it can happen with shoes, necklaces, and plants—all my wisdom abandons me. So it abandoned me in Riga when I was faced with a necklace of pale-yellow amber, perfect, clasped by a medallion in a nineteenth-century oval silver frame, and a bracelet with the same medallion. Pietro was surprised by my sudden request: he had the credit card; I don't have one because of the stinginess I just mentioned. Besides, fewer financial documents, less annoyance. I justified myself:

"I'll give the bracelet to Laura."

Once in Turin I kept the necklace hidden away in its case—I gave the bracelet to my daughter, promising her the necklace post mortem—and I didn't look at it until the following summer. Then I put it on to go to Torre Pellice, where, during the synod, a small "women's archive" was inaugurated. Among other women, I was scheduled to speak briefly. A friend noticed my necklace and asked if it was a family heirloom. I didn't deny it, I said, "It comes from Riga," and I couldn't explain further.

7. Courland

The winter began with storms, with rain and wet snow, while the war dissolved into itself. Had it happened just recently? Had it happened three hundred years earlier? No one talks about that here. A war ended, crumbled like a rotted vessel falling from the hands of fate.

But no one talks about the war here, here we talk about human beings: about Friedrich Ramm and about his wife, who flourished in secret stillness; life led them to live and to die according to what had been fated for them.

The shards of the Great War tumbled through the world, rubble covered fields brimming with hope; the German troops retreated from the Baltic lands.

They hastened toward their homeland and didn't turn back. They marched in groups large and small, some scattering, others in martial order, but all in a hurry, driven by a single desire. On their wretched, painful path they obeyed this desire like a command; it was the only one they knew.

They saw ahead what belonged to them: a house, a woman, children, and life. What they left behind didn't matter.

Their march was difficult; dangers pursued them, preceded them, and attacked on their flanks. The German frontier was still distant, their nostalgic longings barely reached it. The Russians were behind them and threatened on their sides. Insurgents were found in every village and every city; they fired from the windows and kept the Germans from finding lodging. Along the Estonian coast a naval squadron, come from Kronstadt, followed the columns and fired heavy grenades into the interior of the country. The men on the ships hit nothing; maybe the heroes of the Russian Revolution in their red berets couldn't shoot straight with the large cannons. There is no memory of their wounding the fleeing army. Yet the roar and rumble of the heavy grenades overpowered the countryside and caused the heart of more than one fugitive to tremble.

It was a column of horsemen. They were dragoons; they rode calmly, as if it were peacetime, long strides and short trots, on guard, lances at their sides. They were not cheerful, but tears didn't fall into their beards. They were on the march, as they had often been. It's the march through life: one time forward, one time back, one time it will have to end.

This is the start of a short *Reiternovelle*, a novel about soldiers on horseback, which is a genre that appears with happy frequency in German literature. Here the lieutenant who leads the rearguard of the retreat from Russia—in the late fall of 1918—is the protagonist of a veiled, unconsummated love story. He detours his platoon for a few hours to a castle, where he looks for the woman he secretly loved, the wife of the estate administrator, and finds her dead—struck by the only shot fired by someone in the mob of insurgents. Or might it have been he himself who killed her in the terror that she would fall into the hands of the scoundrels in revolt?

It's the old story of desperate, melancholy military tenacity and hidden love, but it's mainly a poetic portrait of a shy, silent woman whose character is revealed in acts of loving compassion toward nature and people.

The novella is entitled *Sorgenfrei*, from the name of the great castle in whose tower, which dominates the surrounding countryside, the tragedy takes place. We can translate the title as *Carefree*. I found it among my mother's books, and I paused at the dedication to her: "My favorite novella, for your birthday. Acki, October 17, 1936."

The author is the noble Benno von Mechow, the scene the Baltic coast. The crude, reserved administrator is a German from Courland. Benno, which was also the nickname of a cousin of mine, is probably short for Benjamin.

I had read the modest, compact story many years earlier. I took it off the shelf again only recently, not because I was interested in the plot, whose outlines I remembered, but to recapture the atmosphere and, above all, the settings.

Reading it the first time I hadn't cared, in fact, to reconstruct the settings accurately; I had situated them somewhere in Latvia, my Latvia, now concealed behind the wall of refusal and fears, my country that extended around me as a child, in forests, swamps, lakes, and silvery beaches. And I repeat the possessive *my* with the single intention of re-evoking that childish attachment that, unlike my sister, I couldn't take with me into adulthood. Disused and ingenuous, the possessive, but entirely faithful.

I had recognized, even smelled, the northwest wind that carried with it the odor of the sea and the chill of faraway ice. I had raised my fur collar and sunk my head into it, in the gesture of men riding against the storm. Beside us, in the gray fields, crows swoop, attentively eyeing the squadron as it passes.

I reread and examine the names of the places. I discover we're still in Estonia; we won't cross the border until the end of the story, at the northern town of Walk, in the direction of Wenden. Wenden, von Mechow writes, where the forebears of the administrator, Ramm, knights of the Order of Livonia, blew themselves up with their wives and children in order to avoid falling alive into the hands of the Russians.

But the battle wasn't against the Russians at Wenden (Cesis, in Latvian) on June 22, 1919: this time the date is precise. Bloodthirsty, furious, they came there to fight, on one side the Estonians with their Latvian allies (a smaller number), on the other the local garrison of Baltic Germans, supported by the German volunteers of General von der Goltz. The Estonians and their allies won. In Estonian, Wenden is called Vönnu, and for years the Estonians celebrated the victory over the hated barons on the same day as the great celebration of St. John.

In the meantime, the Red Army, with its own Latvian volunteers, the famous Riflemen, advanced and retreated in the Baltic lands. A month before, in May, the Reds had had to clear out of Riga—my father with them—defeated at this juncture by the usual Baltic Germans with von der Goltz's volunteers, Latvian assault troops, and units of White Russians.

The three Baltic republics originated in that chaos. That counted more than the orientation of the diverse factions. Even today there are fresh flowers at the base of the monument to the Latvian Riflemen, in Riga. There are three figures, immense, in red granite, with visored caps and big winter coats down to the ground, in front of the Museum of the Occupation. Which refers not, as one might expect, to the German occupation of the Second World War (except minimally) but to the long Soviet occupation. In the Communist Riflemen who mediated with Lenin, the Latvians recognize the virtue of having contributed to their hard-won independence.

And, not coincidentally, my only bond with the history of my country was the festival of freedom—in November, I think—when lighted candles were placed between the double panes of the windows of Riga: the Christmas of our republic. Of earlier events I knew nothing. At most they might be part of the landscape, a background to the soldiers on horseback, although of an indefinable era, the peasants always in revolt, the rabble inevitably drunk—it doesn't matter whether Estonians or Latvians, Communists or patriots—who left the black prints of their dirty bare feet on the white ceilings of the kitchens in the castle of Sorgenfrei: they had good balance even when drunk, heads down, legs up, supported by their comrades.

When I was a child, and the knights of the Order had left the scene for the moment—but for how long, given their age-old reluctance to give up the ancestral lands on the Ostsee?—the Russians had remained enemies. They were such natural enemies that any other enmity—and there were many: the Estonians were brigands, the Lithuanians Catholic, the Swedes self-important—was reduced to insignificance in the gigantic shadow of those who, named in a low voice, could descend on us at any moment. This, in truth, didn't scare me much. I had fears that were far more real: the devil lurking in the dark corners of the cathedral, witches who peered out from behind the immense trunks of firs, the frozen lake where our slightly hesitant steps made long cracks in the ice, and, in summer, under the water lilies on the opaque surface, little waves with dubious intentions. Not to mention that the Russians were, so to speak, always in my house. I had been told that my grandmother's family came from Vitebsk (which to my grandmother as a child must certainly have seemed as Russian as Riga, at the time part of the Russian empire!). And my Papi read his Russian newspapers, grumbling. Also the Russians had evidently wronged him; in spite of that, he was more Russian than Latvian, and perhaps that explained his being so outside the rules. Not me; I was Latvian, it was much simpler.

I was speaking a little earlier about the possessive long abandoned in the forests and swamps, on the edge of the lake amid the swaying, rustling reeds surrounding the boat that cleaves them as it passes, and yet still it annoys me if I'm introduced as Lithuanian, a definition that certainly sounds alien to me; I don't recognize myself in it. I'm Latvian, for goodness' sake—I mean, there's quite a difference.

Then I examine on a map the three tiny republics up there: their names so closely resemble one another when pronounced in Italian that they get confused—but they are Lietuva, Latvija, Eesti—and I sadly resign myself to correcting Lithuanian to Latvian. How to defend the authenticity of Courland and Livonia, suitable at most as the background for a fable or, worse, an operetta?

Besides, not even I was capable of placing those regions precisely in Latvia, and the existence of Latgale was unknown to me. My geographic notions were as uncertain as my historical ones.

The borders of my Latvia were not sketched, and they enclosed, I now realize, an area much more extensive than it was in reality; they penetrated north into Estonia and south into Lithuania. To Estonia I left the capital Tallinn (at the time Reval), but I took Dorpat (Tartu), and if I had been asked the capital of Lithuania I would have answered—ignorant but prescient—that it was Vilnius, since I situated Kaunas in my country. I couldn't swear that in that Latvia of mine there was not also Memel—unrecognizable today, however, as Klaipeda—having jumped out of Lithuania to settle in Latvia, on the Baltic Sea, "my" sea, not far, in fact, from Libau. Probably the German conversations I listened to were tinged with a certain Hanseatic haughtiness that I wasn't able to discern. What was the Hansa, anyway? In the end, I wasn't at all German; I clung unhesitatingly to my rather abstract, but unequivocal, Latvian nationality.

I had slightly corrected both my historical and my geographical notions when, on Sunday morning, Pietro and I set out in the car for Courland. I had understood that my Jewish ancestors came from there, were Courlandian, but I wasn't following their traces, which, for the moment, were still too vague: rather, I would have liked to find, near Kandau (Kandava), Waltershof, the estate of the Baltic barons where Sisi and I had lived secretly with our governess for six months in 1935.

As I passed through the lobby of the hotel to join Pietro, who had gone to the garage to get the car, a song stopped me on the threshold. The tall, blond, pale-skinned men and women, appearing almost two-dimensional with their broad, flat surfaces—that was how I recalled the Latvians—whom I had already met in the elevator were practicing, I think for a concert. A moment of sudden exhaustion overwhelmed me, similar to what I'd felt occasionally in the days before, but this time I was happy. I didn't look at the group singing, at the large, pale, blond bodies that in a certain way appeared unfinished, yet to be shaped, and I sank into their voices, pitched in gradations that came together in a celestial harmony. I would have liked, for a moment, to forget, and forget myself. Sit there on the floor and listen in peace.

We left the city by intuition; there were, obviously, no street signs. That defect is a relic of the customary caution of the Soviets, always on guard against possible invaders who, of course, follow street signs on their march. I had luckily informed myself by consulting the map and was more or less able to orient us.

So I had also discovered that Kandava was in Courland, a short distance from Tukums. We had spent the first weeks after our flight in a large castle in the forest near Tukums, at the time Tuckum. I've already written about the thick walls and maybe also the tiny yellowish spark in the wolves' eyes at twilight on the edges of the forest, but certainly not about the Christmas Day walk in the woods after it had snowed overnight. Above our heads immense branches, fringed with fresh snow, extended from the firs, forming a continuous vault as far as you could see. I had never been in such a beautiful place; rather, I had never noticed that there could be places outside me, such a powerful, endless immensity that ruled on its own account, heedless of us fleeting passersby. In my childish imagination the forest seemed enchanted.

What was tangled up in my mind that morning I didn't remember until many years later. It was Christmas vacation, and I was spending it with my sons and their young families. I was climbing along a mule track, again wintry, up the mountain above our house in the upper Val Susa. I was used to walking for hours, desperate and confused; my husband had died suddenly three months earlier. At a fork in the road—to the right rose a white cliff, to the left a white slope descended—I suddenly found myself recalled not by thoughts but by repressed sensations to the forest of Tuckum. I felt again the painful, profound, and torturous, if momentary, unease of having betrayed my father.

I had proposed to Pietro that we stop along the way in Mitau (Jelgava), which I was curious about because it had been the capital of the grand duchy of Courland. The future Louis XVIII, driven out of France during the Revolution, had lived in Mitau as a guest of the tsar. Mitau was no longer there; it was now Jelgava, reconstructed—so to speak—by the Soviets after the war, with the uniform streets and lifeless apartment buildings, one just like the other, we had seen on the outskirts of Tallinn the day before.

It was hard to find your way in the city, really as if someone had played with the cardinal points: you looked up at the sun that appeared in flashes between the clouds, and suddenly you found it behind you; you thought you were entering a square, and a large, shabby building barred the way. Every so often the modest but dilapidated façade of an Art Nouveau building emerged. Pietro said, perplexed, that he had never encountered such disorderly reconstruction. But maybe it only appeared haphazard, and was following some architectural criterion by which the buildings were arranged in this way to limit damage from bombing. To me it didn't much matter; I was still unaware that Mitau could have anything to do with me.

Outside the malignant jumble of the inhabited area of the city, we came upon an enormous Baroque building, painted red and white, which had been designed by Bartolomeo Rastrelli for the Grand Duke. It loomed, presumably untouched—horrible, I said—on a small island between two branches of the river. It appeared to be empty—it was Sunday—and we wandered around. In the back courtyard we found a woodpile of incredible proportions. It was as high as the highest windows of the extremely high first floor and extended more than halfway across the courtyard. Peasant Latvia had prepared the only material in its possession to warm the University Institute of Agriculture, whose headquarters are in the building, and with the same quantity of wood had presumably warmed the exiled family from France two hundred years earlier.

After passing through Mitau, we continued the journey amid forests and countryside that appeared to be deserted and neglected compared with the fertile countryside of Piedmont. I told Pietro about the fourteen-year-old baroness who every morning, alone on her sledge, left the great castle for her German lyceum in Tuckum, driving the horse. I wouldn't have been capable of driving a horse with a sledge; I had envied her, as always, in secret melancholy. Suddenly we saw a storks' nest atop a telephone pole.

"You should take a picture," I said to Pietro. "I've never seen a storks' nest on a telephone pole. The creature must be crazy."

I was a little embarrassed for the stork, but the craziness was widespread: along the road the poles, one after another, were topped by storks' nests. But were there no longer pillars beside the farm gates? I was told later that storks habitually build their nests now on telephone and other poles, content with the artificial buzz, while once they liked the company of humans.

I didn't intend to go deep into the forest to find the castle; I hadn't the least idea where it was, and I didn't at all remember the short journey by car to get to Waltershof. I followed our pilgrimage with my finger on the map; I had told Pietro that I still had a precise image of the small river that ran behind the house at Waltershof, and when we arrived at a small stream and Pietro said, "Here we are," I shook my head. No, my little river was narrower and from the shore tall grasses curved toward the clear water. Soon afterward, I said, "This time yes," just a moment before seeing the sign, which seemed to me brand-new, "Kandava."

I proposed to Pietro that we look for the baronial estate across the bridge over the small river in the middle of the town, which was also brand-new and shiny. After a hundred meters we stopped beside a group of houses I didn't recognize. We got out of the car; it was drizzling, and I wrapped myself in a cape and looked around. It wasn't the right place. I saw a tall, robust farmer coming along a country lane, and I went toward him. I spoke to him in Russian, because he was Russian, it was obvious, and he answered in Russian:

"Walteri," he said, "конечно." Certainly.

Using a stick, he drew on the dirt path the route we should take, and meanwhile he explained to me that Walteri was beyond the large complex of the Technical School. We were close, he said. In the relief of having understood and having made myself understood I hugged him, moved, as if I had found a relative. We arrived in five minutes. It was no longer drizzling. Pietro stopped the car under some giant trees at the edge of a small courtyard enclosed between the wings of a low brick structure rounded at the corners. The first floor wasn't even four meters up; steep roofs sheltered the building, covered with worn dark tiles on the left side, newer on the right. Next to the wall of the right-hand wing a young man was working at a bench, a ladder was leaning against the house, a young woman was bent over a flowerbed. Three or four hens were scratching nearby.

I spoke to them in Russian as well, explaining that I had lived there as a child. The woman answered, not particularly surprised, and pointed to the first floor on the left: certainly I had lived up there. The wing appeared to be abandoned now, under its worn, rough cladding. Immediately an older woman emerged from the central section that looked onto the courtyard and, friendly and curious, asked me in Russian if I was there on behalf of the old owners. They had returned many times from Germany to see the house that had belonged to their forebears.

As she questioned me closely—where I had come from, how many children I had, how I had traveled—we walked toward the stream, but we stopped while I wrapped myself in my cape. It had started drizzling again in scattered drops. The peasant woman, wearing a large, short-sleeved T-shirt, stood bare-armed in the rain. She talked and talked, and I followed as well as I could. Pietro took pictures. He had said, incredulous, "Are you sure?"

It seemed to him impossible that the old house, fallen in on itself, with big cracks in the walls, surrounded by empty sheds with caved-in roofs, was the estate I had told him about.

(In the course of later research, I found that the Waltershof estate was noted in the land registry as early as the first half of the nineteenth century.)

Trying to answer the farmwoman I turned to look around and, though not recognizing it, I recognized it. There were the fields where, holding a branch, and proud of the responsibility, I drove before me thirty white geese. Beyond the courtyard was the barn with some twenty cows; one gave twenty liters of milk a day and was much praised. I didn't remember where the stable was; there, next to the barn, in the pigpen, I had seen the sow nursing a dozen pretty piglets.

One morning our father had arrived unexpectedly in a car, right in the middle of that courtyard, with his lawyers and the driver; he had found us, and Sisi and I had to hurry back inside the house and shut ourselves in the little room behind our room, otherwise—they had warned us—he would take us away.

There was our room on the ground floor, and upstairs, in a small room in the tower between two roofs, lived the crazy baron, who ate only potatoes cooked in the ashes for fear of being poisoned. We'd go and see him; he'd offer us potatoes cooked in the ashes and read to us yet again Pushkin's fable about the goldfish and the fisherman. The farm—what remained of it after the "reform," which was sometimes alluded to with a sigh—was managed by the baroness. The children were in Germany studying.

To get to our room, we crossed the small living room behind that rounded corner, at night carrying a flickering candle. Would the French ghost of the place surprise us? There was no electric light, I recall; the young blond peasant woman who was ironing in the big room in the right wing was using large irons full of coals and, meanwhile, was telling me about the spirits of the forest: "You have to be careful not to step on them when you walk, or they get angry."

I didn't ask the Russian peasant woman if I could come in; I was discouraged in part by the flowerbeds edged with stones—I found them fussy—in front of the steps at the entrance to the living room, but certainly nothing remained of the French living room and the Sèvres porcelain. Undoubtedly even the ghost had departed in 1939. I considered myself satisfied, in any case, even if I continued to marvel that places really existed, with lights and shadows, in a space of their own and—here at Waltershof I perceived it for the first time during my return to Latvia—in a time independent of mine, places that had remained so long in my memory that they lost plausible substance, becoming figments purely of my mind. Here a history had happened—history had passed—that wasn't mine.

Looking today at the photographs of Waltershof—among the most beautiful of the trip—I see places immersed in a gilded light, the light that the autumn leaves of the tallest, unidentified trees shed on us amid the sparser and sparser drops. Maybe an echo of the chorus heard in the hotel lobby persisted in my mind: the fact is that the desolation and silence of the old, decaying house, the empty barn, the collapsed roofs, the disused oven in the courtyard seemed to belong to my detached serenity. I didn't wonder where the children of the children of the Latvian peasants were now, whom I remembered as being everywhere, busy and noisy. Besides, I already knew, and accepted in their obviousness, the few poor Russians, the few hens, the garden of cabbages. The day had for me a completeness.

And it was sustained for the rest of our journey in Courland. We stopped in Kuldiga, intact, untouched by the war or the Soviets. Pietro took pictures of the beautiful little squares, the house with a trellis, the graceful Art Nouveau houses restored and repainted, the justly famous street named "of the mountain" in the weak autumn sun, the early-nineteenth-century thatch-roofed cottages. For what bizarre reason are there in flat Latvia, not infrequently, "mountain" streets? So that the small hills evoke an unconscious memory of ancestral mountains? In the modest, very clean cafeteria where we had something to eat, the few customers and the girl at the counter spoke Latvian. Immersed in my touristic laziness I looked and didn't think. I took note of nothing, so I don't remember the names of the other towns we passed through.

I was longing to arrive at the sea, at any beach we might come to as we drove through pinewoods and over white-sand dunes, but I let Pietro choose the route.

On the left side of the Gulf of Riga, at the very top, the map and the guide indicated a nature preserve, Slitere; a fairly wide road led to it, marked in red. This, in fact, was there, although still unpaved. Passing through the outskirts of Windau (Ventaspils), we continued on the unpaved road, which we expected at any moment to become a real road, but it didn't. As usual, we traveled alone, jolting for forty kilometers amid forests with their graceful borders of heather, under a clear windy sky, pinkish-blue, which indicated the proximity of the sea. Arriving, finally, at the top, we found no nature preserve—there was, of course, no sign—and, turning our prow to the east, we set out along the sea, toward Riga.

I felt that Pietro was getting tired (he the tireless); we drove through tourist resorts that were not luxurious but well kept, I saw again the villas in the woods, along with new sports equipment. I didn't dare remind Pietro of my ultimate goal, a stay at the beach. Riga seemed unreachable, beyond the interminable Courlandian coast. Anyway, at a certain point he stopped; it was twilight when we got out of the car, next to a broad deserted beach. It was broad, it was deserted, it was pale, it was just like all the other beaches glimpsed between the tree trunks as we traveled along the shore. It didn't even have the power to be a symbol, and still less did the sea, over which hovered a faint odor of gasoline. A light cool breeze blew, and I walked as an old woman toward the water's edge, where harmless, milky little waves broke. The picture shows me with a slight grimace on my face.

Finally, in the dark, following new and clearly visible

signs, we crossed several branches of the Daugava to enter Riga, announced from a distance by the many lights of a great European city. We ate in a so-called Italian restaurant, not bad, but worse than the preceding evenings.

During dinner Pietro, recovering rapidly, spoke about the Jugendstil houses, about the sea—he said we ought to go back. Why not invest in Latvia—it was supposed to be good business, there was a future there—buy an apartment in the city, a villa at the beach? (*Brrr.*) I said, "yes, yes," the fact that he liked the country and wanted to return nearly moved me.

At night in my hotel room, before going to sleep, I greeted from the window the black edge of my grandparents' house. The next winter I discovered that their last address was not Baznicas Iela but Brivibas Iela, not far away, I think.

But at the end of my Courlandian day, saying goodbye to their house, I wasn't yet worried that life in Latvia had moved on while I, in turn, lived in another place and in another way; I was satisfied with the effort made, and, above all, the encounter in Rumbula, two days earlier, remained central, the only event that really happened. The rest, empty of people, turned back sixty years, had proved to be ordinary, devoid of melancholy or passion.

Picking up von Mechow's story (the months of mourning had passed and I was preparing to write about my return to Latvia), I paused, as I said, on the dedication to my mother for her birthday in 1936. The book had been given to her by Acki, the dark, kind handsome son of the German friends who hosted her after she separated from her husband. It was Acki who, two years earlier, in December of '34, had opened the back door of their apartment the morning of our flight. I was supposed to say to him that we were looking for Mamma—in case a witness had been required in the future, I think—but I couldn't say a word. Smiling, he helped me then by asking a question, which I could answer with a nod.

I had left him in the doorway, the kind and handsome boy whose photo I found in the attic in Torre Pellice, with the Greek dedication "κἀλός καγαθός Αγοστός." He had dedicated the sad, dreamy novella to his parents' fascinating and unhappy foreign guest, on whom, perhaps, he had a crush. In 1939, at Hitler's summons, he had returned to the country of his ancestors, along with his parents and fellow citizens, leaving the Baltic "homeland." He didn't even have time to miss his native land; a pilot, he died during the war. Some others, also German, and Baltic, went back with the SS in '41.

But I don't want to end this account of the trip to Courland talking about him or about Waldtraut, my classmate, who before she left had sent me a signed photo saying good luck. Instead, I want to end by writing about the small round child, the daughter of the Latvian peasant who was ironing with the big irons full of coals and telling me about the spirits of the forest.

This child, whose name I don't remember, was around six and played with us. When spring came, we were often in the woods in the pale-green light of the first buds. The child chattered nonstop, she was a liar, clingy and vain, she followed me when I fed the geese. She had tried to make us believe that she had two fathers, who came to see her, in turn, on alternate Sundays; she declared that her surname was her mother's. I don't know in what German-Latvian muddle we understood each other, but at a certain point Sisi and I decided to get rid of the small, round, intrusive girl; we managed to convince her that in half an hour she would be able to walk to Italy, land of every delight. We walked her toward the woods, and I see her still today (I was a notorious coward and was already repenting) on a little bridge, with a small bundle in hand, as she went off among the trees. Nothing happened, of course; she returned, I suppose, soon afterward.

Not so years later, when, between 1945 and 1949, some hundred and thirty thousand Latvian peasants, including perhaps her, her mother, and her two fathers, were deported, along with wives, children, the elderly, to the Soviet Union so the land could be given to the Soviets' agricultural cooperatives. Those who were "amnestied" in 1956, and managed to return, were scarcely more than a quarter of those who had been dragged off. As testimony of their exile, they brought back the photographs and objects that would be conserved in the Museum of the Occupation: sackcloth clothes for children, rough canvas masks to put over the face as protection against temperatures of forty below zero, felt boots full of holes, a letter written on birch bark, the memory of the big wooden boards—here reconstructed—where, sleeping squeezed into the thirty centimeters of space assigned to each person, they dreamed of their small fields, carved out of the enormous possessions of the Baltic barons by the agrarian reform of 1920.

8. Letters (a)

> Alas, I can say little more than this in reply to your questions. What I have been able to give you are the memories of a seventy-three-year-old about things said forty to fifty years ago by a young woman in her twenties and early thirties recalling the incidents of her childhood.

So ends a letter of August 3, 2000, from my brother-in-law, Stan; I'd decided to write to him and ask if he remembered what my sister Sisi might have told him about our time in Latvia. Like everyone who knew her as an adult, he called her Annalisa.

I felt a confused need to talk about my father, if only by asking questions, and, in the meantime, I realized how long I'd been silent.

Stan was the only interlocutor I had left; as I gradually headed toward old age, first my mother had died, on the threshold of eighty-five, then my sister and, soon afterward, my husband, both much younger.

Someone, with a swift movement, had spread a red veil over Sisi's beautiful, thin but smooth and serene face; someone lowered the lid of the coffin. I embraced my husband; weeping, I said, "It's over, I won't see my father anymore."

He seemed to reappear in the deaths of others, as if it were his moment, to gesture to me, to summon me back to the narrow street in Torre Pellice where we had seen each other for the last time.

With my brother-in-law, from whom my sister had been divorced in 1960 or thereabouts, I had maintained a very sporadic but affectionate correspondence. When he came through Turin, we would have dinner together and talk. Although he speaks and writes Italian correctly, I had asked him to answer in English, to get a more fluent and nuanced impression.

> Annalisa told me some of the basic facts about your family very early, and about your father in particular. From her I knew that your mother and father had divorced when you and Annalisa were small and that your father had been an unfaithful husband. I knew also that a dispute over your custody made the divorce contentious and that, amid the contention, your mother hid you near Riga, then took you back to Italy. Then, before the German takeover of the Baltic states cut you off from him, your father came to Torre Pellice at least once when you were living there with your grandmother, trying to get you back. Annalisa supposed (when I first knew her), and was then convinced (later), that your father died a victim of the Nazis in Riga's ghetto.

Naturally these things were not told to me in the matter-of-fact way in which I have just put them down. Annalisa was indignant about your father's treatment of your mother. She believed that your father had greatly wronged your mother, and her implied and only explanation of the wrong was self-indulgence on his part. Her indignation was not surprising, but I am still surprised by how little there was in her story to suggest that either she or you had been hurt by what happened in your parents' marriage. The home that she recalled was a comfortable home and her Riga was a romantic place, with snow-covered houses, lighted candles in every window at Christmas, and a hinterland dotted with the estates of the Baltic barons. Two anecdotes showed your father as a man who cared about his children, wickedly as he might have behaved otherwise and rascally as he might have proceeded. In one he tried to bribe (her? The two of you?) to stay with him with the gift of a pony; in the other he involved an unsuspecting priest in an effort to get you back, pleading the horror of his daughters being raised by Protestants. The flight away from your father and his family seemed less an anxious time (as Annalisa described it) than an exciting one, a game of hide-and-seek almost, where you stayed for a while in a Baltic barn and then took the long train ride to Torre. Years after all of this, what happened to your father still mattered to Annalisa. I was present when someone (I have forgotten her name) told her that he had died in the massacre of the Jews in Riga. She took the evidence—word-of-mouth testimony from some survivors—as fact, though of course it was hard to evaluate . . .

Most psychologists seem to agree that our attitudes toward our parents influence our attitudes toward many other things. You are right to say that Annalisa was strongly attached to your mother. She certainly respected her greatly, and I can remember no criticism she ever made of Clara that was more than an amused comment on peccadillos. Her attitude toward her father was, in my view, a very ambivalent one. She couldn't forgive his treatment of your mother. She was pleased by her English godmother's counter to her reference to this treatment: "My dear, your father treated your mother badly, but he was a charming man!" And I think she admired your father's readiness to put himself above the rules when it pleased him, even though she never said so in so many words.

When I wrote to Stan I was carefully going through the letters my mother had saved, and, as I've said, after returning from Latvia, I had begun to look for traces, whatever they might be, not so much to narrate (I could only repeat myself, I knew) or to verify as to follow blindly that call to turn back that in Rumbula had become a living sound.

Among other things, I found on Sisi's Latvian baptism certificate, which I hadn't known was among the few remaining documents, the name, completely new to me, of the Strand, or beach, where we spent our vacations. It was Jurmala—I had never known it—and naturally I looked for it on the map and found it.

The certificate itself, with its date—my sister was six when she was baptized—led me to reconstruct the fact that that very summer our father must have spent some vacation time with us; in fact, the dog that Mamma had promised to give us if Sisi agreed to the ceremony—so, at least, she claimed—ran after him in the garden of the villa. I distinctly see the puppy trying to grab the leather sole of our father's slipper: he was out in the garden in his bathrobe, as he often was in the morning. Maybe from the same summer, though hazy and indistinct, comes the image of a dark, tall young man in a striped bathing suit, who runs, leaping, into the waves. He's laughing.

I leafed through our letters to Mamma: the first were in a fluent German that, despite the spelling mistakes, revealed a daily habit. We didn't know other languages; I read French but didn't write or speak it. The next letters we wrote to her, when we were in school in Italy, were in a less assured but more correct German—already checked with the dictionary—evidently to please her, since it was important to her that we not lose mastery of our original language.

Reading, I found myself clumsy, stubborn, and ambitious; Sisi seemed to me more direct and bold. She liked wild strawberries, chocolate, going to the stream to swim (every spring she pleaded for a new bathing suit), bicycling as soon as she was given a bike for her birthday. I had contributed to buying it with my piggy bank, aware of (and not at all humble about) my good deed, which won me, as usual, neither praise nor recognition.

At least, I said to myself, I could write about Sisi—and for a while I toyed with the idea, and for that reason, too, wrote to my brother-in-law—about the vital, greedy, quick-tempered child, about her secret sadnesses that I was well acquainted with. But here, precisely, was the difficulty: I couldn't get me out of it; we were the two of us, inseparable. One couldn't exist without the other.

As an adult, I didn't see her regularly for years except when she visited from the United States; nor were we close afterward, when she was divorced and returned to live in Italy. I would have been able to portray only the child, as she appeared now to my grandmotherly eyes. The traces left in my memory were unstable, and, besides, I'd already drawn on them in *Distant Fathers*; the documentation was scant.

In what way, I wondered, could I insert the petty acts, the insignificant events reported in our correspondence with our mother, anecdotes about our adored cat, into a portrait inexorably dominated by the giant shadow of the last months of our father's life, by his death, by the death of his family?

And yet, skimming our old letters, I found here and there phrases or terms I hadn't noticed before. At times, perhaps, an attentive gaze could discern a latent story that seeped out between the lines, but faint, not enough to bare the unconscious scar that Stan was surprised not to have detected in my sister's stories. Was it worth the trouble to insist? To what degree could what two little girls wrote at the time reveal their thoughts and feelings, bound as they were to their mother by a very strict complicity? The absent father had to remain unmentioned as far as possible. To this complicity above all, it seems to me, the old letters bear involuntary witness.

I finally resolved to transcribe some pages in their original form (translating, of course, if necessary), and certainly the very few in which there was any reference to our father. I wouldn't intervene except to make connections and, where necessary, summarize. I wouldn't try to impose a narrative thread on a story that had been withheld and that I could intuit in flashes but didn't feel I could recover by recounting. I would, however, talk about our father; I would try to understand, peering between the lines like one who reads but not like one who writes.

The following letters were written between September of 1935 and the fall of '38. The first are in German; the children are living in their grandmother's house in Torre Pellice, during what to their father might still seem the usual summer vacation. Mamma has left, by herself, to go back to work in Riga.

Sisi writes:

My dear Mammina! I got your letter and was very happy. The presents were great. We already got the book and read it all. Thank you. Now I have a lot of things to tell you! Please go to school and get my gym stuff and ask for the address of Svea Seeberg. You can get her address through Fraulein Egin. Please don't forget it. Love and kisses. Your Sisi.

The presents are for Sisi's birthday, September 18th.

October 24:

Dear Mammina, how are you? The bandit hasn't arrived yet; we're saving the money we get during the week, we already have 12 lire. Grandma is still sick. What book should we buy for Grandma? A novel or what does Grandma like? Bögi's letter hasn't arrived yet and the mountaintops are already all white, covered with snow. On the other hand it's very nice and today we brought the flowers in with Elvina. I made a new pair of pants for my doll because she only had one pair. We're playing together again.

Our uncle hasn't written for a long time. Grandma is reading us a book in Italian, *Bottoncino*. I corrected my writing. You already went to get my gym uniform and Svea isn't Schaffe but Seeberg. Today I wanted to write in Italian but I didn't have the time or will because I already wrote two pages and two lines were still missing and they would have been three. Today I'm not writing well because in Riga it's already nine thirty. And I'm writing on the table Grandma uses when you're sick . . . Grandma is scratching Mini's back. Lots of greetings and kisses. Sisi

Bögi is the children's governess Ingeborg, who lived with them in Waltershof; their uncle, named several times, is Roberto, their mother's brother.

November 20:

My dear Mammina, how are you? We went to Lala's wedding, it was very beautiful, I'm amazed I don't have a stomachache because there was so much to eat. I had a banana, three dates, and a bunch of grapes. Do you want us to keep the notebooks we're done with to show you? The bandit is in Rome. We have fifteen lire! How much do you think Grandma's book will cost? Our new coats look really nice. Mini is now too lazy to write letters.

You have a lot to do. Tante Lotti got your telegram. We're fine and hope you are, too. Our classes are going well, as I told you my writing isn't very good. Lately I've only gotten high marks, isn't that good?

It's strange that the bandit hasn't arrived yet, but he should get here soon because how long can he stay in Rome? We have grapes every day. We carried the train at the wedding. There were around thirty people. We had bonbons and each of us carried a bunch of white carnations. But now I don't have much more to write because it's five to nine and I have to go to bed. I'm adding the letter for Tante Erna.

The Tante Lotti the children write about sometimes is a friend of the family, the daughter of Clara's godmother, who took care of them when she came to stay in Torre Pellice.

November 21:

I still have some things to write to you. In the first place bring us our hymnal. Bring us a lot of sweets and come soon. When will the trial be over? Here we've had the first snow. Mini has decided to write. Is it very cold in Riga? Here not yet. Every Thursday we go to class in the afternoon and also today we have class at two. Your daughter Sisi gives you a kiss.

After around three months of lessons, Sisi in Italian:

Dear Mamma: We're fine. I'm writing that little letter for Mini who doesn't feel like writing. Today it's been raining all day. School is going very well only with my writing it's not going very well. We can already speak Italian a little, though we can't understand all the words, but it's already something that we can say all the things we want. I don't have much time today it's already after eight thirty. Grandma's foot still hurts, we hope she gets better soon. We didn't go to November 4th because that man was supposed to come. Grandma made a nice sweater for Mini. Greetings from your Sisi.

From the same period, the following letters from Micki, obviously longer and more articulate than those of her younger sister and so not always transcribed here in their entirety.

Torre Pellice, September 18:

My dear little Mammina! We just got your letter, so Sisi and I are very happy: we haven't received any letter from someone, we hope that for someone it will be a good joke when you arrive without us. I'm very glad when I think about it. Sisi was very happy with her presents, naturally it wasn't as cheerful as if you'd been here. Grandma made a magnificent cake. Sisi got a package of candy from Tante Lotti and at home another one. You can imagine the joy of the glutton. I'm sure she's already eaten ten, naturally she carefully gave me one of those with mint since she can't stand them, right now she's taking another one, tomorrow there won't be any more as you can easily imagine knowing Sisi. Uncle leaves tomorrow. Please go and get my gym things when you have time. We're studying well. I hope you don't have too much work. We had a slight cold but now it's gone, only uncle caught it.

Grandma will write the rest. This is the longest letter I've ever written in my life. Sorry if there are a lot of mistakes, write me a long letter. Your little daughter who loves you very much, Micki.

Say hello to everyone.

October:

My dear little Mammina, I have a lot to tell you. We're going to Sunday school now and we already have two new friends. Grandmother bought a New Testament for each of us. Sisi, Giovanni, Marisa, and I took a magnificent walk, we had our snack outside on a small island in the Pelici. It was magnificent, we each had our own rock in the middle of the water. I naturally, always unlucky, ended up with one foot in the water and got all wet and we went home early; but at Marisa's house they ironed my sock until it was dry then I put it on and went from there. Grandma didn't realize anything, luckily she doesn't know German otherwise she would have read the letter and would have found out.

October (at the top of the page there is a small flag with the Italian colors):

My dear little Mammina: I wish you a happy birthday. I hope this letter finds you well. The next one I will write in Italian. I'm already at that point, sometimes I read without mistakes and I'm already able to read all your children's books, naturally I don't understand everything but it's already enough... Our teacher says I'm good at numbers. We learned a lot of new poems... Grandmother enrolled us in the Piccole Italiane[3]... I'm fine, I'm eating a lot and make mistakes. Greetings to all. Your little daughter who loves you, Micki.

Undated, probably November:

Dear Mammina, I have a lot of things to tell you. In the first place I wasn't good, Grandma will tell you everything, I'm begging you again, write to Grandma that I will correct myself. Grandma doesn't believe me anymore I'm begging you please. School is going very well I have all 10s and 9s.[4] I read without mistakes and I can already speak Italian. Yesterday we went to the wedding it was very beautiful. Tante Lotti thanks you very much for the kind telegram. A pile of telegrams arrived, they were all read out loud. We carried the train, there was a lot to eat. I can't tell you everything. Sisi has already written everything. Today the first snow fell, everything is white... Please send me my doll or I will be bored. You forget everything we write you but don't forget that.

In the meantime, the "bandit" must have come and gone again.

3 Piccole Italiane: fascist youth group for girls.
4 The highest marks.

December:

Dear Mammina, how are you? We're fine, we're going now to the Piccole Italiane, it's fun we go for walks and sing songs. We have a lot of new friends and play well. Sisi isn't good at all and always says bad words. But at school she's very much improved. Only one thing doesn't go well, she forgets some letters, she is supposed to write *conjugation* and she writes *conjation.*

But I don't want to write just about Sisi but also about me. Because I am not a model of good behavior, I also have my flaws my old flaw is to sulk . . . This flaw Sisi doesn't have. Otherwise things are going well. I'll tell you right away which doll to ask Bögi for, the doll she brought to the doll doctor. You don't know anything about the . . . I won't say the name because you know already who I want to talk about.

I'm writing another letter to Tante Erna.

At the bottom of the letter Micki drew on a pole an Italian flag that says "Italia."

Undated, probably January:

My dear little Mammina, how are you? We are very well, a little while ago we were at the fascist Epiphany, we got an orange, a cookie, and a photo of Mussolini. We've been very good in recent days. Sisi is a little sweetheart, she doesn't fight anymore and sings from morning to night. The preacher who preaches now in our Sunday school is very nice, he gives everyone who recites the lines well a little book. Sisi already has a book but not me, because I'm afraid of reciting. I get shaky with fear about exams but hope to pass them. Say hello to everyone. Your Micki sends her love.

January 28, 1936:

. . . Today I don't have much to tell you. Sisi and I had a fight, because she always acts like she's in love with Elena, a girl who lives nearby. I got very angry . . .

It will take time before I write to Waldi.

Waldi is Waldtraut Burmeister, a schoolmate of Micki's in Riga. She and Micki must have corresponded occasionally. The picture of Waldtraut with the dedication, sent before her departure for "exile," is dated February 1939.

Undated:

We were at the February 17th celebration and we got an orange, a sweet, and a book of *Histoire Vaudoise*.

February 17th is the holiday celebrating the granting of civil liberties to the Waldensians.[5]

---

5 On February 17, 1848, civil emancipation was granted to the Waldensians by Carlo Alberto, the ruler of Savoy, and every year on that date there is a celebration.

Spring 1936:

I like history a lot we're at the expedition of Carlo Pisacane and we do compositions without mistakes and the teacher says I'm one of the best students . . . Please ask Bögi where a doll of mine ended up she brought it to the doll doctor and since then I've known nothing else please please ask her about it.

Micki asks yet a third time about the doll in a later letter: "You forget everything but don't forget this." The doll never arrived, and even now Marina misses her. When she was in Riga with Pietro, walking along the Schützengarten, she glanced at the place where the doll doctor's workshop had been, on the edge of the park. The shop, obviously, was no longer there.

March 22, 1936, Torre Pellice

Yesterday we went to the station with the Piccole Italiane, so-and-so was supposed to come but he didn't, we walked for three hours and when I got home I was very tired. I haven't yet gotten the Sunday school book. I'm not sulky anymore and I'm doing very well in school.

In the spring of 1936, Sisi:

Dear Mammina. How are you? What are you doing? I'd like to have a book please buy me *Das Sternenkind* or *Mutter Natur erzählt*, they're both by

Karl Ewald, buy me the one you think is better and have it be just mine, if they're too expensive buy me *Tiere unter sich* because that is cheaper. Here it's really nice, today we went for a walk on the mountain and it was really nice. We get *Wir Mädel* [We Girls] every week and it's very interesting. I'm putting a letter for Svea in mine. I don't have much to write to you. Things are going well at school and I'm taking the exam for high school. Do you have too much to do? And do you have news of the beast? Mini in the past few days is horrible unfortunately we fight all day. Kitty sleeps outside every night; your little Sisi kisses you.

In June of '36 Micki and Sisi take the admission exam for what at the time was called the lower high school. In the fall they start school and now almost always write their letters in Italian.

November 11, Micki:

In composition I've had crazy good luck. Think, for the first two compositions I got nines and I was the only one . . . School is going well in everything, I'm not afraid anymore [in an earlier letter, in German, she had written: "because you know your timid little bunny"], only I don't like physical education because they just play games and the kids from the lower school are there and the girls from the high school and they always scare me a little.

Everything is fine with our kitty . . . he's dressed like a Piccola Italiana. He's very affectionate and loves grandma a lot, and also she is very inclined to be nice to him, probably because he's a male and males, cats or men, don't make babies . . .

I went to the anniversary of the victory and march on Rome with the Piccole Italiane. That man's arrival doesn't worry me at all. He can come when he wants, I'm not afraid, a coward can't ever harm anyone, when someone is present.

Andrea the boy who is here is a true idiot. I always have to help him with his lessons and I really like teaching a boy who is older than me and also from the town, while I'm a foreigner.

Andrea is the young lodger who is spending the school year in their grandmother's house.

In the same letter Sisi writes:

Dear Mamma. For now no visit has taken place.

When the visit did take place, Sisi, November 21:

Dear Mamma. How are you? Here it's still pretty hot. Our teacher is very harsh and gives terrible grades and even Micki gets those grades from him and I can't stand him . . .

That man bores us enormously, and I wish he would die this winter. Poor grandmother is in a flutter. He gave us a watch for Micki, a pen for each of us, and a camera to share . . . Tante Lotti came and we went to visit her yesterday.

We're very well only that man bores us enormously, and today he said he was staying here for ten more days which as you can imagine has really scared us. Unfortunately another boy in our class lives at the pensione Gelli and he always tells him how much homework there is to do and so we can't make things up in order not to see him. Otherwise everything's fine. Greetings and kisses come soon. Annalisa.

Excuse my handwriting but I'm in a hurry.

While Micki doesn't comment on the visit and doesn't mention her father until the following September, Sisi writes about him in the next months.

February 1937:

I hope that man is still sick and seriously.

March 1937:

What's the weather like in Riga? We copied the letter for that man onto a postcard.

Spring 1937, undated:

That man wrote to us only we couldn't decipher the letter. Should we answer him?

April 1937:

What's the weather like in Riga? [Sisi asks about the weather in "hot" Riga in every letter.] Do you have news of that man? Could you decipher his letter?

Summer over, end of September, Sisi, after her birthday:

That man didn't send even a postcard, but it doesn't matter.

On the same date, in German, Micki:

Today we wrote a short but nice letter to Grandfather. In order for us to write to the other you have to tell us what we should write.

In another letter that year as well, Micki refers to having written to the grandparents and to Sisi's having received a very affectionate postcard from Grandfather with greetings for Mamma.

Another year passes. Sisi in September of 1938:

Uncle wrote me a short letter for my birthday... Geymet [friend] a postcard. From that man nothing.

The same fall, Sisi:

Today the weather is splendid and in Riga? Uncle has exams the 10th of this month and probably he'll bring me a ballpoint pen. They had us make a statement about race, and for us it was a big pain, all because of that man!

In the following years "that man" disappears from the two girls' correspondence. It may be that he no longer wrote, certainly he no longer has money to travel; from the divorce documents it turns out that he lives with the German Ilse and their child in Majori, supported by his parents. Micki and Sisi had been informed of the birth of the child. Both seem used to the new environment; their letters contain news that is mostly about school from Micki, about bicycle trips and promises to study from Sisi. While they're attending what was then called the upper high school, for two years Micki signs her name Marina, seems more self-confident, presents ideas for stories and plays, reports on readings, comments on conquests made by Sisi, "that dark beauty." Sisi gets mad and writes above the line, "it's not true."

We're now in 1939. Why, Micki asks, don't we get the weekly *Wir Mädel* anymore? Mamma, without any explanation, cancelled the subscription. The girls don't understand what the change in the journal's management means, with the installation of a certain Trude Kameradin, who first of all had urged readers to abandon ridiculous nicknames like "Papa's little kitten" or "Bavarian violet." Marina recalls a horrible drawing in which a dark little man with a black mustache clings to the hem of the skirt of a big buxom blonde.

The two girls have finished the upper high school; Micki has found a nickname for her sister, usually called Dicki; now it's Old Moses, or, more often, Mosino, Little Moses, the Jew. Sisi sometimes signs her letters with her nickname. She's even "Mosino the wandering Jew" in one.

Mosino the Jew doesn't study much, is lazy, doesn't like math, but her compositions are very good. She always manages to finish, transforms low grades into passing marks ("Mosino was promoted," Sisi writes). She rides her bicycle and skates passionately, in summer goes swimming in the Angrogna and is furious that Grandmother forbids it on the pretext that she's the only girl in the town who does it. Mosino uses whatever material there is in the house—uses, Micki confirms, even curtains and sheets—to make clothes for herself. She has twice as many as her sister, who is often slow to notice that she's been robbed. Mosino the Jew goes to catechism at seven in the morning, but nonetheless will refuse to "be received" (officially join the Waldensian community in a solemn religious ceremony), as her sister was the year before. In high school she prepares a report on the Jews; she seems to be amused by finding Grandmother's house—Micki and Sisi are living somewhere else during that period—full of Jewish evacuees.

We get to the autumn of 1941. The war appears in the girls' letters only in the censor's stamp, and sometimes in the relevant black stripes of the redactions—so something was written!—and in facts gleaned from the identity card of whoever was responsible for sending them.

The following letters are from 1941 to 1943. They are addressed to Mamma, who, starting in the fall of 1940, was working in Bulgaria. The tone, often affectionate, becomes more confiding, as if Mamma were a contemporary, although from the replies one can deduce that scoldings often arrive: Micki and Sisi are insolent, they do what they like without asking permission; Micki, says Grandmother, is a "Bolshevik." Uncle, who tries to ingratiate himself with his mother, alludes to his nieces as "*infernales petites de Clara.*" The girls tell their mother a lot, with an affectionate lack of restraint. As for the "necessary" lies, those which in German are called *Notlügen*, lies to avoid unpleasantness for those who tell them but also for those who hear them, Micki naturally sees to them.

Early autumn '41, Micki:

Dear little Simmi [from now on they both used this term of endearment for their mother, made up of *salamino*, "little salami," and Mamma], I don't have much to tell you. I got a 9 in science with praise from the teacher . . . She interrogated me in art history and I made a good impression . . . Don't work too much, take care of yourself, and arrange to get here at Christmas and then go to Riga.

In September of the same year Micki wrote:

Dear Simmi. It was about time. Finally your news: but you could tell more. We're waiting for a letter from you to us.

In that period we've twice seen Riga and Latvia

at the movies. We recognized the Cathedral intact among the burning houses. Then Kandau, which we would not have recognized if they hadn't said the name. All the houses destroyed there, too.

Saturday we had a costume party. We had a lot of fun, since in less than a month we'll have school.

October 20, 1941. Sisi:

Today it's two weeks since we've been going to school, on my account I'm very satisfied (how nice of me) with the teachers and also the class in general is bearable . . . Listen, *salamino*, do us a favor: go back to Latvia and take us with you, since the cool pure air of the mountains is becoming too rarefied after an extended vacation of six years! Doesn't it seem right to you? Think how we, Micks and I, have spent years where we understood almost nothing, making long journeys, and now we have to remain here to rot (as terminology it's very distinguished). I have a crazy desire to travel and return to Riga. Come on, be a good girl, Simmy, and contrive to get out of your hole and return to the Baltic . . . Besides I have a great desire to relearn German as before; I think it will be useful to me.

The two sisters don't seem to have any idea of what is happening in Europe, and the reasons that their mother had to flee Latvia. Apparently—their mother, after all, gave very few explanations—they consider it an ordinary "change of post." Which of the two would have had the idea of returning to the Baltic? Probably they developed it together; although every so often Sisi complains about her sister, they are closely allied in those years.

Micki, as usual, must have chronicled in "literature" the few known events. In fact Sisi writes, in April of 1942:

> Micki has at times lately been really intolerable and I don't envy that poor guy who's fallen for her . . . ! Today, however, it seems to be going better and she's content with singing out of tune under her breath: God save Latvia, etc. etc.

Micki was composing, or had just composed, an ode in approximate hendecasyllables that began, "And now you weep blood, my homeland . . . " and ended, " . . . your green victorious waves."

Christmas 1941, Sisi:

> Hooray for the year that's about to begin. 1941 might have been very lively, but 1942 has to be better, purposeful, and well employed . . . I finally have my coat; it's as warm as fur, I love it.

End of October or early November, also 1941, after one of what Sisi called "Micks' tall tales"—that is, the imaginary arrival of a letter from Milan sent by a schoolmate Micki was in love with—Micki writes:

> We had two spiritual sessions: the medium was me. He predicted a very bright future for me as a writer . . . He answered our question saying that your ex-husband and our *signor padre* was still in Riga and was sick and that Irene was with him. Who knows.

The father reappears like that after three years, named in person, without epithets; there's still a slight embarrassment, in that "*signor padre*." But hadn't he in truth already reappeared, carried over from his real existence to another, entirely new and unexpected? And with him Latvia and Riga, where Micki and Sisi dream of returning? There, in fact, "the bandit" remained, but, it seems, he was no longer feared; another father separated from him, splitting off into a version that was not only different but actually opposite.

To the first, certainly, the daughters attributed the letter with the request for help that arrived at the end of the summer. They, in fact, knew that he was capable of inventing any sort of "tall tale" and playing any scene. In one, recounted by their mother (who, besides, very rarely mentioned him), he had appeared one evening at the end of the street in Riga where she lived—they had been separated for a long time now—and, upright, motionless, silent, staring at her from a distance in the twilight, had, she said, made a show of weeping.

Gradually, however, another father had found a place in his daughters' hearts. As the years passed, the two adolescents realized that they had fit in only partially in Torre Pellice; they had remained, in the end, foreigners, and felt the uneasiness of an abnormal family situation, and so that other father—a Jew who commented ironically on his defect and then, like Mosino the Jew, gloried in it—also personified for Micki an innate spirit of adventure and misadventure. The sad, sarcastic father who said to his wife, "Remember, they're Jewish!" took an unconscious, singular revenge.

In the small Protestant world, which they experienced as closed and snobbish but didn't know to be a safe haven, Micki and Sisi were therefore "Latvian and Jewish."

In the spring of 1942 Micki writes:

> The two best compositions in the class were Dicki's and mine. Not bad for two Latvians.

On November 8, 1942, after some reflections on her own unorthodox religious opinions, she writes:

> These are also Dicki's ideas. For two little Jews not bad. I wonder what your ideas are on the subject. You see I know you so little, because when you're away you're a creature more mythical than real, you're the Mamma, not even as a truly existing being but as the personification of a symbol. I'm already seventeen, it's time for me to know that symbol, isn't it, Simmi?

Marina doesn't recall that her mother picked up in any way on either this last reference or the repeated reference to being "Jewish"; besides, she no longer has the letters from her mother, destroyed like all the others in the hands of the daughters. In one of her own letters she finds the reflection of some maternal worry over the fanciful confusions of the older daughter. In January 1943 Micki writes:

> As for my Slavic soul I don't know if it's more Slavic or Jewish or Turk. The fact is that I really am made like that. I get as excited just as easily as I then get discouraged. I have a dangerous penchant for dreams that are pointless. I have none of the qualities you speak of in the Latin soul and to tell the truth I don't regret it at all. I prefer labyrinths to the open plains. I have a crazy taste for intrigue and large and small deceptions.

In an earlier letter, from November 1942, Micki compares her own way of being, similar to that of "my father Samuele," to the mentality that is displayed in the "Waldensifying and preachifying" tone of a Waldensian youth, the previously cited "poor guy who's fallen for her."

In April of '43 she discovers in the Bible the name Gershon, which her surname comes from. A name that, she writes, goes back to the "highest nobility of Israel."

The following letter, from the fall of 1942, which

concludes this series of epistolary quotations, is evidence of how poorly defined and confused things seemed, thanks to day-to-day reality, along with the news, which in any case was scant and biased.

> Occasionally at night, when we go down to the Waldensian Youth Union, we hear the hum of engines in the sky, and we line up and sing "Sole che sorgi" or "Vincere," shouting as loud as we can, and Lau and I, who always use very strong language, shout, "Ugly pigs!" with great feeling. What can you do, it's the only protest we can make! And we are still doing pretty well, others are worse off. We hope they pay quadruple what they've done here.

The war entered Micki and Sisi's day-to-day reality for the first time with the English bombing of Turin in the extremely cold November of '42. The fascists of 1944 were not yet there, those of '42 appeared normal, the "they" were the English; they were enemies and so was the small British plane that flew low to machine-gun a farmer on a hay cart on a country road. As for the Germans, they were enemies if they invaded Latvia, but they spoke the beloved language of childhood.

When the years of the war had passed, the silence from Riga and the subsequent confirmation of her father's death seemed to have finally joined "that man" and "my father Samuele." Nonetheless, the tears Marina hid in the palm of her hand when she left for Latvia in September of 1999 indicated perhaps that on the other side of the wall awaited her, still unresolved, the repressed and postponed encounter with "that other," the father who remained in Riga.

9. Letters (b)

The following letter from Margarethe Raz, the Swiss wife of a cousin of my father's, doesn't need any special introduction: it speaks for itself.

I don't know the exact relationship between the Raz family and my father. I have a precise memory of being with my sister at their house, in Hagensberg, the neighborhood on the other side of the Düna, where we lived that year. I also remember that their house, with a shaded courtyard where we played, was more modest than ours: Margarethe Raz cleaned fish in the kitchen; we had a cook. For a long time the smell of raw fish for me remained linked to a horrible story about the death of twins crushed under something, told evidently with great effectiveness by our cousin Irene, a know-it-all, who was a year older than me. Irene meant to impress me, I remember it clearly, and she succeeded perfectly.

Many names are mentioned in the letter; I don't know the people they refer to but my mother must have known them.

[Jan. 12, 1957]

My dearest Clarette,

That's what we called you, didn't we, in better times? You can't imagine my joy at your letter.

I read it weeping with joy and sadness, everything came back. We had a frightening experience, and, the truth is, the world cared very little about it. The world was on its knees before that devil (those devils, more precisely) in human garb. Say what you like, the Russians were truly simple souls compared with the Nazis. With an individual, in fact, one could in some way adjust, only a few of them were actually members of the Party; as for the Germans, 99%, it's undeniable, were Nazis.

We got through the war fine, in the cellar at the end. We closed the one store since we had the other in Slokastrasse; we lived in Elvinenstrasse near the Lassenhof station; of course, the sleepless nights were difficult, but after ten days it was over. The old city of Riga was partly destroyed by the bombs, including the steeple of the Petrikirche, where there was an observation post, and the palace of the Black Skulls. Our house, the boulevards, the Brivibas, the Opera—all undamaged.

In three days the Germans emptied the shops. And then we were allowed to witness a double miracle: if the Latvians had welcomed the Russians with flowers, they did the same with the Germans, greeting them with the Hitler salute. Immediately the anti-Jewish laws arrived. The Latvians lent a helping hand. They evicted the old owners from the apartments where they had been the Jews' servants and installed themselves. The Jews were permitted to do the cleaning. On October 25th all the Jews had to move to the ghetto.

After the arrival of the Germans I had kept my husband hidden in the house, then he found refuge with a Jewish family in Hagensberg, and at night we brought him food, etc. Until the day my family said goodbye to me, and it was no longer possible to bring them food in the ghetto; to see our relatives there we were forced to walk around, on the other side of the electrified barbed-wire fence, and despite the Latvian guards a few meters apart, with their guns leveled, we could sometimes throw a package over the fence and exchange a few words. You were in trouble if you were caught; any contact with Jews was on pain of death. The ghetto was, of course, very crowded; it was situated in the Moscow suburb. Without ceremony they had expelled the Old Believers, and opposite the Russian church was a gigantic gallows on which a naked Jew was usually hanging for the "edification" of the faithful.

In the ghetto, in the so-called shelter, I saw your ex for the last time. My husband was the supervisor of the institution; there were a lot of them, for the most part schoolrooms, where each person had space for a mattress, the people at the back had to step over those at the front; 130 women worked in the school kitchen, it was all calm, marvelously clean. There

I saw your ex with his daughter. The woman had returned to her "homeland," and he had taken the child with him. Both perished in the mass execution of October 30th, along with most of my relatives.

Lilly had already been "liquidated" earlier; then Leo, taken away on the first night by the Latvians, was killed. Hirschmann perished then. Also the Sachs family; Dr. Springfeld gave himself an injection. My sister-in-law Dora and her second husband were killed along with their friends. Ellen and Willy made it, but Willy was shot shortly afterward for stealing a piece of lard; Ellen died later. For days we knew nothing of my husband, until he emerged from his hiding place and we were in seventh heaven because he had made it. Ah, if we could have predicted everything we would have hoped for him a swifter death. Sixteen hours they had to work, the poor men, in the freezing cold, with rations that, after nine months, led inevitably to total malnourishment. As for us, they gave us the same rations, and what they provided was of poor quality. You went to the black market, you stole! We learned both things perfectly. In the morning we didn't know if we would make it to night and at night if we would make it to the morning. My brother-in-law Stach became strange, went crazy, and was killed, like all the insane people.

On March 18 of '42, while I was visiting some foreign Jews who until that moment had been left in peace, I was arrested and for three and a half months went from one jail to another in Riga. Irene had no idea where I was; for three weeks she looked for me, until a former classmate in the Latvian *ginnasio* told her at the prefecture where I was. And then came a terrible period that Irene got through heroically, as even our acquaintances said. Twice a week she brought food to her father (at risk of her life); once every two weeks she brought me underwear and food with an official permit. Meanwhile she went to school (unauthorized, as she is half Jewish, but respected by the school administration because anti-Nazi), got her diploma, second in her class, gave German lessons, got food, etc. In short, she accomplished superhuman tasks. On June 25 of '42, I was suddenly freed, without a trial, without charges; I was weak, down to 48 kilos, full of fleas and lice, with fragile nerves, heart and lungs in bad shape, arthritis in my left knee that had begun when we left.

At this point came the tragedy of losing our husband and father; the cause of his death was pneumonia, with subsequent cardiac paralysis, resulting from inhuman treatment: roll calls in the night in the courtyard in -35 degrees Celsius, in pajamas, and other "jokes" like that.

Now the only one left alive was Percy's youngest brother, Rolf, who ended up in prison for unknown reasons; there, through a guard, he managed to get in touch with us. The Swiss Embassy had earlier offered us a passport; my only sister had obtained it without knowing if we were still alive, because as long as the German occupation lasted it wasn't possible to communicate with the outside world.

After February 8, 1944, since Felix no longer needed our help, we accepted the offer, and the SS were, in an ironic twist of fate, forced to deliver the passports to us; we left July 13 of '44, at six in the morning. Each of us carried two suitcases and a backpack, this was what was allowed; everything we couldn't put in boxes and send remained in the apartment; only a single box arrived. I didn't even believe that we ourselves would ever arrive; the partners of mixed marriages didn't in fact have permission to expatriate, why us? We traveled through Berlin-Basilea and arrived without delays, safe and sound, at midday on July 15, 1944.

And here, dear Clarette, the value of friendship is again demonstrated. In Riga we were "wives of a mixed marriage" (there were more than 300 mixed unions with Jewish husbands and around an equal number with Jewish wives; in the first case divorce was obligatory and the man went to the ghetto, in the second the woman could stay with her husband after castration). The Latvians, especially the police, took care of carrying out these prescriptions; a Latvian prof. saw to the operation. The way the

> Peck-Schwefels passed together through whatever troubles, helped each other, risked their lives for each other, I have to confess, was truly wonderful, even if immensely sad. . . .

When I left for Latvia I didn't remember this letter except for the few words "had taken the child with him. Both perished in the mass execution."

It was the only information I had, I didn't know the other details; I hadn't even realized that the cousin had been precise about the place—the big shelter for the poor and the old—where my father had been admitted with his daughter. If I had read more closely, I would have gone with Pietro to Ludzas Iela, in the Moscow suburb, where the biggest of these homes was. I would have asked how my cousin had been able to enter the ghetto, or if my father's presence in the home had been reported by her husband, Felix. Without a doubt, I would have been equally surprised by the esteem given to my cousin Irene, as an anti-Nazi, by the administration of the Latvian school; I still put all Latvians in a single category.

And I hadn't even read the next letter; here the cousin, evidently answering some questions from my mother, explained that neither she nor her daughter could remember what had become of our relatives, I suppose my aunt and my cousins. She wrote that in all likelihood they had suffered the common fate. She repeated her bitter judgment of the Latvians in general: "Did you know the Latvians so little that you don't remember how anti-Semitic they were, and also their greed for money?"

This book is littered with "I don't know"s and "I don't remember"s. So I scarcely remember my mother's gray, bewildered face as she spoke to us, faltering: the conclusive proof of my father's terrible fate had reached us from Switzerland. Certainly, in her broken speech the word *terrible* didn't appear, yet the fact that she had written again to the cousin for more information and hadn't opened the third letter reveals, it seems to me, distress in the face of events whose extreme cruelty she hadn't suspected and would have liked to forget. At Torre Pellice, after the war—I now remember—she went one day to Villa Olanda, where at that time a group of refugees from the Eastern countries were housed, among whom, it was said, were some from Latvia. One of them had whispered to her that they had all died, they had all died, even "the Gersoni of the leather."

As for the moment when I actually held the letter, my daughter declares she was very struck—she was young, she doesn't remember exactly when this happened—by the sight of it in my hand. The pages, she says, were large and translucent, similar to the sheets of paper used for air mail letters. So it was definitely the letter in question. According to her, I had said, "Now I know how my father died."

In *Distant Fathers* I claim that my mother never showed it to me and that I had found it among her papers after her death. But maybe she had given it to me—her loyalty was absolute, her method of lying was to be silent—and I, glancing briefly at the writing, had perceived only the few words that remained in my mind, rejecting the rest, which at the time didn't matter to me. My father had been killed with his daughter; nothing else could concern me. For obscure reasons, those few words "had taken his daughter with him" moved me. He hadn't abandoned her, his little child, wild and chaotic as he was; he had taken her with him. His daughter.

That I, too, was his daughter, that my sister was, seemed to have been cancelled out by the meeting with our mother in the park, in the late fall of 1934, when she persuaded us to secretly leave our father, to join her and flee with her. The meeting, after many months of her absence from home, was certainly agreed on with our governess Bögi. It's not very likely, I reflect, that it was truly the sudden watershed moment that memory restores to me now, while I struggle so to retrace the twists and turns in which my child's heart was lost.

What is a happy childhood or an unhappy childhood? It is, I think, a childhood seen through our adult eyes. As children we don't know, even in conditions of poverty, hunger, cold, if we're happy or unhappy. We live in a motionless present, not unlike the one in which old people live inertly. If we cry in fear and call to our mother, we're unwavering in our cry.

If I look back through adult eyes it seems to me that Sisi and I had, all in all, a happy childhood, if not very happy. The discord between our mother and father was part of that happy childhood, frozen in the perpetuity of the present, and barely obscured it. Darkness didn't fall suddenly after the meeting in the park but gradually came to shadow our life.

That day, in the first hug, I smelled—I wrote in *Distant Fathers*—the delightful odor of Mamma's fur coat. She had stayed away before for several weeks—the previous winter?—and we knew, my sister and I, that she hadn't wanted to return because of the disagreements with our father. Anyway, we never witnessed—I want to repeat it—real fights between our parents. Violent as the fights may have been, they never happened in our presence.

We're with Mamma, on the train standing in the station. We've gone to say goodbye to our father, who's leaving. He's standing, thin and tall, in an elegant winter suit that, I remember very clearly, is new and soft. In a low voice my mother says some things, reproaches him, he shouldn't go. I look at him from below; he doesn't answer and I realize that he's nervous. Maybe he's smoking. He, too, has a good smell of cologne and cigar. I'm sorry Mamma is scolding him; she's always right.

And here I repeat, yet again, "I don't remember." I don't remember, that is, exactly what Mamma told us in the park. Would she have talked about herself? Would she have said that she couldn't and wouldn't stay any longer with our father? Of course, she must have said that he wouldn't let us see her anymore; in fact, he hadn't permitted it in the long preceding months.

That he was, *therefore*, bad. It seems unlikely to me, though not impossible, that she had already suggested to us that our father was holding us hostage to force her to change her mind. The hypothesis, certainly likely, was later sustained many times by our grandmother in Torre Pellice. Maybe Bögi also alluded to it. It contained in itself the inexorable assertion: your father doesn't love you. *That* remained a hard certainty locked in our mind forever.

Our father didn't love us. A hard rock locked within us by a bolt that no one bothered to open.

So, with him dead, and dead with him every hope of finding him, I was forced out of necessity to return to where he had lived with us as children; I had to pray at Rumbula; a phrase finally spoken by someone else had to unlock the bolt that barred my tears. In mourning not only for him who had died but also for the love that was taken from us, from Sisi and me. And was taken from him.

A few weeks after I returned from Latvia I was sitting in a restaurant with my friend Carlotta. She asked me about my trip, and I said I needed some help from her husband, Hens—by a strange coincidence the son of Baltic Germans from Riga—to decipher some phrases in a letter (the one from the cousin) written in German script, and in fact he later helped me. I said it had been very painful (or something like that) to go back to my childhood. I mentioned my father, with the usual awkwardness. She, then, quiet and sweet, observed, "Naturally, he was a bad husband but a good father."

Of our very early happiness I have only indirect evidence. I have a few photographs, three letters, some birthday messages.

I have a photo of myself at around two, with short, slightly wavy hair, not yet curly, face upturned in a luminous and happy gaze. I have a photo of my mother kneeling, in a full dress, a long pearl necklace around her neck, a hint of joy in her beautiful, gentle profile; I'm leaning against her. In another picture, a tiny one, she's sitting on a bench, fat and smiling, the usual elegant hat on her head, her coat unbuttoned; behind her, in the distance, Riga and the Düna in 1930.

His serene presence is reflected in our faces; with him we were happy.

I know I will never have answers to many of my questions, yet I wonder if there wasn't a reflection of long-ago childhood happiness in my sister Sisi's homesickness for the Latvian homeland that, for good or ill, was the homeland of our father. There, where she never was granted a return, we lived together with our parents, and in reality we had had to separate from both, if in different ways, after that meeting in the park.

In the summer of 1934—our mother was in Italy—we spent about two months with Bögi in Inschenhof, in a hotel on the shores of a lake. I looked on the map to see if I could find the place: the names are now all Latvian, except for the cities and towns that have the old German names in parentheses. I found a lake called Ineši, ninety kilometers from Riga; might it be the lake of Inschenhof?

I write to Mamma, June 20, 1934:

Dear Mutti! When I started writing the letter,

unexpectedly we had a visit; Papi, Grandma, and Grandpa came, they brought candy. Papi brought candy with cream [I use the Baltic term *Schmant*]. Then we went to have coffee. Then we went in the car for a little ways because Papi came in the car. We walked back.

After describing our trip there, I sign the letter "Micki."

Sisi, in lopsided handwriting that presages the famous bad calligraphy that she later apologizes for constantly and will have her whole life, tells about the wild strawberries we eat every day, chocolate, swimming, and shorts we could wear from morning to night.

Bögi, the governess, communicates to "dear Madame" that we eat with a good appetite, that later our grandparents will come and stay in a room under ours, that "Herr Gersoni comes to see us almost every day, the 22nd he leaves for England."

July 3, Micki:

My beloved Mutti!

I have many things to tell you; first of all I have to say that I have a girl friend and a boy friend. It's true, I had a fight with Bella, but Arne is very nice. We already wrote you a letter but you say you didn't get it, so we're writing to you again. I still have a letter to write, that one I'll send to Papi. Arne and I made a house for ourselves, Sisi also made a house. Grandma arrives tomorrow. I forgot to tell you that Grandpa took a room. We went fishing with Arne's father, and every day we go out in the boat, which is really nice. But imagine, I have worms, 12 of them. But now I have to write the letter to Papi. Your little daughter Micki who loves you very much sends you love.

Sisi, with her big lopsided handwriting:

We're very well: we're very tan, we eat a lot.

Bögi asks her to forgive Sisi, who is very lazy and doesn't want to write, and she gives the news of the grandparents' arrival. "Herr Gersoni is in England."

Papi and Mutti traveled often; we were used to their absence and, besides, confident of their return.

Some weeks later Micki writes to her dear Mammina:

I haven't written to you for a long time and I also have a lot to tell you; first of all, soon it will be my birthday, please don't forget the presents. Papi comes often. Our Ingo has become a big rascal, once when we were in the city, Alvine bought a big fish and put it in a basin. Our Ingo approached very quietly and stuck out a paw toward the fish. He ended up right in the basin and got all wet.

When Mamma returned from Italy, she didn't come home. In September her letter of farewell to our father arrived, and that night he ran through all the rooms weeping and lamenting, "I've lost you, Clarette!"

In one picture we're on the lakeshore; I'm in the background, with a big ribbon at an angle in my hair, leaning over the low bushes, picking something. In the foreground are two young women—but which of the two is Bögi?—with two little girls and a tall, very handsome little boy—my Finnish friend Arne, evidently. The one who refused to let me verify *de visu* that the little sack visible under his swimming trunks was a permanent attachment. The liar.

In the envelope that Mamma saved—she saved, in a disorganized way, everything, whereas I, while organizing, destroyed—I found some Christmas dedications: German poems or short prose passages copied by Sisi and me for our "beloved Mutti."

There's one, this time not for Christmas but written out probably to show Mamma how good I was at Gothic calligraphy, which is dated May 13, 1934. In very tall narrow letters Marina assures her mother that as an adult she'll give her even more beautiful gifts. At first I couldn't understand the words; I climbed up steeples and descended from them; I went from the top of the letters to the bottom, from the bottom to the top. I couldn't have written it!

10. Courlanders, Kurischer

I don't remember our grandparents' visit that summer in Inschenhof at all, but I remember perfectly the soft lapping of the reeds against the sides of the boat. And also the smell of the water and the hollow, tender sigh of the water lily as, torn from the swampy bottom, it rose into my hand. Of our father's frequent visits, I remember—as I've already recounted—the storm on the lake that suddenly turned lead gray as we were returning on the hotel boat from the other shore, where we'd taken him to get the train or a taxi to the station.

Of myself I see again only the figure of a little girl on a small dais in the hotel lobby: I am supposed to recite a poem, lines about a garland of white lilies I'm wearing in my hair. I'm really suffering and almost refuse to get up on the dais. My flowers are not in fact lilies, I'm afraid I'll be laughed at, I don't care about the people who applaud me (it's obvious, I recite very well). Would my father have been in the audience? Would my grandparents have applauded me? When I'm so preoccupied with myself, the words and actions of others barely touch me, and I don't even remember them.

I've been floating forever in the broth of my memories, and I don't feel an excessive unease.

By what whims of heart or mind are our memories guided? At my age I could imagine them now purified and corrected by adult rethinking; instead, to tell the truth, they sometimes seem confused by later sensations, like those first stamped in my childish brain. I startle in front of a simple white house, pale birches in the front yard, the cries of seagulls overhead. Here, I say to myself, here. But did whatever jolts my uncertain memory happen then, in lost childhood, or here, during the long years spent in Italy? Nor do I know what it is exactly, only that it's something familiar. It could even be someone else's memory, absorbed into that vague confusion I carry with me. Every so often, reaching in at random, I extract from the broth the little that matters, for the most part affections and impressions. If I narrate my own experiences, they rise into my hand like the lily pads uprooted from the mud, accompanied by a mute gurgling, with no echo. There's no one with whom I can compare them to give them more definition.

But I'm attentive to the memories of others, which filter into my mind as they're told, becoming, that is, mine. My mother tells me nothing; Grandmother Anna plays the piano and sighs, it's her way of speaking; my father tells stories and my grandfather, too, tells stories.

My grandfather describes how he bought furs in Siberia to resell and become rich and marry Grandmother, who wasn't poor like him but from a well-known family. He never told me we were Courlanders; this I learn in Riga from the courteous director of the museum on Skolas Iela, who also called into question the *i* ending of Gersoni.

At first my research into my ancestors focused exclusively on the variation between our *i* and the *y* of Marina's surname. I would have liked to discover common forebears. She had many relatives: the Gersonys had left Latvia around the time of the First World War, her great-grandfather in the early twentieth century. Meanwhile we consulted each other on a possible, distant kinship, I began to call her "my little cousin Marina." I informed her immediately of every new discovery. In her most recent message, she told me not to talk to anyone else; with our fixation on the Gersoni/y they would end up considering us both crazy.

So when I got ready to investigate I was in a playful mood, I was having fun; the Courlander forebears were hidden in the impenetrable night of time, and I wasn't gripped by the hunger of the bloodhound, which drives me to follow and check and dig into others' facts to represent them in my story as accurately as possible. With the paternal forebears of Courland I felt no familial or historical bond similar to that which, for good or ill, joined me to my maternal Waldensian ancestors.

How many times on an outing had I wakened at dawn, in the mountains, in the valleys, and seen in the east the herald of the sun in the sky that lightened from mother-of-pearl cold to the warmest yellow while the roosters crowed! Bending over the stream, I had drunk water that tasted of iron and stone; as I walked, the soles of my boots had tramped the familiar rocky path traversed by my mother's distant fathers. Walking with Pietro in Riga, I was surprised by the gilded light of sunset that appeared between the leaves of the trees in the parks: it was new. I didn't remember the autumn sunset in the city; *my* sunset was the milky one, of summer, on the beach. Certainly it wasn't enough to revive an ancestor in the twilight of a Friday.

For me, no relative existed before Grandfather Maurice; my Gersonis began with him.

Before leaving for Latvia, in September of 1999, I had proposed to Marina that she travel with us to Libau—she hoped to be able to—and look in the cemetery of present-day Liepaja for possible Gersoni/y graves. I didn't think we'd be able to discover traces of real forebears anywhere else.

"The only sure thing," I said to Marina, "is the fact that our people crossed the Red Sea together."

"Note, they're Sephardim," she said, but she didn't remember where she'd got this certainty. I liked the idea that our common ancestors had been driven from Sepharad to Latvia, but Spain was so far that that journey seemed pretty unlikely.

"We'd have to find someone to come with us," I said to Marina, "who knows Hebrew."

My Bible, inherited from Grandfather Coïsson, was obviously French.

I didn't yet know that on the old Jewish tombs there were no surnames, that usually the name of the deceased was followed simply by the name of the father.

I walked through the empty streets of Riga and the emptiness surrounded me; emotion got in the way of thoughts and recollections. Here and there I picked up crumbs of my past, very little; of the Gersonis nothing remained in my father's city. His life sank in my broth, leaving behind nothing of himself but the faint wake of my childhood memories.

And yet the scent of the lilac beside his parents' house was his. Did he swim in the branch of the river that separates the island where the house is from the mainland? And for that, and for other rebellious acts of disobedience, had his father sent him away to the Lutheran pastor who raised him instead of his parents? His the sea, his the forests, his the cafés, and his the horseracing track—did he bet there? His the streets of the city, so happily frequented at night and in who knows what company. His the country roads of Courland and Livonia, traveled on during excursions in his favorite luxury cars. His the houses of cousins and friends. His the forebears, unknown to me, whom he, of course, could trace back.

Even before I started this book—I was still circling around the title at the top of the blank page—my son Paolo, doing research on the Internet, found for me a series of documents about Libau, the lovely Libau of the early twentieth century, with some autobiographical articles by people who had lived there and emigrated in time. The recollections didn't go back to the era of the probable birth of my grandfather in the city—from which he would depart to make his fortune in Siberia—but there was an email address for someone who had helped gather evidence and information. So I asked Paolo to write a short email to Harry Hurwitz in Israel, asking for possible information. The game continued. From Harry Hurwitz I got a quick and very polite response. For years, the few survivors and victims' children who had escaped the slaughter had been collecting every bit of evidence, every archive note, lists of names, addresses, book titles, as if to fill, at least with the scant memories that remained, the immense abyss that had swallowed up their families. Among other things, two pages from a phone book arrived: one from Libau, in 1930, bore two Gersoni surnames, properly with the *i*; one from Riga, from 1940, with the names of my grandfather, my mother, and a Lidija Gersoni. From researcher to researcher, I reached the address of the Latvian Archives.

When, at this point, I decided to send a letter to the head archivist, Irina Veinberga (the same surname as my Grandmother Anna), and included in it the only certain date I possessed, that of my father's birth, I realized that I was gradually turning onto an unexpected road, walking back not toward an ordinary story ready to be narrated but toward the unknown distant fathers of my paternal family.

I felt some relief in occupying myself with them—I had meanwhile started writing—and began to feel curious. I could have told the story and unloaded the oppressive burden of the stark testimony concerning the slaughter. Although they had arrived in Courland after earlier slaughters—certainly, impossible to have any illusion—they had, at least, arrived. Some of them had managed to raise children to adulthood and these, in turn, had had children and, surviving generation after generation, the Gersonis at the end of their wandering had their last child, my father.

It took my forebears more than a year to retrace their steps from east to west to get to me. Irina Veinberga had replied to my first request for information with a polite letter. The archive was able to go back to the grandfather of my grandfather, she wrote. The family was from Mitau, so they had lived in Courland as far back as the early nineteenth century.

I clearly remembered my grandfather telling me that he had come to Riga from Libau. The Jews did not in fact have permission to live there; they got it around 1850. As in Riga, so in Libau the senators of the Baltic nobility did not grant permission and did not turn a blind eye: they were not Russian. When, at the last partition of Poland, in 1795, Courland—divided, small as it was, into a nearly independent grand duchy but subject to Poland and the Polish possession of Pilten!—had been entirely subsumed into the Russian empire, the tsar allowed the cities to maintain their earlier privileges, among which was that of keeping out the Jews. Yet the Jews were licensed to sell their odds and ends, and, with a permit for a limited stay, lodged in a special area outside the city—in Riga it was the Moscow suburb—but then out with beards, sidelocks, overcoats, and slippers! Horrible to listen to the linguistic jumble in which they communicated with each other; it was obviously useful for deceiving the ignorant Latvian peasants and the servant girls, who might also need those odds and ends. As for the many Jewish timber merchants who came down the Düna on rafts, there was no need to worry: they did not live within the walls since they slept on their boats. And some of the more prosperous merchants were able to get a passport. In the end, many of them had a hand in the commerce that enriched the city.

So when one morning in 1742 Empress Elizabeth, going from her bedroom to the chapel, decided on a whim to expel the killers of Christ from all of Russia—she stated aloud that that blood-stained money didn't interest her—the senators of the Hanseatic city, despite their own Lutheran biases, had tried to oppose it. Peter the Great had, alas, added Livonia, with Riga, to the empire. To the senators, the thaler of the Jews, as long as there were plenty of them, didn't seem blood-stained. But the Russian sovereign, that bastard, wouldn't turn a blind eye despite their protests; fortunately some years later she closed them both, and the German Catherine, who had secretly kept her Lutheran ideas, ascended the throne. She allowed three Jews to live in the city; thirty-three others were immediately added to these, thanks to the deplorable Jewish habit of taking along relatives from the first to the third degree. They became *Schutzjuden*, protected Jews. More, for the moment, the empress couldn't do—she wrote in her memoirs—since her imperial power was just then suspended between the suspicious death of her husband and her future glory. The Jews expelled by Elizabeth had crowded into precarious shelters on the borders of the empire; they died by the thousand, but they also survived by the thousand. Another of their deplorable customs was early marriage: this filled in the gaps left by those who were lost.

At the start of the nineteenth century, in Libau, among the fourteen *Schutzjuden* (with the "dependents" they formed a group of forty-nine people) there were no Gersonis. Nor were there any Gersonys, who turned out to be not from Libau but from Hasenpoth. But what nonsense had those lying grandparents told us?

For the whole year during which I waited for my forebears from Riga to arrive, there was a contest between the *i* and the *y*, won by the Gersonys, who, thanks to an American cousin of Marina's, reached the goal of the genealogical tree eight months before the Gersonis; as time passed, however, the latter became more learned. During the wait, I had nothing else to do but educate myself. I was no longer content with vague notions.

The American Gersony, a second or third cousin of Marina, excited at the news that he was about to become a father—late but generously—of triplets, had asked Irina Veinberga for his own genealogical table. I don't know if he had paid in advance, but his forebears had reached him without obstacles. And they were from Hasenpoth, today Aizpute. I can't imagine what the Latvian Archives thought of us, with the *i* or the *y*, gripped in the same period by a sudden mania for ancestral research, him in New York, me in Turin.

In fact, on the map, the moves within Courland were frequently as short as a few kilometers, but the survival of the Jews was often linked to tiny factors, later revealed as essential, which could vary between localities just a few kilometers apart; the gap between two families after barely two generations could turn out to be enormous. Equally fragile was the duration of even the most solid patrimony. Wealth accumulated thanks to expedient marital arrangements, good luck in business, and personal skill could dissolve in an instant, pushing back into poverty those who had managed to rise. Certainly the ban on the possession of real estate contributed to that precariousness, but also, sometimes, the innate Jewish tendency to speculate, whether on a batch of whalebone or a suitcase of French bonnets.

The Gersonys who happened into Hasenpoth had undoubtedly arrived in a place that was more favorable than the Gersonis of Mitau had. Hasenpoth, inserted into the Polish wedge of Pilten, was the administrative capital. In Courland the local history of every town contained within itself other very local events, but, unlike a matryoshka, the external history didn't necessarily resemble the history that it contained within. The province of Pilten—a plot of land in the west of the country—had been a bishopric; the bishops didn't look too closely at the bloodstains on the thaler of the Jews; and the more money they managed to extract from them the happier they were. Thus their Jews enjoyed privileges that the Kurischer, the Courlanders, usually didn't dream of. The Hasenpoth Jews, in particular, had been granted exclusive rights to import through the contiguous ports of Libau and Windau lemons for the holiday of Sukkot, the festival of huts. In that way more than a few thaler also entered the pockets of the Jews. Was it possible that the Gersonys might be among the importers? If I think of the oranges Mamma acquired through the Italian diplomatic mission in Riga, which, lined up on a high shelf, we admired as if they were gold, I can imagine the opulence of those fortunate citrus merchants.

In the sixteenth century a bishop in financial difficulties had sold the bishopric of Pilten to the king of Denmark, who gave it to his brother, who began fighting with the Polish king, and so in succession they gave it, sold it, disputed it for twenty-five years, until, with the mediation of a prince of Brandenburg, the king of Poland bought it, Jews included, with their ancient privileges. None of the princes in the fight had ever set foot in Pilten, much less in Hasenpoth, where the citrus importers continued to prosper. Every year at Sukkot a citron decorated the wreath hanging on the symbolic hut, also the symbol of a fragrant south lost forever. The winters in Courland were long and cold.

Once I had received the very brief and surprising news that the Gersonis were from Mitau, I decided that I finally had to consult the *Geschichte der Juden in den Provinzen Liv und Kurland* [History of the Jews in Livonia and Courland, 1853], by Rabbi Wunderbar. According to my approximate calculations, he would have been the rabbi of my great-grandfather with the still unknown name. When all my attempts to obtain a copy of the book through the so-called normal channels failed, I decided to ask the Latvian National Library how much it would cost me to have the holy man travel from Riga to Turin. Two weeks later I found in the mailbox an envelope with a photocopy of the text and a request for payment in postal orders of only 12,600 lire. Not for nothing is the name of my great-grandfather's rabbi Wunderbar!

The small book—eighty-six pages, dedicated to his excellency the usual Russian prince with many surnames ending in *ski*, governor general of Livonia, Estonia, Courland in the year of grace 1853 of the kingdom of His Majesty Nicholas I—proclaimed that all the misfortunes of the Courlander Jews were now over; to begin with, they would be called not жидов (*zhidov*) but евреев (*yevrei*)[6]. Before Courland became part of the kingdom of his gracious majesty the tsar, their experiences had been variable and often unhappy. The text, in the elaborate but natural German of a cultured person accustomed to using the language, employed documentary sources and took advantage of the author's direct knowledge of the history of the Jews in those countries since the late sixteenth century.

The date 1561 marked its official beginning. The treaty that authorized the subjection of Lithuania and Livonia to Poland even had a codicil regarding the Jews. In those countries they were forbidden to be merchants or to work as excisemen or tax collectors, but, and this is important, it established the ambiguous norm destined to regulate their life in the Polish possessions and, later, also in Courland for centuries: almost everything was forbidden except a temporary stay. They had to pay very dearly for their passports (they were foreigners and remained so for a long time), but although notoriously sober they had to survive, so they ended up practicing every possible prohibited trade, including working as

6 In Latvian *žīdi/ebreji*; in Italian *giudei/ebrei*; in English perhaps something like "Yids/Jews."

distillers for the nobles from whom they rented—at a high price, of course—the necessary taverns.

So Rabbi Wunderbar told the story; yet ancient tombstones seen by the author bore witness to a Jewish settlement preceding the critical date of 1561, and in reality, one might suppose, there had always been Jews passing through, trading, selling, buying, surviving.

While I rapidly leafed through the book, reading here and there, I paused first on the surnames, in search of an ancestor. There was a fine list of the most notable Jews of Mitau, who in 1794 signed a petition to the grand duke to obtain greater freedoms. Between one prohibition and the next, and periodic threats of expulsion by the regional Diet, the Kurischer had constructed a synagogue; they had already had the cemetery since the first decades of the century—the dead had to be interred somewhere—and now they would have liked to have some civil rights like the fortunate Jews of Hasenpoth. There the Jews could even vote in the elections for city councilors, if not be elected themselves. In any case there was no Gersoni among the prominent men, nor did I find one among the rabbis and scholars cited at the end of the book.

Last on that list, not out of modesty but in alphabetical order, Rabbi Wunderbar appears, with his many, many books. He's not concerned, like the more mystical or imaginative rabbis, with quantifying the number and rank of the angels or of the probable urns in the temple at Jerusalem: no, he's a man of his time; he writes an elementary German grammar for the Israelite youth, a topographic guide to the city of Mitau, more than one text on ancient Jewish medicine, including the macrobiotics and dietetics of the ancient Israelites; he's interested in Buddhism and the sources of Goethe's *Faust*. If he gives in to the Jewish vice of calculation, he counts the lines of the Pentateuch. He appears, all in all, satisfied with the religious condition of the Israelites in Courland: they can be divided into three classes, one or the other of which is the majority in any given city. In Bauske, Jacobstadt, Friedrichstadt, Pilten, and Subbath, most are strictly orthodox—on average, unfortunately, rather ignorant. In the first two cities you would even encounter individuals from the Hasidic sect. In Grobin, Libau, and Goldingen, the Jews have, with the requisite exceptions, let's say, more superficial beliefs. But in Hasenpoth and Mitau, how many scholars there were, how many scholars of great fame and irreproachable traditions!

The list of religious and charitable institutions benefitting the city of Mitau, not for nothing the Courlander capital, is long; it includes a dig at his predecessor, Rabbi Friedmann, who built in Mitau a synagogue and a "fairly decent" bath for women, at his own expense, anyway. There's no lack of schools: there's a community school for the poor (Talmud-Torah) and a good ten private schools. Since 1805 an association for the education of young people, supported by private individuals, has taken care of instruction for poor children; they will be able to study religion and language, and then work as apprentices. There is another association that helps prisoners, providing religious assistance and on holidays proper food, and is sometimes able to buy their release from the government, if they've been imprisoned for debt. This last association has a difficult time, however, since the wealthy Jews of Mitau are not sympathetic to the cause of the incarcerated. There is even an association that supports artisans in difficulty. People live quite well in Mitau under his gracious majesty Nicholas I, if only in the opinion of my great-grandfather's rabbi.

What were the Gersonis doing in Mitau in the early nineteenth century, if they weren't among the notables or even among the scholars? I didn't find them among the latter, either, in any document. Nor the Gersonys. They survived, that's all. Maybe as small-scale merchants or artisans, shoemakers, tailors, stone breakers, workmen, shopkeepers. They weren't concerned with the long diatribes that, at the end of the preceding century, had divided intellectuals on the advantages and disadvantages of the assimilation of the Jews. They were men like any others, declared the adherents of French ideas, provided they laid aside their awkward garments, shaved their beards, and converted to the most civilized of languages, German. They were useful to the country, they stated; they increased its wealth, therefore it was just to grant them the rights of citizenship, schools, property. The adversaries replied: What are you talking about, they were useless, harmful, took work away from honest Christian merchants; the rite of making sacrifices on the altar to their god in an incomprehensible language was repugnant, and then why did they bury their dead in such a hurry? There wasn't even time to find out what they had died of! People whispered about those occult rites—very secret blood rites—and in Russia the rumor, at times, became a public outcry. Where had that little vagabond disappeared to; the one who'd been seen near the synagogue on Friday afternoon?

Rabbi Wunderbar considers it possible to explain to the Christians in "Christian language" what to them appears strange or reprehensible. Are we or are we not in an era of sensible rationality! How many centuries had it been, really, since the Jews stopped making sacrifices on the altar!—ever since the destruction of the temple, when they had been scattered throughout the world. In all likelihood it had been a misunderstanding of the peculiar handling of meat according to Mosaic tradition. Our enlightened Rabbi Wunderbar doesn't even want to think that the same custom—blood, however it's treated, can evoke mysterious impressions of violence suffered and inflicted—is at the root of the superstitious, tenacious popular belief about human sacrifice among the Jews.

At what point in the course of the century had my Gersonis, mixed up in the crowd of fellow Jews, shaved their beards and put on the *Berlinese* outfit, like others, without ever hearing talk of, say, Moses Mendelssohn or reading his German translation of the Bible? Certainly, before the cholera epidemic of 1848, which some of them had escaped, families must have departed for the Russian colonies of the Chersonese, but mine hadn't (I found no Gersoni or Gersony among them); given that they'd managed to make it, why leave? Maybe, even earlier, at the start of the century—my great-grandfather was not yet born, though maybe his father had just been born—some detachment of the Grande Armée had passed through Mitau; maybe some important Napoleonic general lodged in the immense grand-ducal palace, and the French, like good revolutionaries making no distinction between Jews and Christians, sacked any house or hovel that was offered to their hunger for loot. I feel that from the Gersonis there would have been little to plunder. Might one of them have resoled the boot of a Frenchman? The French promised justice—it was said that in Paris Jews had been granted the status of citizens. But was it better to live under the injustice of the tsar and keep the Pact with He who cannot be named, preserving one's own customs, or lose both to gain Napoleon's dubious equality? So they must have thought, pounding the nails into the sole.

While I was finding out about the books, my son Andrea, convalescing in Rome after a long illness, devoted himself to genealogical research on the Internet. He provided me with people named Gersoni/y in every corner of the planet and from every epoch: botanists, racecar drivers, psychologists, writers. He sailed out into the ocean of history and geography with such frequency and skill that the world appeared inhabited everywhere by Gersonis. For a while, in the absence of mine, I imagined an anthology of Gersonis, who hadn't yet arrived from Riga. There the Latvians, polluted by decades of Soviet occupation, had lost in the accounting office my honest and punctual payment, and didn't answer solicitations by email, letters, or phone. Why not tell the story of Hirsch Gersoni—becoming Henry in America—who, having converted for love after a mésalliance with a Lutheran woman, had emigrated, reconverted, to the United States? There he had been a vice-rabbi and a translator from the Russian. He was Lithuanian, however, from Vilnius, although he had the Gersoni tendency to marriage *extra moenia*. Most of all, I liked Clementina Gersoni, a Brazilian who, protesting against the demolition of houses in her neighborhood in Sao Paulo, had released into the air, over the heads of the police, a flock of white doves. Somewhat bizarre, the Gersonis, always.

One day, emerging from his ocean of research, Andrea sent me a small item that seemed to hurl the anonymous history of our forebears back toward a famous date: he had found a Gersoni in a list of Sephardic Jews from Morocco, reported in a book published in 1976.

Thus in 1492, expelled by the Catholic Isabella, some of the Gersonis really had headed north and, driven from country to country by intolerance and by the poverty of the European ghettoes, had reached the limits of what was then Ultima Thule, the immense Muscovite empire that barely allowed Jews passing through to cross its borders. There must have been few Jews heading for the prohibited Russian frontiers compared with the many others who, having crossed the Mediterranean, had chosen less uncomfortable goals, settling under gentler skies in Italy, Turkey, Morocco. So Marina Gersony was right; ours had come from their second homeland, from Spain, removing the mezuzah from the doorpost and keeping the house key in their pocket. For a long time, they hoped to return to Sepharad.

A few days later another item arrived from Andrea that might indicate the route our people traveled to the east: in the middle of Lithuania a small town bore the critical name. Gersoni it was called, or Gersonyay. Here we go again, an *i* or a *y*?

I, too, then set out on their route, gripped by the hunger of the bloodhound I mentioned above. I had realized that few of my Gersonis were recorded in history, and they were hard to identify among thousands, so different from my mother's Coïssons, few among few. Andrea concerned himself with them, too, and had given me the surname of the couple of forebears who in the early eighteenth century had lived in Angrògna: their descendants continued to live there, as stable as my Gersonis were vagabond, very few among thousands.

The reader will already have realized that I'm gradually introducing into my pages, in a straightforward way, the names of those who have been with me and helped in the work (first of all my children), with advice and research, with information, and with lively and affectionate listening—I told my friend Silvana the story while we were swimming in the sea in Sardinia. As if, like me, they were protagonists of my history—I didn't want to place them, in the customary way, at the beginning or end of the book. So I will also cite Gino Moretti, who occasionally sent me from the United States photocopies of texts that, following my experience with Rabbi Wunderbar, I rightly thought couldn't be found in Turin, carefully trimming the margins to make the package more compact—the books are very large.

To Gino I had recounted letter by letter the progress and setbacks of the book. He had liked Henry Gersoni so much that he asked permission to write his story; I had refused, suggesting that he instead call a great-grandchild, Henrietta Gersoni, discovered by Andrea among the various Gersonis. The woman had slammed down the phone; it was impossible to find out if she had anything to relate about the Lithuanian Gersonis. I had sought information about them in vain from a very courteous cultural attaché at the Lithuanian Embassy. Both she and a young guide from Vilnius, a specialist in Jewish research, had politely doubted that one could uncover any Gersoni who was unquestionably my personal ancestor—it was true, and I already knew that there were some hundred and fifty variations of the surname in the tsar's empire! I seemed to perceive even some slight disapproval in the voice of the girl with the Russian Jewish surname, the guide I telephoned in Vilnius. She reproached my snobbishness: Who did I think I was, with my Gersonis?

And yet, on the list of the hundred and fifty variants, the Gersonis, those with the *i* (the *y* didn't emerge; the hypothesis that it was a matter of transcription became ever more likely), occupied, with the Gershuni, a place of their own: they bore a surname derived not from Gershon but from the plural of the Gershonites, the same ones I had found in Numbers 3. There's our *i*! The place indicated on the list was in fact Riga.

All right, I said to myself, then I'll follow them among the multitudes of refugees who left with mezuzah and key in pocket from very Catholic Spain, mixed with other multitudes of Ashkenazi fleeing to Poland and from there to Lithuania and from there to Courland. I will never know at what point along the age-old path they lost the house key; I will know only that they never lost the Sabbath, or Passover, or, naturally, the *i*.

In Courland, in Kuldiga, I had seen the little houses leaning one against the other on the famous "mountain road," tranquil and familiar in the sun of an autumn afternoon—at one time they'd had roofs of rough shingles with straw pressed into the cracks—and I had already imagined the place in the serenity of a Sabbath, like a goal finally reached.

Their journey had doubtless lasted centuries, with sojourns, some long, some short, depending on the opportunities a place offered; in a year they had moved from Amsterdam to Bamberg, in ten years from a village in Pomerania to another village just across the river. Unlike the peoples of the countries they passed through, they couldn't pay attention merely to daily events but always sought to know what was happening in the capital and to be aware of it before the news appeared on placards displayed in the square or in the sermon read from the pulpit in the Gentiles' church. The merchants reported to them, a cousin arrived with his wife and in-laws, the son-in-law of the rabbi who had ties to someone in Warsaw, Danzig, Vilnius.

In Poland their subjection to the Polish kings was much more direct than that of their Christian fellow citizens. They suffered wars and plagues just like everyone else; but their daily life seemed to depend, without intermediaries, on the sovereign himself (by others seen only on coins), who, almost staring them in the face one by one, decided their fate like the biblical Nebuchadnezzar on the rivers of Babylon and Ahasuerus in Persia.

When, step by step, maybe with the house keys still in their pocket—or they had stopped for some decades in Amsterdam and had left them there to a couple of descendants—the Gersonis reached Poland, passing through the ghettoes of Germany, they had begun to speak in "Jewish-German"—Yiddish—with the busy local Jews, who, in Poland and neighboring Lithuania, had for centuries enjoyed the intermittent favor of some Casimir or Sigismund. These sovereigns didn't dream of imaginary cities (like those who in Italy and France wrote of "ideal cities," concerning themselves more with government than with subjects) but had in mind their future State and very soon granted the industrious Jews the right to stay and to trade everywhere, and even a viable defense in trials with Christians. They could make loans with interest and collect taxes. They could also use the Christians' public baths. Finally, some of them, provided they had the necessary capital, were entrusted with the responsibility of a government official. The legend goes that, like the Persian Ahasuerus, the most important of the Casimirs had none other than a beautiful favorite Jewess, who bore him two sons and two daughters. Oddly enough, her name was Esther.

Only a few were truly fortunate, and no Gersoni, it seems; most got along as well as they could, always detested by the priests, by the lower classes, and by the bourgeoisie, yet certainly much better off than before, considering that, in a century, thanks to the Casimirs and the Sigismunds, their numbers increased in Poland from 50,000 to 500,000. They dealt in wax, cloth, furs, cattle, trinkets, jewels, perfumes, pots and pans, they were employed as stewards for noble landowners; half the artisans in the country were Jews. They knew how to wait during periods when, between a Casimir and a Sigismund, a more superstitious Augustus ascended to the throne, who decided to temporarily abolish their permits. But they were so useful that you couldn't do without them, and Rome was distant.

The Gersonis had been gone from Spain for some sixty years when Rome came closer. The papal nuncio began to appear every other morning at the royal palace to tell of hosts that, pricked by a sacrilegious Jewish hand, had begun to bleed, and protested that Jews were everywhere, and you were compelled to cover your eyes continuously, in order not to see the impious killers of Christ coming and going freely on the streets. The Sigismund of the moment observed, cautiously, that he had never known there to be blood in the hosts. Behind him the nobleman Leszek Wiśieski suggested to the king that he remind the nuncio of the papal bull of Innocent III, which absolved the Jews of the charge of ritual sacrifice. The noble Leszek, obviously, knew nothing of papal bulls but suffered from gout and had a doctor, Salomo

Sanchez, whom he couldn't do without, and who tirelessly repeated to him the story of these papal bulls. All he needed was for the scheming Roman monsignor to deprive him of his Salomo! The translator translated from Polish to Latin, and the nuncio changed the subject for that day. He suggested, however, that, as a start, one could revive the old ban on the Jews' wearing clothes like the Christians': that way, one could at least avoid them on the streets.

At the same time, whether because of rumors about a new period of restrictions or because they were struggling to get by, the Gersonis, whose grandfather remembered the story of his own grandfather's departure from Toledo, where they had had to lock the door with the key (the almond trees were flowering in the garden within the high stone walls), started traveling again. As for their personal past, they scarcely knew that they were not ordinary Gershons; they were Gersonis, and their *i* went back to those Gershonites who in the Temple, among other responsibilities, took care of the house of the tabernacle. The language they now spoke no longer contained Spanish words. From Sepharad, only a few recalled the expression *sangre judía* and some recipes that were no longer usable because of the lack of ingredients; indeed, where to find almonds and figs? Even the German expressions, learned along the road to the east, were changing. And so from one marriage to the next the names of the children were modified, a Jozeph became Jossel; a Gerson, Gershen; a Jehuda, Juddel. They remained a group of related families, even if, here and there, following the chance of new bonds or the opportunity for a more stable situation—so to speak—branches separated from the main tree.

The winds of banishment drove them farther east every year. None of the children by now remembered the words of Isaac Abravanel: "When our brothers learned the terrible news, there was among them great mourning, a profound terror, an anguish without equal, such as hadn't been felt since Judas, since the people of Israel had been led into exile by Nebuchadnezzar. They tried anyway to keep up each other's spirits: 'Courage!' They said, 'It's for the honor of our faith and for the Law of our God, which we have to safeguard from blasphemers. If they let us live, good, if they put us to death, we'll perish; but we won't be unfaithful to our Covenant. Our heart must not retreat, we will depart invoking the name of the Eternal, our God.' And so they departed."

They continued their wandering eastward; from Lviv they moved to a village near Grodno, from there to Lithuania—but they didn't call it Lithuania; for them it was always the land of the Polish kings—and after a brief sojourn in Vilnius, where one grandfather remained with a son, daughter-in-law, and grandchildren, they went beyond Kaunas, to Kedainiai. Here there were maybe a dozen Jewish families; in a *kloyz*, a house of study, the rites could be celebrated, but most important here, for the first time in their age-old journey, they had what after due consideration could be considered a stroke of luck.

A poor cousin of the Tyckiewicz family, the most aristocratic of the local nobility, rented them a stable on the road that led from Kedainiai to Krakas: there they would be able to distill liquor on his behalf and sell the product, and rent from him two horses for a small post station. The road wasn't much traveled, but some took it if there was danger of bandits on the normal route to Panevezys. They could keep what was left after the rent.

They fixed up the old building, distilled, pocketed a little from the distilling, bought a horse, then another; next to the tavern one of them opened a forge and shod the peasants' horses. They had a field of rye and a henhouse. One son had seen a barber working in Vilnius and became a barber. Or no: he had learned to fashion wooden cups, which were used in the tavern and liked by the peasants. None of them drank what they distilled, not because of the poor quality but, simply, because they didn't drink.

They were isolated in the countryside, which was very green for a short season, white and frozen through the long winter nights; they suffered from hunger in the first winter, but then they learned to brine cucumbers, to preserve cabbages, turnips, apples, to smoke or salt fish. With their rye they made bread in the oven in the courtyard. The bread was black, and over that black bread—they could imagine it white—they pronounced the Sabbath blessing and on the first day of Rosh Hashanah they scattered crumbs in the small river nearby.

They were as if on an island in the heart of Lithuania, which they believed was Poland. The grandchildren of the grandfather who had stayed in Vilnius saw the Swedes arrive; those who had remained in Lviv were slaughtered by the Cossacks;

one who was more enterprising, and had gone ahead, not to return, barely escaped the plague that spread out of Moscow one summer. The Gersonis, in their unnamed place between Kedainiai and Krakas, had children and grandchildren, and managed to remain there for more than fifty years. One of them became famous in the region. He knew how to make whistles, and they were magic whistles: they returned a lost cow to the barn, kept the foxes away at night; if a pretty girl passed, they whistled a song that made her turn to the player of those notes. Because, obviously, the whistles themselves were playing the notes. The Gersoni who made them was short of stature and broad-shouldered; in the countryside, but also in Krakas and in Kedainiai—his fame extended as far as Kedainiai—they called him Geršunok. When a large part of the family moved to Courland he remained, and his descendants later called themselves Girshon.

The Gersonis stayed so long in their refuge in the middle of Lithuania they forgot the meaning of the words of their prayers; like women they repeated them by heart without understanding them. But they continued to celebrate the Sabbath and Passover and Yom Kippur on the tenth of Tishrei—they never forgot the names of the months and the holidays—and brought their children to be circumcised in Kedainiai and the dead to be buried in the Jewish cemetery in Krakas. These customs disturbed no one: it seemed that, for the first time in many years, their being Jews fit in perfectly with the surrounding fields, with the forest across the little river that flowed not far from the house, with the streets of Krakas, where there was talk of building a synagogue. In the future—they had a future—their children would learn the meaning and not only the sound of the prayers. Also Kedainiai would become the center of a *kahal*, which, the grandfather remaining in Vilnius used to say, wasn't without inconveniences: indeed, there was a danger of doing business only with Jews, and then whom would they lend money to?

We don't know why—if it was because of a bishop in Krakas or a rabbi in Kedainiai or, rather, because of a succession of years when it didn't rain or rained too much or snowed in June and the impoverished peasants no longer came to the tavern—the Gersonis, with their *i*, their children, wives, grandparents, and newborns, attached two carts to two horses and went back on the road. In the countryside near Mitau, the capital of the grand duchy of Courland, they could find distilleries to rent; there was a great movement of Jews in the area. The grand duke, it was said, preferred to stay in Danzig, and the lords were so busy fighting among themselves at the annual Diets that they only occasionally concerned themselves with the Jews. The latter were not forbidden to stay, although, as usual, there was no explicit permission; besides, to tell the truth, at the time distilling was prohibited. Well, they'd see.

They had remained on their island in the heart of Lithuania (which they called Poland) so long that the three houses there retained the name Gersoni, today Gersone.

I found them again in Mitau, in Courland, when the documents from the Latvian Archives finally arrived. I had given the archives my previous address, where the mail was delivered to a porter's room. So I returned home with an envelope that at the moment seemed thin; I had imagined a thicker package. I opened the wrapping and from between large sheets of paper four photographs slid out. Suddenly, after sixty-five years, incredulous and astonished, I saw again the faces of my grandfather, grandmother, father. They were excellent photos, even though they were made for passports.

I barely glanced at the genealogical table: my great-grandfather was Jankel David; at the top of the tree was a Gersoni with the name Levin. The first date indicated was 1796.

For the whole day I went back and forth between the kitchen and the living room, where I had opened the genealogical table on the typewriter and on top of that placed the photos, two of my grandfather, one of my grandmother, one of my father. I considered their faces; I knew them but didn't recognize them. They had appeared as if spontaneously, so surprising that they seemed to exist on their own account, strangers to me. I couldn't sleep that night; at one point I got up and went back to look at them. They were still there, I contemplated them like a Native American who believes in the life of the figures represented.

My grandfather, portrayed in two pictures—one from 1919, the other from 1927—stared at me with burning, proud black eyes in a hard face, pale and stiff in the first photograph, more melancholy and gentle in the second. My grandmother hid within the indolent gaze of eyes slightly sunken along the sides of a straight nose, a little wide at the nostrils. I didn't recognize her except in the tall, thick hairdo; despite that, she was oddly familiar to me. I began to realize that my features bore some resemblance to hers, while a hint of something indefinable in my grandfather's expression brought me back to him.

With stubborn indifference my father exposed to the photographer's light his forehead with a markedly receding hairline on the left, and a full, smooth, capricious face. Closed off. The large, noble almond-shaped eyes were distant. He was wearing what looked like a skimpy Russian military coat with a small collar. The photo is from 1921, so he had just returned from the Soviet Union. I dreamed about him—for the first time—some nights later: he was standing a few meters away, wrapped in a black cloak; he turned toward me and summoned me with eyes that I remembered, Grandfather's burning black eyes, which my father himself didn't have in the photo. In the dream I said to myself, "Now I can dream about him."

In the following days I began studying the genealogical table; I didn't look at the whole but lingered randomly on one or another of the forebears, as if I had to make their acquaintance gradually. Even then, however, the birth date of Juddel Gersoni, my grandfather's grandfather, struck me. He was born in Mitau in 1796. According to Rabbi Wunderbar's book, 1794 was the date of the petition to the grand duke from around forty of the city's leading Jewish citizens. I picked up the book again; could I get from it some more precise information on my Gersonis in Mitau at the end of the eighteenth century? Maybe the father of Juddel, Levin, had married in those years. The cousins Abraham and Joschel had come to the wedding, and also grandfather Gerson. Joschel was about to leave for Hasenpoth, where his fiancée awaited him.

Meanwhile the heads of the wealthiest families, with their most important relatives—a son, a grandson, a widow with a son-in-law—respectfully asked the grand duke, this I remembered, to grant them the same rights that their fellow Jews in Hasenpoth had already had for some time. They assured the sovereign not only of their devotion, which was natural, but—and this I didn't remember—also of their full grasp of the needs of the city of Mitau. They declared that they were ready to meet those needs: it was true that there were too many Jews in the city, two hundred families—the signers represented around forty of them—too many for maintaining balance in the market and the houses. They offered to reduce the number by a third. How they would bring about the beneficial expulsion of the superfluous Jews wasn't explained.

Calculations followed, oddly vague given the known mathematical ability of those who presented the petition, as a result of which that third became, splitting hairs, almost half. With the Jewish population of Mitau thus reduced, they could live there in harmony and to mutual advantage.

That self-interested offer—was the grandfather in Vilnius right when he stated that, where there were too many Jews, the risks were more than an inconvenience?—had no follow-up. Shortly afterward all of Courland went over to Russia; the grand duke returned to Danzig, the grand duchess to Berlin. Cousin Joschel married his fiancée in Hasenpoth, and a German official, in the census taken by the Russians in 1807, transcribed the surname with the *y*. Rabbi Wunderbar doesn't comment on the singular offer of the notables, occupied as he is in praising the munificence of the most eminent signer, his benefactor Borchum, who on the day of his daughter's engagement had wanted to lay the first stone of the synagogue in Mitau that he had financed. The future bridegroom, Wunderbar recounts, then had the honor of wearing the uniform of court councilor in Hasenpoth.

With the arrival of the Russians, the Jewish tailors—there were a lot; four out of ten Jewish artisans were tailors—had more to do. The Russians were crazy for uniforms.

Was my ancestor Levin Gersoni, with his newborn son and three other family groups bearing the same surname, expected to be among those expelled from Mitau? Or were they among the useful *zhidov* who were about to become *yevrei*? Was he already a tailor, as later his grandsons Abraham and my great-grandfather Jankel were? In any case, my Gersonis were residing in Mitau at least from the second half of the century; the German census official who recorded the family in 1834 had written in the heading of the report, in a Gothic script that Hens deciphered for me: "Artisans in the city."

Whatever they were, their conditions must have been very modest but to a certain degree solid. The families of Abraham and Jankel lived together, maybe on the Judengasse in a house with a shingled roof. Certainly they strained their eyes sewing, especially in winter when the day ended at four in the afternoon and they were compelled to work near the lamp. But, to judge from the eyes of my grandfather and father, they had excellent vision. I know only what the documents tell me about them, though I have one more small clue. In the 1854 census—the Russians took censuses constantly, in order to procure taxes and soldiers—the nitpicking German bureaucrat on duty had terrible handwriting, and had the names filled in on the document by Abraham Elias, the head of the family; the latter wrote in the names of the family members and signed on the back with a fine clear signature and light, even flourishes. The *s* of Gersoni not Gothic but Latin. Next to the barbaric letters scratched by the German bureaucrat, my father's great-uncle wrote like a European. It amuses me to think that the indecipherable Gothic signs were the same as those used by Immanuel Kant in letters to his brother, who was living in Mitau.

My father, we know, did not inherit that beautiful calligraphy. But maybe my grandfather inherited from his father the tailor a special care in dressing; in the first photo he's wearing a jacket that fits perfectly, from which the immaculate tips of an elegant white collar emerge, and a glimpse of an impeccable tie; in the second he wears a jacket or overcoat with wide velvet lapels.

Where the Gersonis had learned to write, and what else they had learned, the documents don't say. Unspoken, for good reason, the fundamental fact: gathered in a loyal, compact family group, they managed to survive the perils of the era, which was much less tranquil than in their rabbi's description. The cousins in Hasenpoth, too, increasingly distant, survived. The men of the family weren't seized and forced to join the "cantonists," the young adolescents whom his gracious majesty Nicholas I, without asking their opinion, destined for twenty-five years of military service. At the end of it, the few who survived were free to live wherever in the empire they wanted, even outside the regions of forced "confinement" for Jews.

The Kurischer, on the western borders of the empire, did not have to undergo attempts at reeducation like their fellow Jews deeper inside Russia, who were driven from their native villages to urban poverty. Thus they managed to avoid the obligatory draft, and didn't fight against the Turks or suppress revolts among the Cossacks. Daughters and sisters were brides or died at home unmarried, sewing on buttons and edging buttonholes. After the wedding, one of them made a journey by steamer on the Lielupe to Sloka, which, one could easily say, was nearly at the gates of Riga. But usually they didn't leave Mitau; on Saturday evenings in summer, they sat on the bench in front of the house and enjoyed the sunset. Faithful to the Kurischer tradition, they performed the rites, precise but not sanctimonious. In the glimmering light of evening they didn't see angels flying—they weren't Hasidim!—but mosquitoes, in dense clouds in the short northern summer.

They cared only about one angel, the angel of death. Notoriously distracted, it might make a mistake and carry off a child instead of an old man with the same name. It is what it is for girls, but you have to pay particular attention to boys. So they were seldom given the grandfather's name; although grandfathers often died rather early, great-grandfathers were preferred when the name was chosen, or even the founder of the family. My grandfather had as his middle name the name of his great-grandfather Levin, and Abraham, his uncle, had a middle name heavy with meaning, Elias. Wasn't the head of the Gershonites called Eliasham?

At first I didn't pay attention to the details of the documents that had been sent to me: the letterheads were printed in Russian on the pages containing birth and other records, on the left the facts in Russian script, on the right the same in Hebrew. In German, the facts of the census and the draft, very meticulous. Even the children's ages were indicated in fractions: there was a child (all males from birth to death were listed in the military rolls) of a quarter of a year, I think, among the Gersony papers that Marina had let me have. The archivist in Riga had translated the most important information; some I checked myself later.

To begin. Skipping the details, then, I got acquainted with the documents and didn't stick to a strict agenda. I wandered in the neighborhood of my grandfather, where it seemed that I could encounter not only names but also people, and especially Grandfather himself. I lingered on the document that attested to the death of his mother, Beile, who had died of tuberculosis at thirty-two, following the death of her last child, Israel, a year old: between this little brother and my grandfather there was a difference of ten years, and maybe other dead children. Grandfather's father got remarried right away, to his sister-in-law, with whom he had four children. The second daughter was called Frume Beile.

Orphaned at eleven, my grandfather didn't practice his father's trade—were the sons of Abraham, the head of the family, tailors?—and his only brother was, according to the report of the Latvian Archives, a "painter" (house painter?); he, leaving the increasingly cramped family circle—a new sibling was born every two years—really did go to Siberia, because in the marriage registry he was "fur trader of the second *Gilda*," also registered in Mitau. In his generation, he was the Gersoni who advanced the furthest, even if the Guild wasn't, obviously, the aristocratic Hanseatic League but the more primitive definition of the Russian censor. Yet he came from Libau, where the whole family had moved around 1870, and where Beile and her child were buried, along with, later, the other Gersonis. Libau, which by will of Tsar Alexander II was becoming an important trading and military port—the waters didn't freeze in winter—offered more opportunities for making uniforms than Mitau.

Thus my grandfather gave up uniforms and became Westernized. On the marriage license he had gone from Mozes to Moritz, the young bride from Hanna to Anna, and by the time their son Samuil married the Italian Clara, my grandfather, witness at the marriage, was the "English" Maurice. The son (somewhat imprudently) bore the name of his maternal grandfather.

I paused, imagining, on the fate of Beile, torn so soon from her children; and I recalled, too, the life of my grandparents, whom I remembered as very intimate and close, in the dark apartment of Baznicas Iela: so attached to one another that they died a month apart—Grandfather in February of 1940, Grandmother in March. Inevitably I thought again of my father's early exclusion from their intimacy, an exclusion that an unexpected change in the last part of all their lives perhaps managed, at least in part, to heal.

In fact the most startling revelations of the papers from Latvia alluded precisely to those years.

I had sent the archives the facts needed to find the birth certificate of little Irene, who, because she was illegitimate, couldn't be registered in our father's documents. I knew the surname of Ilse, the German nurse, his companion and the mother of the child. The archivist Lena Polovceva, to whom I am grateful for the careful research and, especially, the photos of my relatives, found the birth record and was able even to trace the path of my little sister's brief existence. In Riga, every building had a *Hausmeister*, a porter and bureaucrat who recorded the list of residents, registering their arrival and departure. Thus I followed from address to address the movements through the city of my grandparents and my father over the years.

Irene was born in 1936, so she was five when she was killed. All three, my father, Ilse, and the child, must have lived together for only a short time in Majori and later, for some months, at my grandparents'. They had moved in '37 and their son had joined them right away with Ilse and the child. In April of '38—Irene was a year and a half old—Ilse left the Gersonis, and the child remained with her father.

It couldn't have been easy for the young woman to live with my grandparents, and besides she was half the age of my father; Grandfather was often imperious, and I recall the harsh voice in which he sometimes spoke to his son. My father, I suppose, spent the day not working; according to the trial documents he was supported by his parents. But, like Sisi and me, Irene surely had, if only for a short time, a grandfather who loved her. She was living with the grandparents when they died. Six months later my father took her to the new apartment on Juri Alunana Iela. It was their last home: they were removed from the corresponding registry on October 15, 1941. Transferred to the ghetto.

I could now consider my research finished, but something held me back. I couldn't leave the genealogical table, the names, the dates. However cursory and conclusive the information I'd received was, I continued to delay; it was almost as if Abraham and Jankel, their wives and children, the great-grandfather, wanted to emerge from the page where I had enclosed them, as I had done with my maternal distant fathers. If I thought about it, the century and a half of life that came before my father's existence didn't precede me: I began with myself—I have to repeat it—my roots were my children. With the story of the Gersonis, what had already happened to me when I retraced the experiences of my mother's Waldensian forebears would be repeated: I was the narrator, that was the only bond. But I realized how inadequate what I reported about them was, how little of their history was really known to me. I would have liked them to escape from my page and tell their story themselves.

I found more information in books and documents. I was helped by the very patient, kind archivist Rita Bogdanova, who had already helped arrange the matter of payment; she searched through registries and lists for additional information. I received a text from Marburg on the Russian censuses; the archives in Kaunas confirmed the place named Gersone, and the Dutch Sephardic "master" the Sephardic origin of the Gersonis.

One day I reread yet again the report from the Latvian Archives that summarized the information that had been sent to me and suddenly I was struck by my father's last address; it was on a street that I didn't know at all, but I seemed to have seen the name before. I checked the page from the 1941 Riga phone book and found it: it was the same as that of the unknown Lidija Gersoni. Who could she be? A cousin or, strangely, my father's first wife?

Rita Bogdanova, questioned by email, sent me the answer the next day: she was in fact his first wife, Lidija Blechman. She and my father had married in 1911 and divorced a few years later. They hadn't had children. I think she had maintained a good relationship with my grandparents; I remember that I met her at a tea at Grandmother's, where she had observed me attentively, dark eyes in a white face. For almost a year from 1940 to 1941 she and my father, along with his child, had lived in the same building on Juri Alunana Iela, though not in the same apartment. Lidija, Rita wrote, had been removed from the building registry on July 12, 1941, probably killed at the start of the German occupation; this my father surely knew, maybe he had even been present.

I don't understand why the scant information that, if you think about it, didn't closely concern me moved me so much, or why, similarly, it distressed me to find on the list of Jews killed in Liepaja (Libau) the names of the relatives who had remained in the city, my father's seventy-six-year-old aunt, a female cousin, maybe also a male cousin. What did I know of them? What did I know of Lidija Blechman? Nonetheless I couldn't stop thinking of Samuel and Lidija's long-ago youthful happiness, there in the tranquil, luminous house on the island in the river, and of the end of the Gersonis of Libau. As if their bodies were still bleeding in my heart.

11. Contemporaries

At the desk in front of me, in class at the Lutherschule, sat a large blond girl; one morning I glimpsed on her paper—we were doing, I think, a geography exercise—that she had been born in Riga the same day and the same year as me. We were twins. She wasn't the Waldtraut with whom I exchanged some letters and who sent me a photo of herself. About this girl, among other things, my mother had written to me that she had become a "master" skater at the age of thirteen. My mother never missed a chance to extol the gifts of my contemporaries, I suppose to goad me into emulating them. Later that praise plunged me into a sad, impotent envy. How could I become a master of skating or any athletic skill, I who wanted only to be left in peace to wander around daydreaming, rather gawky on my long legs?

With my school twin I wasn't really, if I think about it, contemporary, except for the class. She left for "exile," I think, like Waldi, in late 1939; I had been in Italy by then for four years. My contemporaries are Italian.

There are, in fact, periods of life that tie us more tightly to those who are growing up alongside us. It happens rarely in childhood, and we're aware of it later only if we grow up with a playmate from then to adulthood. As children we are singular units, closed within ourselves; we observe through the keyhole the secrets of adults in their room. Other children, in turn, spy in the same way on the same room. The experience is interior and individual. Or at least it was for me; the only contemporary I recognize as a child was, of course, my sister.

Those who brought up children in the same years as me, who worked with me, and, as happens in every generation, remember certain dates, are, undoubtedly, contemporaries.

Maybe we who were born between 1920 and 1930 remembered those dates only occasionally, as we struggled to climb out of the poverty of the postwar period to well-being, became parents, moved, traveled the world, went to meetings, paraded ideas and banners, won or lost elections (were those of us destined to lose them, I wonder, more intimate contemporaries?), and yet the dates stay fixed in us forever, transmuted, as we age, into symbols. Even if we began to forget some name or the details of some event, we never forgot our dates.

A month ago, a tall man was standing in front of me in line at the post office, holding some bills to pay and a blue pension check like mine. He stood erect in a leather jacket and at one point he turned to look at the line. He was an old man with a well-shaped face, pale eyes. A handsome man. I'm often uncertain about people's age, and besides, it doesn't matter to me whether I know it. If they're old I lump them together.

We began chatting, the handsome man in the leather jacket and I; something led me to my usual complaints about the bad habit of using Anglo-Saxon words in Italian, and using them badly. I cited the locution "Turin Marathon" that appeared on the buses at the time of the annual race, a locution that made me indignant. My companion in the line grew animated, agreeing with me. He spoke Italian with a very slight Piedmontese inflection. He said, as if with relief, in a reference to Mussolini, "It was better when someone else was there."

Aha.

I said, sternly, "Well, no, I have some ugly memories about that: he burdened us with that disastrous war."

He shook his head and was quickly silent, resigned.

"Yes, that's true, but . . ."

He wasn't even disappointed; he had already heard the argument repeated plenty of times.

We went on to talk about grandchildren.

Thinking back I realized that I, too, had been resigned, had given up on adding anything: the words had all been said, on one side and the other; each of us remained in our own irrevocable past. Each of us had grandchildren, here we could agree.

So we were contemporaries, in a way: he, however, on the side of the tyrant, I on the other, not because I'd decided but on account of fate. After the ruinous war, whose disasters he didn't deny—but, he muttered, this democracy of theirs, it's nonsense: we need facts, facts—he always on one side and I on the other. And yet we don't entrust reconciliation to the grandchildren—*après nous* the matter will be closed—to them we entrust the future and our faded dates.

In conformity with the law of nature, my contemporaries diminish year by year. Sometimes I go to a funeral: "He was born in '22," "Just imagine, he was only from '28," "You know, he was born in '25, like us." Would I go to the funeral of a fascist?

In fact it's taken an effort to get used to the funeral rites of the Italians. Gianni, my husband, didn't spare himself a single one. I found it a little ridiculous myself. Certainly, I said to myself, the funeral of a close relative, if you have one—but the funeral of a friend of the neighbor, of the wife of a cousin you haven't seen for thirty years, of the grandfather of a colleague's nephew?

And then there's the rosary and the viewing of the body, and the thirtieth-day Mass. It never ends. Watching on television the crowd applaud as the deceased passes by under his magnificent wreaths, I feel like a tourist contemplating a barbaric ritual. But those wreaths . . . I try in vain to consider them with the proper Calvinist detachment, what a waste! I reflect: I could have one sent to me by my children at every birthday, without any ribbon. If nothing else, I would enjoy them while I'm alive.

So, for love of Gianni, who went to every funeral farewell, I also go to funerals now. I take part, I try to understand. Our Italian children are loyal to the custom of their country, and dutifully go to bury their neighbor.

Perhaps there is consolation in being together, in speaking of the dead person. Among us, in truth, one doesn't die, one "passes away." And once dead, everyone's perfect.

Those who are buried have done no wrong. The pact of the sham Italian funeral has an innate, profane native wisdom, a requirement for order and harmony. We respond to a duty, avoid irritating Hades, confront, confide, say, "See you next time," or, "Farewell."

A year ago I drove with my daughter to Settimo Vittone, on the border of Val d'Aosta. We were going to see the family of my daughter-in-law Raffaella. Her father had died, my grandchildren Alice and Giovanni's grandfather Mario. He had died at home after a serious illness that had forced him to endure several hospital stays. He was lying in a long coffin. He had been a tall man, big, broad. If he was in a room, he became the center of it.

He was tall and imposing, and in 1994 he suddenly found himself in the floodwaters of the Dora. He had gone down to the river to check the solidity of a building he had constructed—he was a contractor—and though the structure remained standing, he had to be pulled out of the water. At home, his wife, Yvelise, had given him a piece of her mind, in vain—he always did what he wanted.

I had seen him rarely, occasional Sundays at my son's house. He and Paolo watched the games on television; we barely exchanged a word. From him my daughter-in-law Raffaella gets her blue eyes, long straight nose, clear gaze.

He knew everything and everyone in his town. He'd been the mayor for ten years, beginning when he was still very young and had just returned from prison. He would have continued to serve as mayor if his wife hadn't achieved a rare victory, insisting that he stop. Working with his father in the family business, not only was he busy administering a small town reduced to great poverty by the war—he recalled, laughing, that he had even had to scrape together the money to pay the restaurant bills left by fascist government officials visiting the Vallée—but he never refused anything, even countersigning the many letters that the town madwoman sent to the devil in person. If he was preparing lunch at home, there were usually no fewer than twenty guests; the ten beds in the mountain cabin he'd built on the Serra d'Ivrea—the broad landscape of the Canavese extended below—were available to any friend who knew where to find the key.

When he retired, he devoted himself to his favorite pastime: he liked to cook and to make jams, homemade delicacies, preserves. I still had, after his death, some glass jars of zucchini in a special *agrodolce* that he had perfected among his last activities as a cook. On the lid was the label "For grandmother Marina," written in the beautiful slanted calligraphy that my mother was taught in elementary school twenty-five years before him. When persistent arthritis finally forced him to ascend from the big cellar where he received countless friends, he had a vast kitchen made for himself on the ground floor, because his wife didn't want him upstairs and was perhaps tired of washing pots and pans. Raffaella would return from Settimo with provisions for the week and the grandchildren ate Grandfather Mario's polenta. He had collected in a booklet printed by a typographer friend in Ivrea twelve local recipes, *I mange d'la Granda*, and here the

Granda, the great, was the grandmother. One of these *mangè* (foods) bore the name of its inventor: it was a cheese sauce to accompany the polenta. Maybe the *fritto* made by Perulin is the legacy of a great-grandfather!

When the arthritis made it difficult for him to bend over in the garden—he competed with his friends over who could produce the most beautiful and earliest vegetables—he had stumps installed among the beds, at a proper distance, and sat there to put in his tomato plants himself.

He lay in the big long coffin, much thinner owing to his illness, but once again straight. Among the instructions for his funeral was a request not to forget to set up some chairs, so that his old friends wouldn't have to stand, as had happened to him at one funeral after another, given that those born in 1920 were beginning to depart.

"Those born in 1920" was one of our dates. It included, naturally, those of '19, '22, '23, and so on. In any case, "those born in 1920" were our oldest contemporaries, who had all been in the war, from beginning to end, from 1940 to 1945. Before the war and after, many had also been in prison.

Grandfather Mario had also left written instructions that eight roses should be placed on his coffin—one for his wife, three for his son's family, four for his daughter's family—and next to the coffin, on a table, the two notebooks where he had recorded, point by point, the 762 days of his deportation to Germany.

They are French school notebooks, to which pages have been added, carefully numbered (loose-leaf n. 1, n. 2, n. 3, etc.):

some are thick paper cut with scissors and some, the last notes, are the blank backs of German forms taken from a town registry. Along with the notebooks, some old banknotes, a small German *Lagergeld* coupon, the few letters received by *Kriegsgefangener* 4698, some loose pages with brief reflections and mathematical calculations, a map of Europe with the names in German. Prisoner of war 4698 had marked on the map in red the route of the thirty-two days it took, traveling by train and including stops in concentration camps, to get from the prison in Alsace to the one in East Prussia. From Forbach to Johannisburg.

I've been reproached by some readers for the apparently rambling digressions I like to put in my books. To me, on the other hand, it seems that my digressions contain obvious references to the material I'm addressing, and I therefore persist in the error by presenting here some pages from the diary of Alpinist Mario Prola of the mountain artillery. It was published in 1969 in a very abridged version by the publisher Franco Mongino, for friends, prison mates, and relatives; it should be republished today in its entirety.[7]

> September 8, 1943—The trumpet sounds the alarm. I return from off duty and find a big commotion: we're ordered to leave for Italy as soon as possible.

7 In June 1940, Mussolini declared war on France and Britain, and invaded France, occupying a fairly small area. In November 1942, as Germany occupied most of Vichy France, Italy expanded its occupation zone. In September 1943, Italy surrendered to the Allies, and Germany took over the Italian-occupied zones. The Italian soldiers, who at first were heading back to Italy as part of their own army, quickly found themselves prisoners of war of the Germans. In this diary excerpt the Italians are in the Savoie region of France.

It must be 23:00 when the captain gives the order to march. We're going toward Italy, on the highway from Moncenisio toward Modane. We're all silent, marching at a good pace, there's a sense that something serious is happening.

At 6:30 in the morning we reach Aiguebelle, forty kilometers from Modane. We're still united and there hasn't been any sign of rebellion against superiors, no sign of desertion; a few kilometers before Aiguebelle, Lieutenant Ivaldi again reprimanded Collomb of the 1st for sitting on his gun, telling him, "You'll be punished."

Suddenly I see the column stop, and armed Germans emerge from the nearby fields and surround us. I see on a balcony at the edge of the town some Germans loading a mortar. Someone shoots, the Germans don't respond, it's tense, I say to Grosso, "We're done for if they fire that mortar, they'll shred us; let's keep an eye on it, ready to dive under the cart that carries the matériel for the 1st division."

Two Germans advance to the head of the column with an Italian who serves as interpreter; after a long discussion with the captain a rumor runs through the column that the Germans only want us to leave our weapons with them and then they'll let us continue on to Italy.

I go up toward the captain and the squad command. There's already a pile of rifles on the asphalt,

I see Lieutenant Bertolino struggling with a German who wants to take his pistol, they argue, the German gets the better of him.

I return to my squad while the Germans approach ever closer with their guns raised. The captain sends word that he wants to speak to the squad leaders; I advance with a sense of fear mixed with rage. The captain tells us that we have to leave our weapons to the Germans, who will take us by truck to Chambery and then repatriate us. I'm not persuaded, and while I'm trying to return and report, a German who in the meantime has come up to me takes my gun and signals me to empty the cartridge box. I leave everything and go back; Grosso, Milono, and the others wait for me to tell them something; I say nothing, I have a lump in my throat and spreading my arms I signal that it's all over.

The Germans lock up the now disarmed Italians in a barracks in Chambery.

September 18—Big news. An Italian officer came; the Germans had us go down to the courtyard with all our bags. The officer, a major in the infantry (probably a former militia officer), made a long speech asking us to sign a pledge to continue fighting alongside our German allies. He told us we would return to Italy to fight against the Americans and the English; otherwise the Germans would consider us prisoners of war. He concluded by asking us to shout, "*Viva l'Italia, viva il Duce*"; no one responded and at the call to leave the ranks and sign, only 16 out of around 1500 went. These sixteen were immediately taken to the guard corps and given a generous ration of risotto. We were rushed back to the dormitory and no one mentioned any ration. It's 20:30, we haven't eaten since yesterday evening, I'm going to sleep.

September 22—Today big news. At 7:30 it was still dark and the Germans made us come down saying we were going home; instead it was only an excuse to make us take out all our stuff. While we were in the courtyard they rummaged through all the dormitories. They took everything; we were left with what we had on and a blanket. I had hidden two pairs of socks, a pair of underpants, a skier's hat. After a morning in the rain they made us go back to the dormitory, each to his own place.

At 2:00 those from the 51st and 52nd Battery who had remained at Albertville arrived. They told us they'd fought against the Germans the night of the 8th and had had some dead. We hope that this reuniting of the group brings us some news.

The Italians have no officers, morale is low, they are put

to work digging trenches; the rations are small, they're finishing their ration tins.

> October 3 (Sunday)—This morning there was Mass again and again Sergeant Longo sang the Avemaria. After the midday ration a major repeated more or less what "Militia" (the major who spoke to us a few days ago) had told us. But he also said many sensible things and it was clear that he was suffering, poor man. Had he been forced to come and speak to us? He exhorted us to sign up to fight and also told us that in a few days we would have a visit from a general. No one signed, and now as the days pass we realize more and more clearly that we are truly enemies of the Germans.

Shortly afterward, stripped of their uniforms, in broken German shoes with iron heels, the Italians are transported by train to Alsace. There they remain to work, numbered prisoners of war. With luck, the bread ration is divided in three, otherwise in five. Once a day, turnips and cabbage. They're in the neighborhood of Forbach. Mario works various jobs, first on a railroad line, then from March 1944 at Stieringen, in a mine. He waits in vain for mail from home. He takes careful notes every day.

> October 9—Early morning, they got us out a little while ago for our needs, usual show. We're still

in Metz. At 14:00, we're in Alsace, in a town whose name I couldn't see. All the houses are black and the countryside is also black; there are a lot of ironworks. At night, we're still locked in the train car, maybe tonight they'll have us proceed.

October 10—At dawn they made us get out, I'd been standing so long I couldn't walk anymore. They brought us to a barracks where we were given a medical exam. Naked in the cold for more than an hour, then examined by the doctor, who has an ironic expression, for barely a moment.

While we were waiting to be seen they went through our knapsacks and took anything of any value. In the false bottom of the knapsack I'd sewn after Prato Sesia, when we had to go to Russia, I'd hidden my watch and money: 1,500 French francs and 2,200 Italian lire, the hat, and this notebook. It's evening, we shared a loaf of bread among four. In the afternoon they numbered us, my number now is 4698, and they photographed our faces, hanging a blackboard around our neck on which our number was written.

We're in a prison that's all red brick, around us are high fences and other prisons with prisoners of every nationality, they all have such faces! The line for the bathroom lasts more than an hour; if someone does it outside, they shoot from the tower. The camp is all illuminated, as much inside as in the narrow courtyards and along the fences. Grosso and Basilio and I settle ourselves on the floor for the night.

October 20—We got our ration a little earlier than usual in the kitchen of the French, on the way a child threw me an apple, I could have kissed him!

November 2—Today I didn't go to work, I stayed in the Germans' building to make lists of prisoners who were to go into the mines. I had only to transcribe the numbers with the name and last name next to them in numerical order. Again an Italian came to the camp to propagandize that we should sign up to fight with the Germans, no one signed. Yesterday evening we recited the rosary, and while I prayed I thought a lot about home, Mamma, everyone.

On a piece of paper he brought home is the prisoner's prayer for his loved ones.

November 8—Again at work. The siren went off three times, hearing the planes we have a sense of joy and hope.

November 17—Today we worked on the tracks 7 kilometers from the camp pickaxing gravel under the ties. I've learned the numbers in German, and my job was to read aloud the number of the iron plates that's on every tie.

I hear the Ukrainian women in the camp nearby singing a sad lullaby.

November 26—This morning it snowed until 11. The work was very heavy, loading and unloading freight cars of railroad materials. The Ukrainian women worked with us, many of them wept, I felt so sorry for them.

Today the siren went off four times, and tonight the anti-aircraft artillery fired a lot. If it keeps going like this I hope it's coming to an end.

December 9—My morale is low. The ration was terrible and yesterday evening I also ate the second kilo of flour gruel [Mario traded the pair of cotton underpants for two kilos of flour] so today I'm even hungrier than usual.

Today marks the end of the third month of prison, when will it be over?

I talked for a long time with a young, educated Ukrainian woman, who spoke Italian well and has been here for almost a year. Her husband is at the front with the Russian Army and her elderly parents are in Ukraine, she has no more news of her family. She was weeping. She told me that almost all the women are in her condition and they are around

500. She told me that they often have to submit to the Germans and even to some prisoners who are in the good graces of the camp commander.

December 13—I can't understand, I don't know if I'm weak or what it is, but today, although the snow is melting, I wept because of the cold.

The cards we wrote days ago are still piled up in the room next to the guardroom. They leave them there right in view to discourage us.

January 10—In spite of the bad weather, work went well. Just now the siren stopped. It's already 22:00. After I got back I had a bath and boiled the dirty stuff, I was crawling with lice and I'm really afraid of typhus.

January 20— . . . If only I weren't so hungry! The Russians who were with me offered 20 kg of bread for the watch, I haven't decided, I'd be sorry to be separated from it. I would trust the Russians blindly, they would never go back on their word once given.

February 6—20:00. I undressed in the bunk. Today a really terrible day. It should have been a day of rest but instead they tortured us all day. At 7:30 assembly and in the courtyard in the snow they made us do training exercises. The Germans took turns, and we had to keep going until it was time for our ration. I still hear in my ears: "*Eins, zwei, drei.*" At three the whistle again and another assembly. I was on my cot and had to go out without socks and with my shoes untied. I just had time to grab my jacket. Training exercises again until late at night and when we returned to the dormitory everything was a mess, they had ransacked our knapsacks again in search of anything that had eluded other searches. The false bottom of my knapsack worked again. Apart from the watch, the trouble would be if they found these two notebooks. At all the assemblies they always threaten very severe punishments for anyone who keeps notes. Will this life end?

February 26—Last night the siren again. Isn't Germany destroyed yet?

I exchanged cigarettes for bread, I managed to get three rations and I've already eaten it all and I would eat more if I had any. It's 20:00, a prayer and a fond remembrance to my family and to bed.

March 20—No mail, no package, so much work and still cold, I'm exhausted and I don't know how long I can keep going.

March 21—A Bergamask Alpinist died, he had been sent to work again yesterday, and couldn't get back to the camp by himself, four men carried him, and he died in the night, probably because of untreated pneumonia. This evening, it was already night, we carried him into the woods nearby and buried him among the many other graves, undressed and without a coffin. His fellow townsmen will bring the news home.

Mario is transferred to Stieringen to work in the mines. The bread ration is larger but the work very dangerous. He is still waiting, in vain, for mail from home.

March 30—By a miracle I escaped a chunk of stone that broke off from the ceiling: it grazed my head and made a fairly deep wound in my right hand, especially at the wrist. Someone is praying for me, I'm sure of it.

On April 14, finally, mail from home arrives: his father, Pierino, writes:

Settimo Vittone, February 21, 1944

My dear son Mario. From your most recent letter I note that you are still without our news, we hope the first we wrote reaches you soon, but in any case I repeat our news. Last November 11 your mother passed away suddenly, I didn't want to give you that sad news but I preferred to tell you myself rather than have you learn it later from others. Sandro, too, is in your situation and maybe you are not so far apart, he also wrote yesterday and, like you, sent a form for a package.

Antonietta will prepare them tomorrow and they'll be shipped right away. I'm working on building a new house for the SACI opposite the Hotel Tripoli, and I'm getting along as well as possible, always awaiting your return. In Figliei [the part of Settimo that Mario's family is from] they are all well and so are the relatives. Aunt Maria would also like to have a form so she can send you a package, but when you can get the forms send them only to us, since we got a pig this year, too, and have some things to send you both. Bear up and let's try to get past this calamity. Affectionate greetings from Antonietta, your father Pierino.

By chance Mario encounters his brother Sandro in the spring of '45, when they're both in East Prussia, Sandro in Konigsberg, Mario in Johannisburg.

April 16—Last night Sergeant Bancolini who commands my company brought me the package and stayed a while to comfort me. Probably he feels sorry for me because he's very kind to me. Today we didn't work, I ate and wept all day.

April 22—The work is always hard, I couldn't find out how the Bolognese who died next to me was buried. I'm afraid they wheeled him in the handcart along with those who die in the infirmary. Tonight I sewed a black band on the gray-green jacket. Poor Mamma!

29–30 April—Last night I had to wash and clean up in the bunk, the fleas wouldn't leave me alone. In the crisscross of my knapsack straps I found about thirty as big as peapods. It makes my skin crawl just to think of it. Working overtime again.

When he could, Mario got sheets of paper, probably in the Germans' building where he sometimes worked. He saved some in his notebooks. On two there are calculations of square roots, of prime numbers. On another two, observations and definitions. One even has two or three words in Greek. Mario hadn't studied Greek: after elementary school, he had gone to a private school in Settimo run by a priest to learn mainly mathematics and drawing. Here I quote only one of his reflections; I don't know when it was written.

The cult of the dead is the religion of the family, and this religion has no need of priests.

A postcard from home is dated January 16, 1944. When did it arrive? The only line not crossed out by the censor says, "We're all fine, ciao, Papa."

May 20—The new tunnel is very low and poorly

ventilated, there's less than half the amount of coal to dig as before, but we work harder because the air is unbreathable.

Will I get out of this inferno alive? I always pray that Mamma will help me.

The summer passes; in early June the rumor that the English and Americans have disembarked on the coast of the Channel circulates. In late July, there are other rumors: departure is starting to be talked about. The Italian soldiers will no longer be prisoners of war but interned Italian civilians. Will anything change? When the Germans ask the prisoners assembled in the courtyard who wants to become a "civilian," only around thirty out of a thousand raise their hand.

August 24—This afternoon the Italian consul came from Saarbrucken and confirmed that we will become civilians starting September 1. He made a strange speech, it's clear that he, too, is forced to behave in a certain way. He asked us to shout with him "*Viva l'Italia*," to which we all responded loudly. He then asked us to shout "*Viva il Führer*" and "*Viva il Duce*"; no one responded. He looked at us and seemed almost pleased by this attitude of ours.

August 30—Two hours of overtime. It's said that the Americans have taken Metz. So then they must be only 60 kilometers from our camp.

September 1—This morning we had the regular assembly, but rather than go to work they had us return to bed. At 5:30 again assembly and departure for work. We worked for half an hour and the order came to return, it seems they want to flood the mine and blow up the elevator shaft. The German who was with me patted my shoulder and said, "*Grube alles kaputt*," that is, the mine will be totally destroyed. I felt sorry for him, poor man, he wasn't a bad fellow and every morning he gave us the miners' greeting, "*Mig auf*," that is, "Come back out."

Returning to the camp, we encountered columns of Russian prisoners who were leaving. We're leaving tomorrow morning, in the camp an indescribable chaos reigns. The sentinels are doubled, they all seem very agitated and often fire shots for no reason. It's 14:00.

20:30—The American tanks are not far from the camp, we can hear their engines, they were shooting in the direction of Saarbrucken, the shots passed over us.

22:00—We were assembled in the courtyard and given provisions for two days. We're ready to leave. The Americans aren't shooting anymore. Are we at the end? Instead, the next day, early in the morning, they depart.

September 3—Today we walked on back roads

for 32 kilometers. The roads are crowded with every type of vehicle: military trucks, tanks, and civilian trucks that are evacuating, also military trucks loaded with wounded. It seems as if this damn war is getting to the end. They again admitted us to a concentration camp, we're always under guard, evidently they're afraid that at this moment of chaos someone might escape. I'm very tired, getting ready to sleep outside on the ground in the cold.

September 7—What are the English waiting for to advance? We're still shut up in this little camp, where before there were 350 prisoners and now we'll be 2,000. Hunger. Hunger.

Mario and his comrades leave on September 13, and travel eastward on a very slow train, until September 16.

September 16, 18:00—For several hours now I've been in a big camp not far from a city I don't know. The journey was terrible, three died in the cars behind mine. At 17:00 we got our ration, I hadn't eaten anything since early yesterday morning. I suffered even more from thirst than from hunger. They never let us get out, we had to do everything in the car. The hunger is terrible. I met an officer from the Alpinists who knew Antonietta's Giovanni. He wasn't able to give me news of him. A lieutenant from the

Alpinists told me that my dear friend Egidio Giugler died in Montenegro, I couldn't keep from crying. What will become of us?

September 22—This morning the wakeup came earlier than on other days. They gave us provisions for three days: bread and sugar and I ate almost all of it. It's 18:00 and I'm afraid of having to spend the night outside. I saw the Jews passing, each with a large stone either on his shoulder or under his arm. Such suffering! With us they haven't yet reached that point!

The journey resumes.

We're stopped at a small station. I finished all the food and also the water I had in my mess tin. We've been traveling since yesterday evening at 20:00, we passed through Berlin during the night, everything was burning.

Night, we're traveling without a pause, where?

September 25—We left the car this morning at 9, we're in Honnestein, maybe in Prussia. Food was given to us only at 13:00, it was more than 50 hours since I'd had anything to eat. When we got out, we realized that a large percentage of prisoners had remained in the cars, they were exhausted and

> some were dead. I hope I don't have to stay here long, otherwise I don't know how it will end.

When Mario Prola reviewed his notes from prison for publication, he added some; they are mainly about the long journey from Alsace to East Prussia and the four months he spent there before the arrival of the Russians. Both on the journey and in the last period under the Germans he evidently had few opportunities to write. Among other things, he and his comrades spent many weeks in makeshift shelters near the front; they were assigned to prepare positions for cannons and to dig trenches for the final Nazi resistance against the Soviet advance. The following are two days from those months when there is no more talk of letters or packages, and the Italians, who are in the countryside, manage to supplement the very meager ration with a dead hare, a stolen turkey, any potatoes not dug up by the local inhabitants before they fled.

> November 17—Today we stopped work a little earlier. It's very cold and snows almost every day, but the snow is very dry and is blown by the wind and piles up according to the direction it's blowing from. I'm still working as a carpenter with the usual friends.
>
> The cannon resumed firing more insistently and at night you can see the flashes of the shells bursting on the horizon. We're all in bad shape, wearing rags,

we've worn everything we had in our knapsacks and we look like bundles. If we continue this life and the cold doesn't subside I don't know how we'll survive. The days are very short, it's always night, it starts getting light at 8 and at 15:00 it's already dark night.

Of the war we know nothing.

January 11—Since day 6 we've been working on the lake sawing ice, we do eight or nine hours of work a day. We make blocks 70x70x2 [centimeters] square (the ice is 70 centimeters thick). These blocks we distribute over the surface of the lake, apparently they're afraid the Russians will use the surface of the lake as an airfield. It's a really nasty job, and also, since the lake is huge, we're exposed to the four winds the whole time and there's no chance of shelter for a single minute. If you're still on the lake when night falls you're gripped by a sense of fear and anguish, sometimes we're 3 kilometers from the shore.

The lake, marked on the German map, is Spirding.

February 8—I will try to summarize the life and events of these 18 days.

On January 21 we didn't work, we foraged in the deserted houses and found a pig and three chickens. The pig Leo killed with a hammer, it must have weighed 30 kg, we immediately cooked a big hunk of it. Luckily the 22nd we stayed in the same place, because eating too much fresh meat without bread caused intense pain in our stomachs and diarrhea. We tidied ourselves up a little in terms of clothes, only we couldn't find shoes.

During the night of the 23rd they made us get up in a hurry and leave Johannisburg. We had everything ready and slept with our shoes tied in anticipation of having to escape. We had gotten a sledge on which we put knapsacks, pig, chickens. In Johannisburg we joined the column that was waiting for us there, and we left for where we'd gone to work at Christmas, that is, the front. The roads were crowded with civilians and carts, soldiers; on the road there was every kind of abandoned goods except food. In one cart we found a package of honey. On that whole day we went more than 50 kilometers. We then sheltered under a shed roof, because the guards wouldn't let us stop, we three spent the night there.

We left early on the 24th, moving through the countryside. The roads were all crowded and for the whole day three Russian fighter planes machine-gunned the columns. They were gone for less than an hour, then returned, descended to a low altitude, and fired from the wings, the tail, and a small cannon in the middle of the nose. Throughout the countryside dead animals, carts overturned and abandoned . . . For all of the 24th we didn't eat because the meat was

> frozen and we had no bread, we only broke up the honey and sucked on it. It was very cold, since we left the lake the thermometer has been under –30 . . . Anyone found waiting for the Russians was killed with a machine gun volley, even if he was German. We walked again for the whole day and stopped before night to cook a hunk of meat.

On January 27th and 28th, after a day of rest in a hayloft, the three Italians, by now fleeing, start walking again.

> We sheltered in a barn already packed with people of all races, and sat silently in a corner, very depressed. As soon as it was night cannon fire rained down in the courtyard; behind the barn, a roof was hit and caught fire, and eventually everyone ran away, while we decided to stay. We were dead tired and numb with cold, always -34, -35.
>
> The next morning, as soon as it was light, Morozzo came out of our hiding place and returned immediately, running, to tell me he'd seen Russian soldiers all around like ants. In fact they were in the courtyard rummaging through the abandoned carts.
>
> We came out and approached the soldiers saying, "Italienschi." They paid us no attention, we also started rummaging in search of things, especially shoes. The soldiers left, and a little farther away we heard the machine guns again; in the courtyard were

a lot of dead, maybe it had been the Russians or the cannon fire in the night. It had been day for around an hour and we had already lighted a stove to cook when other Russians arrived. An officer searched us, I came out for a moment and when I was about to go back inside (the officer and some soldiers were wandering through the house) a soldier took me for a German and fired at me from 30 meters with his gun, I flung myself down and had the impression I'd been hit. The officer and the soldiers were coming out, they came over to me, meanwhile the one who had fired ran over gesticulating and wanted to shoot again. The officer grabbed the barrel of the gun and held it up, they argued for quite a while, then the soldier left. For me it was as if I'd been knocked out, I lost heart, I couldn't stand up, they told us to go back, we got ready, but I no longer wanted to go, I kept saying to Morozzo and Leo that it was over for me and I wanted to stay there, they persuaded me to go with them.

We left in the direction of Rastenburg. In the first town we went through we could still hear shooting, German soldiers who were found were killed. I had a lot of trouble walking. We had with us a Russian civilian whom the soldiers called *statpolca*, and he saved us, otherwise we would have met the same end as those we saw along the roads, lying in grotesque positions. There were dead of all nationalities, especially German soldiers. There were also women young and old, generally certain parts were exposed.

All the villages were burning, and gradually as we approached Rastenburg the devastation increased. In the city the streets were overflowing with the dead. In a smashed shop window there was a naked young woman, her belly riddled with bullets. The Russian tanks passed over the dead, no one cared to clear the streets.

In Rastenburg, a city larger than Ivrea, we didn't see a single German except the dead . . .

They made us walk more than 40 kilometers. Always the same sight, dead everywhere and total destruction. We reached the outskirts of Angerburg, where we lodged in houses that were still standing, we three Italians, with the French and a group of Poles. We stayed there for a day, and they took our names and prisoner numbers. They asked us for documents, we had only the piece of paper the Germans had given us when they said we were civilians. The Russians collected it, but what saved us was the money from the concentration camp that we had in our pockets. From the first day, all the Russians we met asked for our watches: "*Ciassi*," we answered. "*Niet, ghimeschi zabrata.*"[8]

8 This was the Italians' attempt to say in Russian that the Germans had confiscated their watches.

The Russians sent the Italians off on foot on the back roads. In two weeks they traveled more than 450 kilometers.

> During the last days we passed through Goldap, a German city on the Russian border, not a house was standing, it was barely more than a pile of rubble and it was hard to get through. A little past the city we crossed a valley where the first German line was, and where the Germans had managed to halt the Russians for four months. It was all black, the trees were lying on the ground with splintered trunks, there were dead everywhere, I saw a head hanging on the branch of a fallen tree. A hallucinatory sight, a thing I will never be able to forget.

Certainly Corporal Mario Prola never, for his whole life, forgot the devastations of the war. He had to wait until October of 1945 to be repatriated. Under the Russians he worked with his comrades. He worked at many different jobs, according to the needs of the moment: he loaded bombs on airplanes and taught an ugly girl to iron an officer's white collars. Unfortunately she wasn't the beautiful Mariora, who wanted to show him that within the uniform there was a woman, and whom he wasn't able to meet again to show her he could do better than the first time. At night, after twelve hours of work, he sat exhausted before a variety show offered every so often by the Russians to the troops and foreign soldiers who were no longer prisoners but not yet free. In the spring he found Sandro, his younger brother. In his diary the word *hunger* no longer appeared, yet upon his return he weighed 54 kilos; in March of '40, when he was called up, at twenty, he weighed 85. This he told his grandchildren. He liked to tell them about any of his "adventures" as a prisoner that might entertain them.

> April 29—This morning I was very busy, I had to make some flower beds with designs in front of the Russian command. I drew a big red star with the hammer and sickle at the center. The commissar was very satisfied, many Russians came to see it, including some officers. On the four sides of the big flower bed I designed an Italian flag with the shield of Savoy, a French flag, a Belgian flag, and a Russian flag with hammer and sickle. I make the drawings with fragments of glass, bricks, and enameled tiles. The Russians are enthusiastic about them.

Surely he told his grandchildren about the return journey, which lasted about a month, back and forth through destroyed Germany.

> October 9, 1945—It was still the middle of the night and we were sleeping when we heard a warm voice on the loudspeaker that said, "Welcome, you are in Italy. I bring you greetings from your mothers, from your wives." I got up to look out, it was dark,

I lay down weeping. Next to me Sandro, Morozzo, and Leo also wept. From the troop trains not a cry, not a shout, maybe they were all weeping like us.

Mario's two comrades had agreed that they would take care of bringing back his diary if he couldn't return.

He lived his whole life in his town. He married in 1949. In the small, ugly, black-and-white photos—our photos at the time were like that—the young bride is shining, her face, her hair, her smile, next to him, who is serious, a little awkward. She comes up to his shoulder, wears a simple dress that one assumes is dark blue, with a broad white lace collar. In the distribution of noses in the family, Alice has inherited the turned-up nose of her grandmother Yvelise, who is luminous in the small wedding pictures. Only black-and-white can give this light to a fresh face, to the blond halo of the hair, to the smile showing pretty white teeth. The colors of today extinguish even brilliant, variegated tones, dazzle them.

And so in his town Mario served as mayor, built houses, had a son and a daughter. As long as he was able to, he went climbing in the mountains to look for herbs. In his recipe book there is an "herb soup." The reader is advised to gather the herbs in meadows that are not chemically fertilized. Bran, *custiunet*, nettles, *erbabuc*, chicory, *lavassi*, violet leaves and flowers, primula leaves and flowers, wood sorrel, blackberry shoots, *riundelli* (mallow). Clean the herbs, wash them carefully, cook them in a small amount of water with a leek, two potatoes, two onions. After half an hour of cooking put it all through a sieve (you can use a blender) and season it with brown butter. Serve on crusty bread.

"Grandmother seasoned it with lard and pancetta."

The Italian name of the Piedmontese *riundelli* was given in parentheses; evidently well-known, on the other hand, were *erbabuc* and *custiunet*! With Raffaella, taught by her father to pick and distinguish "the herbs," I counted some thirty-five, with the most varied uses; from arnica to juniper and *urie d'levra* (bladder campion), Mario knew them all, the herbs of his land. I kept as a memento of him the list compiled by Yvelise and Raffaella; I returned the glass jars.

He struggled to die; life had a hard time leaving his large body and his large heart. He was carried in the massive long coffin on the shoulders of his friends and relatives through the town to the cemetery, according to his instructions.

From Gumbinen, where the Russians had taken him to work, he had brought home some stationery with a public telephone number on the letterhead; there he had written the names and addresses of his prison comrades, who had entrusted him with sending word to their families if necessary. They are mainly Alpinists from the Val d'Aosta, but among them is also an Attilio Bianco, of Stella Cilento, Salerno.

He, too, is a contemporary.

12. The Gold of the Latvians

During the five days I spent in Latvia with Pietro, I had some brief experiences that in memory I can't immediately situate in a precise frame of time and place without first re-examining and assessing them. On which afternoon, for example, was I walking quickly, following Pietro, who went ahead of me with his long strides, talking on his cellphone? I remember only that we were near the Orthodox cathedral, in the gardens not far from the Basteiberg, from whose summit, in winter, we went sledding down toward the frozen canal. The others had fun; not me. I wondered, naturally, if the ice on the canal would hold—wouldn't it crack as soon as I, trembling with fear on my sled, slid over it?

Pietro was busy making contacts all over the world: I didn't dare ask him to keep going, at least to the summit, let's call it, of the hill, from which you went down a street and arrived at another street—or was it the same one?—where my father's office was. I wandered without worries. Behind the cathedral we happened on a young man peeing noisily, I don't remember if against a wall of the church or an adjoining fence. We walked twice around a massive red granite plinth, stripped of the statue that had stood on it: a tall man, in bronze, with a funny, very tall hat on his head. It was Barclay de Tolly, the tsar's general, born in Livonia but, despite his half-French name, of Scottish origin. The monument was an homage not to his cultural and ethnic diversity—in any case common in the Baltic—but to his successful skirmishes against the invader, that is, Napoleon.

Yet I'm able to picture without hesitation the only episode of our journey during which I was afraid.

It was Saturday morning, and we were leaving the city to go to Tallinn. We headed for the Brivibas; there were no street signs, of course, that could orient us toward Estonia, and probably we turned too soon, thinking we were taking what on the map was marked as the direct route. We came to a sandy area, rather unpopulated, and, reaching the shores of a marsh, realized we'd taken the wrong road, so we turned back, still in the midst of sand and conifer forests. At a certain point we saw on the left, below the level of the road, a group of cinder-block sheds, and on the right men at work amid big piles of what looked like reddish-brownish sand. They were loading it onto railcars stopped on the tracks. Other men went back and forth between the sheds and the open area beyond the road.

"Look there," I said to Pietro, "is it peat?"

"Yes," he said.

"There," I said again.

"Yeah," he said, and got his camera.

"Don't get out," I said. An absurd fear had gripped me; I was afraid of being caught doing something forbidden.

The men moved calmly; some turned to glance at Pietro, who was taking pictures from the car.

Below street level, a twisted rusty guard tower loomed over the sheds, still covered by a slanting tin roof, not years but decades old. The sides that had supported the stairs had by now disappeared, and they were hanging in long, corroded spirals. The men went back and forth, calmly. I could add that one was whistling but it would be false: I remember the whole scene in a total, profound inner silence. Evoked by a satanic will, a specter had appeared amid barracks surrounded by a barbed wire enclosure, a specter that only I saw and the others didn't, and it would have remained ghostly if Pietro's photograph hadn't offered proof.

Investigating later on the map, I thought it likely that that place was one of the many *Kommandos*—the name used by the Germans—in the peat bogs along the entire coast that were under the authority of the great concentration camp of Kaiserwald, constructed in 1943. Prisoners transferred from the camp worked there during the season between April and September.

The tower hadn't been destroyed; the workers moved around that grim monument as if it didn't exist. It's not possible, I said to myself, it must be a later Soviet ruin, maybe from the years after the war. But had there been gulags in Latvia? I didn't think so; the Soviets deported prisoners many kilometers away. And then—all the more reason if it had been Soviet—why hadn't they knocked it down?

The silent indifference in which the men came and

went between the sheds and the railroad yard wasn't new to me. I had already felt it, even if only at a distance, reading and imagining.

At the trial, in Hamburg, of Viktors Arājs, who had commanded the Latvian fascists, the witness Leopold Schlesinger, head of the SD (*Sicherheitsdienst*), the Nazi intelligence agency, recalled that in August of '43 a wind from the west had blown a horrible stench over the city. He asked his Latvian collaborators what the cause of it could be, and they answered, sneering, that the stink came from the pyres, outside the city, on which the corpses of the Jews were burning. He should have known.

That testimony on the Latvian side was an exception; the west wind blew away not only the stench but also the memory. In the following years the Latvians—when not forced—generally refused, in a stubborn, arrogant way, to admit that they themselves had had anything to do with the extermination of "their" Jews. Wasn't there defiance in the silence that accompanied the tranquil coming and going of the workers in the peat bog?

An official-unofficial, public-private refusal, a game of numbers and innuendoes that had a single aim: burying—very appropriate verb—the mass killings of the German occupation in Latvia. In the face of that refusal I felt that I was a revenant, a "returnee," as the French call those who return from the world of the dead to the world of the living. I alone was able to truly recognize the spectral guard tower; the tower didn't exist and, in the end, I no longer existed, either.

On November 18, 1999, the newspaper *Die Zeit* published a feature on Riga and Latvia. It described, among other things, the Museum of the Occupation, lingering on the numbers of the deportations and executions of the Soviet "Terror." The director of the museum, Valters Nollendorfs, observes that "the experience of the gulag is the trauma of the Latvians." We read: "Faced with the indignation of the self-critical German visitors Nollendorfs is puzzled." The German reporter then provides detailed figures regarding the slaughter of both the Latvian Jews and the German and Austrian Jews who were transported to the concentration camps near Riga and eliminated. But, he concludes, "evidently for the Latvians the horrors of Stalinism are closer than the infamies of fascism."

Throughout the entire article the writer's sympathy for the industriousness with which Riga tries to recover from the damage of the Soviet occupation is evident, although the harsh discriminatory measures that the Latvians have used to get back at the numerous Russians who have lived there for decades are also manifest. But in the next generation, at the latest, Nollendorfs confides, the Russians will be part of society. They will be naturalized. "The sooner we adjust to the idea that they are now established here, the better."

A year later, on November 6, 2000, the journalist Tim Sebastian interviewed the president of Latvia, Vaira Vike-Freiberga, on the BBC program *Hard Talk*. The interview touches on the current situation of Latvia, the hopes of the Baltic countries to enter the European Union, Putin's observation that the "oppressive and repressive Latvian government apparatus increasingly targets the anti-fascist resistance fighters." The reference is to the war crimes trials of some Russians, former Soviet citizens, that were just held by the Latvians.

Here are some passages from the interview. Vike-Freiberga, who, like Nollendorfs, comes from "the emigration"—the Latvian citizens who managed to flee their country before its annexation by the Soviet Union—responds with composure and decisiveness. As for the judicial proceedings, she says, there are three recent articles of Latvian legislation that allow for the prosecution of war crimes against humanity and genocide. However:

> T.S.: Now, Madame President, I'd like to read you what Efraim Zuroff, the head of the Simon Wiesenthal Center in Jerusalem, said: "Not once, of their own volition, have the Latvians prosecuted anyone for the murder of Jews, in great contrast to the energy with which they are trying to bring Communists to trial."
>
> V.V.-F.: There is a very simple reason for it. The people who committed crimes against Jews were tried, executed or sent to twenty-five years of labor in Siberia immediately after the war.

The journalist insists: What does the president have to say regarding the Konrāds Kalējs case?[9]

The president says that Latvia delayed asking for Kalējs's extradition by Australia because sufficient evidence needed to be gathered. The Latvians didn't act, even under pressure from the U.S. Justice Department; the argument is absurd.

> T.S.: Forty-one war criminals have been pardoned since Latvia achieved independence, according to the Simon Wiesenthal Center.
>
> V.V.-F.: Forty-one individuals have been pardoned among the many thousands that had been accused of a variety of crimes under the Communist system, which made out blanket accusations against all sorts of people. If you owned two cows rather than one, you would be . . .
>
> T.S.: No, no, no.
>
> V.V.-F.: Yes!
>
> T.S.: But we are not talking about cows here; we're talking about the murder of ***** Jews [the figure, even here, is given in its entirety]. And there were two Latvian SS divisions, weren't there? So there was a huge degree of complicity with the Nazis, wasn't there? [In fact there were two divisions within a single legion.]
>
> V.V.-F.: There was a degree of collaboration on the part of some people, much as you have in any

9 Kalējs was a Latvian soldier who was a Nazi collaborator and managed to avoid arrest for many years, living in Australia, the United States, and England.

army. When an occupying army marches into a country there is always collaboration.

. . .

T.S.: The Holocaust historian Raoul Hilberg said: "On a per capita basis, the Latvians were represented as heavily as any nation in the destruction of the Jews."

V.V.-F.: I think he should review his statistics. I do think that the Germans, rather, were the ones who started the process. When they came into Latvia they set up their camps. They sent in people from other countries. I think that if we're talking nationalities, then one should review one's figures.

T.S.: Why was it that Latvian Waffen SS veterans were allowed to march through Riga this year?

V.V.-F.: We have a city, Riga, the capital of a country which has recovered its democracy and the right of people to assemble, if they ask for a permit to do so.

T.S.: Even the Waffen SS? No other country in the world allows them to march through its capital.

V.V.-F.: We did not have the Waffen SS marching through. We had a group of people who had participated in the Second World War. On the 13th of October we had a group of people from the Red Army, the people who conquered Latvia and subjected it to fifty years of oppression. They marched freely through the streets. At the Victory Monument they put down red flowers. They sang their own *čas-tuškas* [popular tunes] and their own war songs. We have a free and open society, but we do not have official Waffen SS marching in our streets. We do not.

T.S.: Maybe not official, but they were members of the former Waffen SS who marched. Are you happy about that?

I know from my friend Verina Jones, who sent me the document from London, that Latvians in England were "outraged" by the interviewer's insistence.

The president calmly lists various groups, including extremists on the left, who have demonstrated in Latvia. She points out that the demonstrations are not initiatives of the Latvian government. She repeats the "right of assembly" for all, as in Great Britain. Tim Sebastian objects that in Great Britain, Nazi marches and Waffen SS banners are not allowed. When, shortly afterward, he declares that only in Latvia have Russians been tried for war crimes, Madame Vike-Freiberga answers, "Of the people who marched into Latvia with their tanks on June 17, 1940, most of them happened to be largely Russian, although of course they represented the Soviet Union."

The long discussion that follows in the interview concerns the current relations of Latvia with Russia and the hope of the Baltic countries that they will soon be full members of the European Union; the agreements, the president confides, should be concluded by 2002.

Then, responding to Sebastian's repeated criticisms concerning the discriminatory laws governing the Russians, the president firmly defends the provision that requires that Russians living in Latvia must know Latvian in order to hold top government posts.

Parenthetically: the Russian protests about the "difficulty" of learning Latvian are curious; everyone knows that Russians seem to learn any language in a few months. Might the obstacle be of a different type? It's hard to be forced to learn the language of one's own serfs! Hard to give up one's own colonies!

> Madame Vike-Freiberga: "In Latvia we have a language that had lost its place in society after fifty years of Russification. The language law simply reinstates the rights of the Latvian language as the state language. It doesn't really go much further than that. It sets up certain requirements for people to use it who otherwise would not. It is analogous to Bill 101 that was passed in Quebec in order to restitute the rights of the French language under the overwhelming majority of an English-speaking continent. It worked in Quebec in order to restore the use of French in the public sphere. It's doing exactly that in Latvia. It's not a hardship to learn a language. I think it's an enrichment."

Responding to an objection from Tim Sebastian, the president says that requiring the Russians to learn Latvian isn't a way of getting revenge: "How do you think you can be paid back for your lost life, for your lost future, for the people who were killed and died of hunger and starvation out in the steppes?"

There is no resentment in Latvia, the president continues; mixed marriages are twenty percent of the total, the percentage of resident Russians who don't know the language has shrunk in the past five years to nine percent. The children learn it in school; seventy-five percent of Russian parents send their children to Latvian elementary schools. Those 60,000 who have opted for Russian citizenship did so by their own choice.

Here is a brief self-portrait of the president:

> T.S.: Given what happened to you personally, the fact that you had to flee the country when the Soviets invaded in the closing days of the Second World War, you would have every reason for bitterness against the Russians, wouldn't you?

The president was a child when her family fled to Canada, the destination of many Latvians who emigrated. During the flight a younger sister died.

> V.V.-F.: I find bitterness is a luxury that a healthy human being can't afford. Bitterness drains your psychic energy. It's a useless emotion. I look forward to the future, I know that people . . .
>
> T.S.: Can you control your emotions so well?

V.V.-F.: Well, look. One can try and cultivate the positive emotions rather than the negative ones.

T.S.: You were a professor of psychology at the University of Montreal.

V.V.-F.: Yes, and much as I grow my garden and cultivate my potted plants on the windowsill, I feel that one has to cultivate tolerance and kindness. One has to look to the future rather than to the past. A neurotic keeps picking at old wounds, and I think that is unhealthy. I think a nation has to look to the future.

The old wounds are very likely those inflicted by the Soviet "Terror." But the Latvians have no resentments, the president repeats.

The interview concludes:

T.S.: You see yourself as a bridge, don't you, between the West and Latvia; you've said so in the past. What of Western attitudes do you want to teach the Latvians?

V.V.-F.: I suppose, in a way, more self-confidence . . . This is a people who for half a century have had no choice. And what I would like to encourage is the sense of freedom that comes from finally, at long last, having choices that we can make.

T.S.: And tolerance.

V.V.-F.: Of course.

"In our view," said Ojars Kalnins, a former Latvian ambassador to the United States who directs the government-financed information institute, "the Second World War ended in 1991, when we finally restored our independence." (*The New York Times*, May 20, 2001).

The perverse game of numbers continues to play out in every official Latvian declaration on the Shoah, almost always solicited, very rarely spontaneous. There's no need to exaggerate; the total of those exterminated should be revised. And see how the numbers themselves cover the massacre; we don't talk about extermination, we don't talk about human beings, still less do we allude to locals in charge—it was the Germans, their business—and if we talk about numbers the discussion shifts, becomes impersonal. Or even, in a horrific comparison, "Those are the numbers of your dead, look at mine!"

In the fifties the Latvian historian Arnolds Spekke (*Latvia and the Baltic Problem*, 1955) called the extermination of the Jews in Latvia "regrettable"—it was exclusively the work of the Nazis; the Nuremberg trials demonstrate this clearly—and avoided the figures. He saved them for the Soviet deportations.

The figures are, instead, helpful to Bernd Nielsen-Stokkeby in his book *Baltische Erinnerungen* [Baltic Memories]. He is a German Estonian who devotes fine pages filled with affection and longing to the Estonia of his childhood and adolescence, and to the history of the Baltic countries. The son of a pharmacist, at twenty he "repatriates" with his family; he takes part in the war, at first mainly as an interpreter, later in the Wehrmacht. After the final stubborn German defense during the sack of Libau he was imprisoned by the Soviets.

He is freed and goes home to Germany, but in his capacity as a journalist he often returns to Estonia—he also likes hunting there. He witnesses the damage caused by the Soviet occupation, revisits the beloved places, can't find his first love—an Estonian girl with a long braid who, more easygoing than a German girl, granted him the first joys of sex—and embraces a Jewish schoolmate, the most intelligent in the class, who escaped to the Soviet Union. To what? To an implicit disaster, not named. The calamity reappears in figures on page 235 and following, and now is explicit, although cited only in reference to the drop in population in the Baltic because of the war. A demographic question, in short. In Latvia, writes the honest German Estonian, the "total number" of Jews killed "in the course" of the German occupation of the Second World War should be included among the human losses. A little farther on, the term "frightful" is attached to the "total" of the Lithuanian massacres (by percentage no greater than in Latvia). Nor does Nielsen-Stokkeby—who, thanks to logical analysis, manages to substitute the phrase "in the course of time" for the true agent of the disaster—begrudge the adjective *horrible* for the punitive expeditions of the SS in Lithuania in 1944.

Given that he is accustomed to judging every event from an unfailingly anti-Soviet point of view—he doesn't dislike the Russians themselves (not to mention the Russian women), especially if they're Ukrainian, like his orderlies, the faithful *Hiwis*[10]—possible variables escape him. Describing a last attempt at Latvian resistance against the invader from the east, in 1944, led by Colonel Roberts Osis, he speaks of Osis the heroic partisan, not Osis the commander of the Latvian police battalions who had been summoned by SS-Obergruppenführer Friedrich Jeckeln to the meeting before the massacre in Rumbula. Did Nielsen-Stokkeby, who worked as an interpreter on the front in Leningrad in the winter of '41 and then fought in Courland, not have information about this man's other side? Or "in the course" of the huge disaster was there only one side, no distinctions to be made? Points of view, fate.

Similarly, the Soviets, in the postwar period in Latvia, judging and sentencing on war crimes charges the Latvian resisters, collaborators with the Germans—these were the trials that President Vike-Freiberga had referred to—considered them guilty not of participating in the massacres of the Jews (though some were) but of fighting as traitors against the Soviet Union; here, evidently, Jews didn't exist, only Soviet citizens. Points of view, fate.

While I was reading Nielsen-Stokkeby's *Baltic Memories* I felt yet again, I have to admit, that divided sense of kinship that, despite my strong reservations, any contact with the world of the Baltic Germans rouses in me. For good or ill I had in common with them a language and a homeland that belonged neither to them nor to me, and that we mourned, although we lost it in different ways.

---

10 *Hilfswiger*, auxiliary volunteer.

During our visit to Latvia in 1999 I didn't feel particularly nostalgic. Nostalgia comes from a sensation of distance, and I lived with emotions that oscillated between past and present; at most I was filled with a kind of surprise: inside I continued to be amazed that I was there, like a tourist on a trip. I was passive, the emotions were someone else's: I contemplated the busy Latvians and their gorgeous girls with the eye of a foreigner. Even as a curious, timid child, I had observed them like that. My sister, at the time, accused me of acting like a snob because I wouldn't speak Latvian with the mailman and the pharmacist. In truth I would never have dared to speak with anyone in "his" Latvian. No, no: the flowers of my garland had to be lilies; my Latvian had to be Latvian.

Monday morning, before we left, I went with Pietro to the big covered markets, situated in the former airship hangars. It was an obligatory stop for every tourist; Pietro, besides, belongs to a generation of eager shoppers. I wondered what in the world he could find to buy there. All I remembered of the markets in Riga was that one rainy day we had gone to the nearby outdoor fish market, beside the Düna. The fishmongers and the stalls were dripping with profanity and dampness.

Driving into the parking lot, evidently reserved for vendors, we were given a ticket by a polite Latvian policeman who, unlike his Estonian colleagues, gave us a receipt for the fine paid, lower this time (alas for my hundred dollars extorted in the Estonian forests!), and explained to us, always politely, the mistake we had made. On the ticket my son's name was written simply as "Piero."

Outside the enormous hangars we wandered through the so-called flea market, among shoddy goods, cheap clothes, paltry objects, pitiable flowers. It was drizzling. Entering, we walked under the gigantic vault of the hangars. We were overwhelmed by the abundance of the products displayed. The quantity and variety of cheeses in the cheese section and fish in the fish section left us amazed. Pietro managed to buy some fish; I didn't dare, they had unknown names, hanging, laid out, in barrels, dried, big, little, very long, tiny. I would never have thought there were so many different fish in the Daugava and the sea. The predominant color was gold. The gold of the Latvians shone in the cheeses, in the smoked fish; for centuries it was the only gold they possessed, these strangers among whom I was born, a foreigner. These peasants who had not had the right to a surname until 1835, who had previously borne the surname of their master, of the estate from which, at any moment, they could be sent away, sold to a new master, separated from their families.

My friend Paša, to whom I was recounting the experiences of my forebears, had said with a smile, "Don't think that the others"—and here "the others" were the Russian peasants—"were better off."

In the markets of Riga the Russian peasants were numerous; mixed in with the Latvians they couldn't be distinguished by their appearance. They were all peasants.

I ventured to buy a tin of little fish with the label in Cyrillic; they had appeared to be (and were) smoked fish, the *Strömlinge* that hung in big garlands, and which I was crazy about, though in our house meant for cat food. In an unusual impulse of affection I also bought a packet of pale raw honey. I don't know why, eating it later, I thought constantly of our months at Waltershof. There was no direct connection, but, whether it was the honey's rough packaging or its homemade taste, something carried me back to that brief period in the country. The experiences that a capricious memory restored to me, unlike Nielsen-Stokkeby's recollections, were not at all poetic. The terrible stomachache after eating black bread, still warm from the oven in the courtyard, which I had covered with fresh butter. The scolding when we had nearly drowned the newborn ducklings, sticking them in a puddle to teach them to swim. The room where intestines hung, dangling on strings, ready for making salamis after the pigs were killed.

On Monday afternoon we got on the plane and left Latvia. I was, on the whole, quiet, content; I had fulfilled a duty. I had gotten over the wall. I didn't ask myself questions, I didn't give answers, I rested.

When I started working on this book I hesitated, as I've said; not only did I not have a clear purpose but, as I had been before our trip, I was afraid deep down of that other return, which I would have to carry out by writing; I was afraid of the work and I was afraid I would have to finally untangle the cruel knot of my personal history. But I couldn't keep refusing to confront the reality of the last day of my father's life, even if I could find the only remaining evidence in the books of others.

Looking for information, I happened on the name of Andrew Ezergailis. He had published a book in 1996, *The*

Holocaust in Latvia, 1941–1944, in collaboration with the United States Holocaust Memorial Museum and the Latvian Historical Institute. The author's last name didn't seem Jewish; could he be Latvian? The book arrived, also from Gino Moretti, in photocopy. I had tried to order it through Amazon, but after a month realized that I would have had to wait forever; I had in fact requested it around Christmas, and there must have been too many orders. Gino, again, got busy and managed to get it for me.

The author had worked on the book for ten years; he had had access to the many documents assembled by the Soviets in the Latvian State Archives, largely kept secret from Westerners. He had consulted innumerable others in the most disparate libraries, from Jerusalem to London; he had had private conversations with compatriots, both with those who had remained in Latvia and with Latvian emigrants. Although in the conclusion of his book he scrupulously lists all its possible inadequacies and all the details still to investigate, the overall picture that the reader can form is very clear and exact. He omitted nothing, no fact, however atrocious. The appendix lists the members of Viktors Arājs's commando (including, of course, Konrāds Kalējs); members of the SD, the Sicherheitsdienst, German and Latvian; the trials of war criminals in Soviet Riga, Germany, and the United States; tables showing the branches of the Nazis' bureaucratic system, grotesque in its complexity aimed at a single linear goal—slaughter.

Finally the silence was broken. In that sense the book, dedicated "to the Latvian Jews who perished in the

Holocaust," is dedicated also to the Latvians. The majority of them, out of inertia, fear, ignorance, peasant distrust and complicity, had been silent, but with precision and rigor the historian Ezergailis tries to redeem what remains of their lost honor among the lies of the powerful, the Germans on the one hand, the Soviets on the other.

And so for the first time I listened to a Latvian speak and with him spoke Pēteris Stankēvičs, Osvalds Lipāns, the Garkalns' little girl, Jānis Franks-Pranks, the twelve-year-old Juris Legzdiņš, Ēriks Pārups, Alberts Baranovskis. They spoke and I looked them in the eye.

While Pietro and I were in Latvia, the only Latvians I had looked in the eye had been, basically, the small tidy airport worker and the kind policeman at the markets. The others were part of an indistinguishable mass. Of course, they were no longer the Latvians of whom my father spoke contemptuously, alluding to the "dictator" Ulmanis, the anonymous ones who sneered at Schlesinger's question about the stench of the pyres, the anonymous who, with whips and clubs, escorted the groups of Jews condemned to death, the anonymous who, locked in their silence, pretended not to know. In spite of that I couldn't keep myself from wondering: Is my grandmother's samovar still in some Latvian house? And didn't the fear that had assailed me at the peat bog emerge from a fear that still dwelled hidden in my soul, fear in the face of the Latvians? Would I have to reckon with them?

What name to give to that reckoning?

The necessity or possibility of "forgiveness" has been

and is discussed endlessly in Italy, the country where I live, the country of my mother, of Gianni, my children and grandchildren, my friends. It has gradually become mine, mediating between affections and language. And in fact for years now throughout the world the word *forgiveness* has been used casually, like a household utensil, dropped into conversation, mentioned in ordinary interviews, proclaimed or denied.

The first time I heard the word burst like an undefended balloon in the silence of a room I was in the audience at the Teatro Carignano, in Turin—definitely more than twenty years ago—in a big crowd of people. Not spectators but people who had come to hear the writer Edith Bruck, who escaped from Auschwitz at fifteen, speak about herself and her books. Tall, dressed in white, very beautiful, she was introduced by the small, thin Primo Levi, speaking sternly from the stage in his clear Piedmontese voice.

Near the end of the presentation, I think, a woman rose—I no longer remember how old she was, but not young—and, trembling, asked Edith Bruck if she had "forgiven." The word in fact burst: it lost power, shriveled, withered, reached no one. Levi or Bruck answered, or they both did; I don't remember what they said, or if their answer reached the woman. They were polite, that I remember—sorrowful, bewildered. The question seemed to me indecent.

(Since then, it has often been said that it's not up to us to forgive; it's for the victims. I myself wrote it in my diary when I was twenty. Besides, we don't own anyone; we don't even own those who are most dear to us, so we are not robbed by those who kill them.)

What more could I add apart from my conviction, firmer every day, about the nature of forgiveness? Knowing how to forgive seems to me the hard-won fruit of a long inner process in which the goals and actions of a lifetime are completed and clarified, and refers only rarely to a specific act; it's the very private result of our inner struggle. This result doesn't emerge from a momentary impulse, which might cause us to lose it at any moment in a new rush of anger, in an irresistible burst of bitterness. It's an act of contrition that should be repeated from minute to minute; even when we're old we find it hard to forgive a childhood slight.

The beautiful young wife of a policeman who was in Falcone's[11] escort and was killed with him was not offering forgiveness when, in the packed Palermo cathedral—crying, as one cries in the sweaty spasms of childbirth—she read, gasping and weeping, from the page that had been prepared for her, the polished, simplifying words of reckoning; they were not hers, which would have been words of fury and desperation.

There is no reckoning except in the bosom of the Lord. So I will not write about forgiveness now, here; I will write about knowledge.

From Ezergailis's book I learned how many ways on

11 Giovanni Falcone, the Sicilian anti-Mafia judge killed in a bombing by the Mafia in 1992.

Sunday, November 30, 1941, my father and his daughter could have perished. I know the names of some of the chosen executioners, Germans, who were active in Rumbula that day, the names of the Latvians and the Germans who in the morning went wild in the ghetto with murderous rage against those who tried to hide, to flee, to avoid being herded into columns. I know the names of the streets taken, the names of the weapons used, and in what ways they were used. But I will never know what really happened. This, too, as it should, lies in the bosom of the Lord.

In late November it was very cold. Osvalds Lipans, policeman in the 6th Company of Riga, received orders to supervise some Soviet prisoners of war who were digging pits. These, shaped like an upside-down pyramid, were thirteen to fifteen meters long, ten to twelve meters wide, five meters deep. Several Germans were supervising and directing the operations. The policeman wasn't told the purpose of those pits, but some days later, while he was again working in the vicinity, he heard continuous gunfire coming from the direction where the pits had been dug. Then he heard that the Jews of the ghetto had been killed. (Deposition at the Arājs trial, in Hamburg, taken in Riga April 12, 1976.)

Peteris Stankevics, from the harbor precinct, arrived at the ghetto, following orders, at seven in the morning on November 30. A column of Jews with their baggage was already lined up in the street. Before leaving for the ghetto

Captain Riks had informed his men that the Jews were to be transferred to another camp. Stankevics recalled, "But when we entered the ghetto we saw another picture: possessions were scattered and in several places in the square bodies of murdered Jews. One could conclude that it was the Germans and Latvians of the SD who dragged the Jews out of their houses, and those who had tried to resist had been driven, beaten, and some killed." (Deposition at the Arājs trial, in Hamburg, January 16, 1975.)

The next testimony is taken from the book by Frieda Fried Michelson, *I Survived Rumbula*, which is sadly famous because it was written by one of three who survived the second "action," on December 8, 1941. No one survived the first.

On the morning of November 30 Frieda could observe from the windows of her home in the ghetto the columns of "the departing" down in the street. Each was allowed to bring twenty kilos of baggage. They had all spent the night before packing and unpacking the suitcases, to get the proper weight.

"It was already beginning to get light. An unending column of people, guarded by armed policemen, was passing by. Young women, women with infants in their arms, old women, handicapped, helped by their neighbors, young boys and girls—all marching, marching. Suddenly, in front of our window, a German SS man started firing with an automatic gun point-blank into the crowd. People were mowed down by the shots, and fell on the cobblestones. There was confusion in the column. People were trampling over those who had fallen, they were pushing forward, away from the wildly shooting SS man. Some were throwing away their packs so they could run faster. The Latvian policemen were shouting 'Faster, faster!' and lashing whips over the heads of the crowd."

Faster, faster they fell, got up, fell, remained on the ground, the crowd, lashed by whips and shoved by rifle barrels, trampled them on the frantic, chaotic march to death.

Along the street (Maskavas), just past the Škirotava station, lived the Garkalns family. Their daughter, then seven, recalled the columns of Jews driven past her house, around thirty meters from the street. She described the scene to Ezergailis: "There was an enormous pandemonium. Some Jews had refused to continue, there were shots, shoves, blows. The column started moving again. A few steps farther on there was another scuffle. There had been some shots and someone had been killed and left on the side of the street. People panicked, wailing began." The child's mother hung blankets over the windows; the child was taken to a room at the back of the house and forbidden to look out again.

They didn't all walk.

Janis Franks-Pranks testified on April 5, 1976, at the Arājs trial, in Hamburg, that as the driver of the blue police bus, he had taken to Rumbula a load of Jews with children and others not able to walk. He had passed by the columns, which were escorted by Latvian police; at the front and back were two Germans.

Does it matter if they were police, SS, SD, Gestapo?

The mother of Juris Legzdinš, who was twelve at the time, was a clerk at the 11th Police Precinct. He told Ezergailis he had learned from her that the German supervising this precinct had boasted that he threatened Lieutenant Grigors of the Latvian police with a gun, forcing him to kill Jews.

Ēriks Pārups, in a conversation on April 14, 1990, reported to Ezergailis an incident involving the police lieutenant Aleksandrs Vilnis, who, after Rumbula, had asked to be transferred to the front. Vilnis hadn't intervened when a German, at the head or back of the column, had forced a Latvian policeman, aiming a pistol at his temple, to kill a young mother with a child in her arms, because the woman had stopped.

Of what happened at the edge of the pits on Sunday, November 30, we have no direct testimony except that of Peteris Stankevics. After escorting the column assigned to him to the station in Rumbula, he had received orders to return to the city. He disobeyed and hid in the shelter of the bushes. Peering through the bushes he saw that the Jews were forced to undress before being sent, fifty at a time, toward the pits. The final passage was a path fifty meters long and five wide that had been marked off, with Germans and Arājs's Latvians guarding, a few meters apart on either side.

Reports of the events of November 30 inside the "big" ghetto came mainly from the survivors among the men strong enough to work, separated from their families and locked in the "small" ghetto. Every witness repeats the name of Herberts Cukurs and the names of Germans from the SD. There must have been a relentless manhunt; rivulets of frozen blood stained the walls of the houses, the stairs, the doorways. Despite the fact that that very afternoon Jews from the "small" ghetto had been assigned to transport to the old Jewish cemetery the bodies of those who had been killed that morning during the departure for "evacuation," German Jews who arrived in Riga two months later still found corpses in the cellars and attics.

Little Juris Legzdinš, going in the late afternoon to look for his mother in the 11th Precinct, met policemen who were completely drunk wandering in the courtyard and the rooms, in total confusion.

In Rumbula intense firing was heard until twilight, at around five—the sun set at three-thirty—but isolated shots were heard until evening. It was probably a matter of finishing off any who had been wounded and regained consciousness.

Alberts Baranovskis, stationmaster in Rumbula, testified to the Soviets in November of 1944 that at 11:00 a.m. on Monday, December 1, two naked women, covered with blood, appeared in the station yard. One had been shot in the neck, the other had a wound in her cheek that had torn out her tongue (they had been shot with an automatic Russian weapon loaded with fifty bullets and capable of firing one at a time). The woman who was still able to speak couldn't utter a word: a Latvian guard rushed at the two unfortunate women and would have killed them on the spot if the wife of a railway worker hadn't intervened, saying there were children in the house. The guard threw the women on a sled and took them back to the forest.

The second action unfolded on December 8. We can hypothesize that Jeckeln had intended to spare the twelve from his guard who were chosen to carry out the mission (and never rotated out) the physical and psychological tension of two successive days of slaughter. In the opinion of SS-Sturmbannführer Ohlendorf, head of Einsatzgruppe D, who testified to that at the Nuremberg trials, the Jeckeln method, called *Sardinenpackung* (I won't translate the German), required of the workers too great an expenditure of energy.

All day on November 30 SS-Obergruppenführer Jeckeln stood at the edge of the pits along with high-ranking officers of the SD, the SS, and the Latvian police. Osis, the head of the police, was almost always present. Arājs, increasingly drunk, took an active role near the pits, supervising and directing his men. Jeckeln invited guests from every level of the German hierarchy: Lohse, Reischskommissar for Ostland, was present, and, perhaps, so was Drechsler, Generalkommissar for Latvia. Jeckeln ordered his own officers to be present as witnesses of the executions. He summoned the police chief of Pskov and other cities in the region. He summoned Stahlecker from the front in Leningrad. They all must have been complicit with him. No one from the Wehrmacht was invited.

The Wehrmacht washed their hands of it. Did they (those disgusting bastards) want the local commanding officer to sign their orders against the Jews? Agreed, no reason not to, what's a yellow star, after all. Did they want a second yellow star? Agreed, what's a second yellow star, after all. They wanted trucks to transport the Jews on November 30? Agreed. They wanted some squads on the outskirts to watch for possible escapes during the transfer? Agreed. The Wehrmacht washed their hands of anything those bastards could do. Washed their hands of it.

Ella Medale, the other woman who miraculously survived, wrote about the second "action." She worked in the hospital in the ghetto.

On December 8 the Jewish staff members of the hospital received orders to prepare the sick to be evacuated. Around noon some SS soldiers entered the building and searched it from top to bottom. In the street were two trucks ready to transport the staff. Ella went to the driver, a young, strong, tall Latvian, and calmly asked him, "Where will you bring us?" He turned and began to weep. "To the shooting . . . The whole morning I have been bringing our people there."

The truck stopped on Maskavas, near the Rumbula forest, in front of a barrier of armed men. Shooting could be heard.

"People were overwhelmed by a sense of inevitability and the impossibility of escape, and proceeded in a rapid flow, without protesting. They threw objects of value into a wooden box, then there was a pile of furs, coats, padded jackets. Then followed shoes, caps, hats, and beyond stood those who were already only in their underwear."

Ella takes off her coat but, as she leans over to put it on the pile, a sudden, chance blow to her back makes her fall and the sharp pain restores her instinct for self-preservation.

"I jumped up and ran to the next guard, a man from the Pērkonkrusts"—an Arājs man is meant—"who had guarded us frequently. He was ashen and hardly could hold his Nagant gun in his hand. He appeared nauseated; I grabbed him by the arm and pleadingly told him: 'Save me! you know that I am not a Jew.'" Ella Medale was very blond and spoke Latvian well. "For an answer, he mumbled something incomprehensible and pointed to a group of policemen: 'Speak to the higher-ups!' I rushed toward them. The head executioner, Arājs, fastened his eyes on me. His face was disfigured, beastlike, and he swayed back and forth, horribly drunk. I shouted again, 'I am not a Jew!' I trembled as in a fever. Arājs waved me away: 'Here are only Jews. Today Jewish blood must flow.' . . . I ran back to the guard. He pointed to a group of higher German officers. They stood there and looked on . . . Some snapped pictures."

Ella Medale managed to convince the Germans that she had been taken by mistake; a Latvian, a neighbor, later provided her with the false information needed for "Aryan" documents. Similarly, by chance, Matiss Lutrins survived, whom Arājs knew personally and spared almost as a joke.

Later, in low voices, the Latvians exchanged information about what had happened on November 30 and December 8 of 1941 in the vicinity of Riga, on the road to Salaspils. We don't know how many of them found out about it, certainly many more than those who talked about it. It was said that among Arājs's men some became alcoholics and eventually committed suicide. It was often repeated, in a whisper, that after the massacre the earth continued to shudder over the bodies of the buried.

Then the snow fell. The place was not yet known as Rumbula, after the nearby train station; the Latvians called it *varnu mežs*, crows' forest.

13. "Who Emptied the Sand from Your Shoes?"

Who emptied the sand from your shoes
when you had to get up to die?

The sand that Israel brought back,
The sand of its exile?

The burning sand of Sinai
mixed with the throats of nightingales
mixed with butterfly wings
mixed with the restless dust of serpents,
mixed with the grains of Solomonic patience,
mixed with the bitter wormwood of exile.

O fingers, you who emptied the sand from the
 shoes of the dead,
Tomorrow you will be dust in the shoes of those
 to come.

Nelly Sachs, *Flight and Metamorphosis*

The Soviets captured Jeckeln in May of 1945 near Berlin. They didn't immediately recognize his intelligent and threatening face; he didn't get photographed, and he appeared in public only rarely. Was he recognized by his uniform? Even if he was wearing a jacket and pants similar in style and color to the gray of the Wehrmacht's, he certainly wore the grim official beret with visor and death's-head, and displayed his rank. For goodness' sake, he was SS-Obergruppenführer, he wasn't a general in the Wehrmacht, he wouldn't turn traitor, not him: "till the bitter end" he had fought to defend Berlin and his Führer. At the last moment, when he was about to leave Riga, in September of 1944, he had ordered all the Latvians—he emphasized *all*—to be sent to the border to dig a gigantic trench to keep the Soviets from entering Latvia.

From Germany he was brought back to Riga. There he was put on trial in the winter of the same year—a short trial, lasting two weeks. The Soviet prosecution wasn't concerned in this situation with arguing about numbers: Jeckeln's far surpassed the figure necessary to justify a death sentence. Before arriving in Latvia, he had been active in Ukraine, at Himmler's request, and later, in addition to Latvia, also in Byelorussia. The prosecution was interested mainly in establishing the exact relations between the Obergruppenführer and his bosses in Berlin. There were no written orders, of course; he didn't dwell much on oral ones. He knew very well that he wouldn't save his skin, better to say as little as possible. He insisted on the orders he had received from Himmler, who in turn, he declared, had received them from Hitler in person. To judge from the reports of the interrogation, he was fussy about the tally of those killed: he didn't deny his own hundreds of thousands, but he wouldn't let himself be blamed so perfunctorily for the thousands killed before his arrival in Riga, in November of '41, a job carried out by SS-Brigadeführer Stahlecker, but largely, he said, by the Latvians themselves, and in any case incomplete.

Stahlecker wasn't there to confirm or deny: in '42 an Estonian partisan on the front in Leningrad had shot him in the head with a well-aimed bullet, sending him to his gods in Valhalla—decorated, we may suppose, with the longed-for *Ritterkreuz*. Despite his scant respect for the Latvians, shared by Jeckeln (who in 1944 had refused, horrified, to provide arms to the "natives" for a possible ultimate defense), Stahlecker would no doubt have supported the argument, later sustained by many German witnesses and historians—and, for different reasons, by the Soviets as well—that it was the Latvians, anti-Semitic and anti-Soviet, who launched the extermination of their Jews.

It may seem difficult today to understand how brazenly and casually the Germans attributed their crimes to others. Fifty years have passed, books have been written—fifty, according to the historian Margers Vestermanis—conferences have been held, the sealed Soviet archives have been opened, and slowly but tenaciously Jewish centers of research have managed to unearth witnesses: by now it has been demonstrated that the anti-Jewish directives and the subsequent slaughters in Latvia started—"naturally," we say today—with German plans and systems. We can still, it seems to me, allow ourselves to measure the Latvians' zeal in following these directives. But what we now find natural wasn't at the time. Meanwhile, the Nazi norm of dissimulating and lying at all costs was an ironclad rule, and so was the need to protect oneself in every way possible; in the language of Heydrichs, the extermination was seldom "elimination" but, rather, "filtering," "reconditioning measures," "purification," "special provisions," "special regime." Not by chance does the German national hero, Siegfried, perform his dirtiest deeds disguised by a *Tarnkappe*, a hooded cloak that makes him invisible. To this Germanic camouflage we should add the lack of written evidence, the Nazis' confidence that they had acted in utmost secrecy (think about the fact that news of the slaughters in Latvia in 1941 did not reach Sweden until the fall of 1942), the usual suppression of possible witnesses, the chaos of the postwar period: everything combined to make it problematic, in the least, to attribute and distribute responsibilities, untangle hierarchies, verify additions and subtractions, know anything with certainty.

As for Jeckeln and his accusations against the Latvians, I believe that—besides his intention to include in his own guilt not only the despised complicit Latvians but the entire population of Latvia, and his desire to mitigate his own misdeeds—he also felt a subtle pleasure. The German term *Schadenfreude*—the pleasure felt in others' misfortunes—here might rather be, with a new meaning, the joy of sticking in your shit those who, by force or of their own free will, provided you with their vile services.

Entering Riga as victors on October 13, 1944, the Soviets managed to arrest in the country some three hundred members of Arājs's commando; they put them on trial, sentenced them, hanged some, and later, perhaps, made use of some themselves. As I've already said, the guilty were charged as enemies of the Soviet Union, not as murderers of Jews.

Besides, even then it wasn't easy to tell. Who in Latvia was left to provide evidence? Certainly not the hundred and fifty ghosts who, concealed at great risk by friends or simply acquaintances, came out of their hiding places a few days after the arrival of the Soviets, and were seen on the streets of Riga. In all of Latvia no more than four hundred Jews were saved this way. But the Latvians who tried to help, Vestermanis thinks, were a good five thousand, even if it was just a mouthful of bread placed every morning on the roadside by Baptist peasants who had noticed him, a seventeen-year-old Jewish fugitive, hiding in the forest. In reality, the scattered groups of Baptists and Adventists were generous, according to their forces. Frieda Michelson, who survived at Rumbula, was hidden in the home of an Adventist pastor. Vestermanis doesn't tell us how many of those five thousand wanted to testify about their experiences.

Besides, who asked for evidence? And once it was provided, maybe by chance, who was willing to use it? Time was needed for the huge calamity that was later called the Holocaust to take shape, for its scale to be assessed. The Nuremberg trials passed judgment on the supreme leaders of Nazism—in that sense the proceedings were hierarchical—but acting under them were innumerable accomplices joined to one another by links in the complicated chain of military and civilian ranks of the Nazi order. Although the voluminous Nuremberg files revealed many of their names, in general only after many years will we find any of them brought to judgment.

Viktors Arājs, the head of the Aizsargi, the squad of the blue buses, was put on trial in 1976 in Hamburg. He had hidden in West Germany under the surname of his wife for some thirty years. Most of the testimony concerning the exterminations in Riga and Latvia emerged from this lengthy trial—"the trial of Lieutenant Jahnke and others"—which lasted two and a half years. In the proceedings there's a photo of Arājs with a group of his men. It was taken in the fall of 1942, on his return from the SS school in Fürstenberg, where he had gone with some compatriots for a training course. We might ask what they were training for, but we can presume that killing the unarmed was not considered sufficient extra credit for those who, even of an impure race, now had to replace the Aryans, more and more of whom were falling on the Russian front. Arājs, with the rank of major and not without courage, later received the Iron Cross 2nd Class. Stahlecker at the time of his death was, among other things, commander of the unit that the two Latvian companies under Arājs belonged to and was leading a punitive action during an anti-partisan campaign called *Winterzauber*, winter magic. Many of the names of the German "cleansing" expeditions—following, clearly, the custom of masquerading at all costs—read like titles in a poetry anthology.

In the photo the commander of the Aizsargi is sitting next to two smiling, gloved SS officers. The others aren't wearing gloves and don't have the runic *S*s. To tell the truth, only Ezergailis, the historian, is able to discern how the Latvians differ from the Germans. At first glance they appear the same in every way. But the German officers smile, satisfied, not the Latvians. The lawyer Viktors Bernhards Arājs has a young, slightly timid, anonymous face. He was thirty-two, he had advanced in his career, he no longer needed an interpreter to speak with his German comrades. Like him, many of his acolytes came from the university *Bruderschaften*, or fraternities, of Riga that had Latin names in imitation of the German ones. His *Bruderschaft*, Lettonia, was the oldest and thus the most distinguished. He came from a peasant family, and had had some difficulty getting accepted.

West Germany was not in general the land of asylum for Latvian war criminals. The few who went on trial there did so because they were involved in other cases against German officers and noncommissioned officers.

Arājs's story offers an example of how in the chaos after the war those who today are called "guilty of crimes against humanity" could be mixed in among refugees and prisoners; it reveals not only the means but also the political interests that in the West contributed to whitewashing the criminals. It was, in fact, the start of the Cold War.

Captured in civilian clothes near Lübeck by the British at the end of the war, he was interned in a camp for military prisoners; he had false documents with the surname Abel.

But after he was informed on by someone, he was sent to an SS transit camp in Eckenfelde and from there to a camp for SS officers in Hamburg and then to an exit camp in Putlos. While he was making up his mind to escape, he heard that a unit for the liberation of Latvia was being formed in Belgium. Arriving in Belgium, he was again interned in a prisoner-of-war camp. On the last day of 1945 a Latvian—I quote Ezergailis: "for two bottles of beer"—informed on him to the British, revealing him as Arājs; he was interned in various camps for prominent SS members. He was interrogated, confronted with witnesses, and after six months released and interned in a camp near Oldenburg for those being repatriated. The English intended to make use of him by sending him to Courland, now Kurzeme, as a spy. But returning alone to Latvia seemed to him too dangerous, and he didn't know Russian, so he rejected the offer. Arrested again in October of '48, he underwent a preliminary hearing at the British Court of the Control Commission. After several hearings, he was released without a trial. Later he worked as a driver for the British military government and lived with his wife in Oldenburg. In October of '49 the judge for the preliminary hearings of the Hamburg court—did some other Latvian need a couple of bottles of beer?—signed an arrest warrant for Arājs, who was living under his wife's surname, Zeibots. The warrant wasn't executed, because he escaped, nor did he return to Oldenburg and his wife. Between 1949 and 1975 he lived in Frankfurt, still under the name Zeibots, with an international passport obtained thanks to the intercession of "friends"—maybe a "brother" from the *Bruderschaft*?—at the Latvian Embassy in London. He worked for the *Neue Presse*.

After a hundred and ninety-nine sessions of the trial he was condemned to life in prison; he died in prison in 1988. Besides Nuremberg, the main trials regarding events in Latvia took place in Germany: 1949, 1950, 1961, 1968 (three), 1985. The places: Augsburg, Munich, Dortmund, Cologne, Karlsruhe, Hannover, Düsseldorf.

The trial that provided the most information, along with the Arājs trial, was the previously cited trial of Grauel and others, at the *Landgericht*, 1968–1971, in Hannover. It concerned the slaughters in Liepaja, and here, too, many Latvian witnesses appeared. But the statements that seem most surprising have to do with in particular the citizens of Liepaja, and come to us unexpectedly from Germans. On October 11, 1941, the *Gebietskommissar*, or regional commander, of Liepaja writes to Generalkommissar Drechsler that the killing of the Jews had caused general bewilderment in the city. The mayor himself, who had almost always gone along, had come to him to express the discontent of his citizens. On January 3, 1942, SS-Untersturmführer Kügler notes in his usual biweekly report from Liepaja that "the execution of Jews that took place during the period under discussion continues to be the main subject of conversation among the populace. The fate of the Jews is widely deplored and up to now few voices have been heard in favor of it." At a distance of fifty years, the indignation of the Latvians, who were not all blind, deaf, and dumb, is thus verified by these unwitting German comments. Again it took a German, SS-Oberscharführer Schrott, to photograph the scenes of an execution in Liepaja on December 15, 1941. The photographs—which were displayed at Nuremberg and have become stock footage—are so clear that some of the survivors could recognize, naked, women from their own families. Equally clear are the figures of numerous Latvians in the SD and the auxiliary police, armed and wearing the identifying armband.

Herberts Cukurs, whose face, unlike Arājs's, was well-known to everyone in Latvia—he was a pilot who in 1934 had flown from Riga to Gambia in a plane he fabricated himself, and a sports hero, whose dubious reputation added romance to his image—came to a more terrible end than Arājs. He was ten years older; he was forty-one when, on the morning of November 30, 1941, he went on a drunken rampage, armed with his Nagant, in the Riga ghetto, randomly killing anyone he met in his path. That Jews were his victims was incidental: he wasn't, in the end, any more anti-Semitic than my Piedmontese grocer; like the latter he enjoyed every so often making allusions to those unpleasant characteristics that some would still consider Jewish. Unlike my grocer, however, Cukurs was brutal, opportunistic, uncivilized as a goat. In the emigrant Social Democratic press, he was judged disreputable; people alluded often to what might be called his parapolitical past in 1919, when, because he belonged to a violent group of the extreme left, he had been expelled from the party.

Ezergailis's book leads to the conclusion that in Latvia—and, really, wasn't it the same in fascist Italy?—proclaiming oneself anti-Semitic generally required a certain intellectual stature: you had to have at least attended high school or, even better, like the members of the Lettonia and Livonica fraternities, university. By carefully reexamining the history and society of his own country, Ezergailis demonstrates the superficiality of the widespread European belief that all Latvians were rabid anti-Semites. The Latvians, he states, were no more anti-Semitic than the French or the English, and certainly less so than the Russians. The Orthodox Church had succeeded in planting seeds even more robust and enduring among the latter (I would say) than those scattered by the Lutheran Church in Latvia. The only pogrom that took place here was the one in 1905, at the hands of Russians; in the same period the Latvian peasants, harassed and maltreated for centuries by the Baltic barons, massacred some of them and burned down their castles. The Germans were so hated in Latvia that Arājs's father had forbidden the language to be spoken in the family, although the mother of the future leader of the Aizsargi was likely of German descent. Hatred of the Germans was not, it seems, sufficient to prevent Latvian collaboration with the "comrades"; once they were installed as conquerors in the country, the Latvians realized there were too many Jews and gave in to the hated former masters. Were they more predictable in their ferocity, more orderly and methodical in their criminality than the Russians?

Thus Cukurs's brutality—he also went wild torturing victims in the notorious headquarters of the Aizsargi at Valdemara Iela 19—was not fed by particular ideological beliefs. During his belated university studies he hadn't hesitated to resort to a Jewish acquaintance for help in studying for his exams, when necessary—he was very ambitious—and he could even make enthusiastic comments about Zionism, but, all in all (and I realize that this might seem a monstrous simplification), he was "merely" indifferent: an indifference that, combined with a cruel nature and genuine manual dexterity, sustained him in his activity as a butcher.

Like Arājs, Cukurs was interrogated by the British, as a prisoner in the British zone, and, unlike the former, admitted some responsibility; in spite of that, he was released and as early as 1946 was in Brazil. Here he lived by makeshift means, so that, twenty years later, an agent from the Mossad—perhaps on a tip from the KGB—pretending he was an ex-officer in the Wehrmacht who had become a wealthy businessman, managed to lure him to Uruguay by offering better opportunities. On March 6, 1965, the police found his mutilated corpse in a secluded villa in Montevideo. Other sources say it was in the trunk of a car. He had been tortured before he was killed and a placard had been placed on his chest with the date of the execution—February 23—crediting him with 30,000 murders and naming him "the executioner of Riga." Certainly he was responsible for a frightening number of deaths, Vestermanis confirms, but not that many.

The man who truly deserves to be called the executioner of Riga, Friedrich Jeckeln, was hanged there by the Soviets on February 3, 1946, in Uzvaras Laukums, Victory Square.

Of his end, and that of Cukurs and Arājs, and their "careers," I still knew nothing when, on September 23, 1999, I returned from Riga to Turin. I was reading the newspapers left out for travelers, and an article in the *Baltic Times* that day surprised me greatly. The headline was "Inquiry on War Crimes Encounters Resistance."

> RIGA—A Canadian investigator looking into war crimes in Latvia during the German occupation encountered some unexpected criticism at a press conference Sept. 15.
>
> Lynn Lovett, a Department of Justice lawyer working in the country's crimes against humanity and war crimes section, merely intended to release the details of her latest investigation in Latvia to reporters.
>
> Lovett spent two weeks interviewing seven people—who cannot be named because of a publication ban—as part of her investigation into a suspected war criminal whose identity is also protected.
>
> Canadian criminal law prevents a suspect from being named until legal proceedings are started against him in order to preserve his privacy.
>
> However, Arturs Malta, who attended the press conference, was more interested in challenging Lovett than learning about her investigation.
>
> Malta accused Lovett of creating a negative public impression about the "Aizsargi," a paramilitary

organization that existed before Soviet occupation and was re-established around independence.

"I am a member of this organization. I can even show you my membership card," he said. "How can you accuse this organization?"

Lovett said the Canadian government has made no accusations against the Aizsargi and that it simply was looking for information through newspaper advertisements about possible criminal activity during World War II.

"I'm sorry if that's the way that you feel, but the way that we've asked for the information in our ad is simply information about and there are many organizations listed," Lovett said. "No accusation is being made against any organization."

Malta wanted Lovett to then address the Russian occupation after the Second World War, but she declined until the *Baltic Times* asked her how she balanced the conflicting histories of Russian and German occupation in her investigation.

"The response I have for that is that the majority of the activities that would have taken place during the Russian occupation would have been undertaken by people who do not reside in Canada, and as our mandate is limited to people who reside in Canada, we're not in a position to do anything about it," Lovett said.

"However, in a more general sense, if we receive an allegation against somebody who committed a crime in any country during the Soviet occupation, we would investigate it just the same that we investigate the crimes about the Nazi occupation."

At the end of the press conference, Malta peppered Lovett with questions about a KGB file regarding the shooting of Jews in Salaspils.

Malta claimed the case against Viktors Arajas, a suspected [sic] Latvian war criminal, was falsified and the KGB material could prove it.

"In this document, they showed none of the Latvians shot Jews," he said.

Lovett explained to Malta that documents found in either the Latvian or KGB archives only form a small part of their case, especially since many of them cannot be examined because their creators are now deceased.

"The question of the truth of the contents is up to the court to decide," she said.

Lovett supplied reporters with few details about her current investigation or the investigations into three other Canadian Latvians. However, she reaffirmed her department's mandate is to investigate war crimes, crimes against humanity and other atrocities, which in Latvia's case happened prior to and during the German occupation.

She said there are 1,200 such cases in Canada, and 100 of them are actively being investigated in countries like Ukraine, Belarus, Rwanda and

Somalia, but she refused to say how many of these suspects are from Latvia.

"On this trip, I've merely assembled one little part of a large file and so once I get home, I'll have to assemble all of my information in order to prepare a report and decide what to do with the case," said Lovett.

Reading the article not only surprised me—were there still Latvian war criminals touring the world?—but it seemed to me a final sign of that secret and watchful fate that had accompanied my return to Latvia. It should also be said that I knew so little of the subject I didn't even realize that the author of the piece, Blake Lambert, probably didn't know much more than I did (or had he been cautious?), since he had attributed to Viktors Arājs, sentenced twenty years earlier (and in the meantime deceased), the term *suspect.*

When I was preparing to write *Un leggero accento straniero* I had consulted the proceedings of the Nuremberg trials to find out about the slaughters in Latvia, with the intention of reconstructing the story of a young SS "ordered" to the Baltic countries in 1941. On the basis of the Nuremberg sentences, I retained the impression that, like the protagonist of my book, very few of the "subordinates" had paid in the end.

The truth is that that didn't matter to me even in a personal context. The murderers of my father and little Irene, of our relatives in Libau, in Mitau, in Riga, for me had no face or name. Nor do they now. The death of my family has in my heart such a weight, a measure so absolute, that it remains there as if self-contained. My pain stays steadfastly with my dead, deep in an abyss in which time no longer tolls its hours. There is no event that can drag it into the light, almost as if there were no connection between the hand that committed the crime and those who were its victims. There can be nothing further.

If I had to represent this sensation with an image, I would say that today, at the end of my book, I see them here around me, each with his or her own face: my father, Irene (resembling my sister Sisi as a child), Benno, Saul, my aunt Betty, even old Nechame with her daughter Raja, whom I didn't know. Their killers, on the other hand, blur; they mingle and hide in a crowd. In reality the killers were not a single person, not a group, not ten, not a hundred. They, too, were uncountable, and, I wonder, if one of them is judged so long after the event, can it be as himself? Is it still possible to reconstruct the actions of one individual among the uncountable? It should have been done immediately, I say to myself. But I hesitate: Was it just, the speed with which the Soviets made decisions, or, on the contrary, was it the procedural slowness of the Germans that was just? And yet, I say to myself, an executioner should be judged. The judgment isn't owed to my mourning; it's owed, as closure, to the order of the world in which I live.

It's not owed to me, I said; rather, I fear the entanglement that is gradually created between personal sorrow and public sorrow. Mourning for the Shoah is a burden so heavy—and lies at the bottom of that timeless abyss I mentioned above—that it can't be imposed in a public rite, it has to remain "ours" alone. Otherwise, facing the enormity of the event, we risk provoking a defensive reaction, and a collective mourning would be entirely rejected, along with the necessary pursuit of justice, which alone is a duty—yes, a duty—of the whole community.

As for me, I wouldn't want tears, I wouldn't want sympathy, I wouldn't even want Israel's commemorating moments of silence, I only want people to know; and so, as I was able, I placed stones, by writing.

I despair, in fact, of a justice that responds to the wish of almost everyone, if not everyone, that it not be discussed. Of a justice not "for Jews" but for the human beings, the *Menschen* recorded on the stele at the entrance to the cemetery in Šmerlis. What's the use, I repeat to myself, of creating a link between private memory and historical memory if the link doesn't connect my will to the public will, if the act of justice—although incomplete and necessarily imperfect, delayed—isn't understood and shared by the collective?

To return to the *Baltic Times*: if I had been better informed, I would have been alerted by Arturs Malta's reference to the acts in Salaspils, which have little to do with Arājs directly but, rather, with Konrāds Kalējs, Arājs's man, who was the Latvian commandant of the concentration camp in Salaspils.

In fact, also in the *Baltic Times*, on January 28, 1999, another journalist, Daniel Silva, had concerned himself with possible Latvian war criminals who lived in Canada; nor was it the first time that the Canadian Department of Justice had sent someone to investigate in Latvia. Canadian law forbids anyone who collaborated with the Nazis to immigrate to Canada, and a war crimes department (particularly active in the nineties, thanks to the minister of justice, Anne McLellan) has tried to discover and, if necessary, try those criminals who entered mixed in with other refugees when, after the war, the country took in many Latvian immigrants.

Thus investigators had already come to Riga to interrogate possible witnesses; overwhelmed by avalanches of documents, Canadian judges had had to put off sentencing in order to get the documents translated. Fifteen volumes of documents in German, Latvian, and English had been introduced into the court in Vancouver in the case of Eduards Podins, *Schutzmann*, that is "guard," at the concentration camp in Valdiera; he had been a Canadian citizen since 1959, and Ezergailis also includes him on the list of Latvian members of the SD. Nevertheless, Ezergailis's book was invoked by the defense to demonstrate the coercion to which Latvians were subjected, compelled to choose between death and collaboration with the Nazis. Many members of the Latvian SS legion, formed in 1943, were drafted by force, Ezergailis writes, especially toward the end of the war; whereas the men of the SD and the terrible Arājs group were volunteers.

In 1997, Konrāds Kalējs, an Australian citizen who had lived in Canada since 1994, was identified as a member of that squad, though without conclusive proof, and expelled from Canada. The case against him had been building over the years—and while I was in Latvia, evidently, people were talking about it—and now, in 2001, he was to be extradited from Australia to Latvia, and there he would be tried for genocide.

So an old man of eighty-eight was summoned to judgment, blind, demented, a "frail" old man with prostate cancer—the defense lawyer's adjective struck the journalists; I find it repeated in several comments—an old man in a wheelchair. He was born in Riga in 1913. It was the first time, the newspapers wrote, that Latvia had tried a war criminal for crimes committed during the Nazi occupation. It was the first time, I would add, that Australia had decided to extradite a man presumed guilty of crimes against humanity.

Official Latvia, on an Internet page in the year 2000, in a small statement from the president's office, expresses its horror at the crimes committed by the Nazis. A far-reaching and honest examination of what happened in Latvia from 1941 to 1944 is necessary, it states.

At the University of Riga, in Room 210, there is a center for Jewish studies; the university also has a Hebrew language course.

The Latvian delegation to the conference on Holocaust-era assets in Washington in 1998 pledged to compensate the victims, using twenty-five thousand dollars taken from the sum due to Latvia from the international fund for victims of Nazi persecution, provided (this is specified) they are in need. That fund has been managed since the end of the Second World War by the tripartite commission that administers the Nazi gold acquired from the sale of goods stolen from the Jews.

I see that there is also a provision for a Latvian commission for the restitution of confiscated real estate. Should I mention the ruins of my grandfather's house on the island? I don't know why, that's the only thing that comes to mind.

Faced with the "Kalējs question," however, even official Latvia has hesitated; if you look closely, it's in a period of adjustment, and the country's basic law is, to be precise, "transitory." The history of the free republic is in reality very brief: free from 1920 to 1934 (the year of Ulmanis's coup d'état), occupied by the Germans in 1941, and handed over to the Soviet empire until 1991.

In Latvia today, Vestermanis writes, the nostalgic elderly, who are not few, and the young radicals of the right (see Malta) still revere Cukurs. A page in Latvian on the Internet exalts him, hero of the fatherland, true Latvian, intrepid sportsman, entrepreneur, writer, modern man. He fired a few too many shots from his revolver, but let's not exaggerate the numbers. Let's add that on the Internet pages on the history of Latvia in English, "the episode" of the ***** Jews massacred there is skipped.

At such a vast remove and with no Soviet (or Latvian) evidence, the truth is that the young don't know anything definitive about past events. Only recently has information about the Holocaust begun to be introduced in schoolbooks and only in the past ten years could books in Latvian be found on the subject. The West has had fifty years, says Vestermanis, to assimilate, discuss, accept, or reject; Latvia only ten.

The revisionist Latvian historian Vidualis Lacis would like those in power who allied themselves with Stalin, and handed Latvia over to him, to be tried along with Kalējs, who, according to him, is guilty at most from the moral point of view—he was a soldier and fought the Communists. Someone who wants to remain anonymous, a "senior" academic, interviewed in Riga on the subject of the Jewish extermination by the journalist Simon Mann, of the *International Herald Tribune*, speaks as if he had received an "order" directly from Nazi Berlin: the Jews possessed all the wealth of Latvia, and so many of them, in that grim year 1940 of "the horror" (as it was called), had collaborated with the KGB! Is it surprising that there was a certain anti-Jewish animosity in the country?

That this account was not accurate, that it might, in fact, present in more than one case even a contradiction in terms, Arājs and Kalējs both knew as, in front of the fire in the great room of the house at Valdemara Iela 19 in the winter of 1941, they discussed a plan to send two companies of the Aiszargi, both under Stahlecker's command, to the northeast border. Kalējs would lead one, the other Harijs Svīķeris, his schoolmate at the military academy.

Arājs loved to relax after the day's labors in front of the cozy hearth. He and his men had established their provisional headquarters in the magnificent house belonging to a Jewish banker, deported by the Soviets in June of 1941. Not all the capitalist Jews, you see, collaborated with the KGB.

When the war was over, Kalējs was a displaced person. As such he obtained, with many others, citizenship in Australia, and he lived for thirty years in the United States with an Australian passport, making a fortune buying and selling real estate. He would have died peacefully in his bed if in 1979 German judges hadn't tried and sentenced Arājs. The name Konrāds Kalējs appeared in the proceedings of the trial.

At that point there was of necessity official interest in him; nevertheless, six more years passed before, in 1985, the Office of Special Investigations of the U.S. Department of Justice began an inquiry that led finally to an appeal before a court in Chicago. In 1994 Kalējs was expelled by the United States to Australia: thus the entire proceeding lasted, Italian style, for a total of nine years. The OSI investigation produced thousands of pages of documents, but resulted only in a civil suit; it did not succeed, in fact, in demonstrating that Kalējs was personally responsible for killings in the Salaspils concentration camp, which he oversaw. He had certainly been part of Arājs's commando, but that wasn't enough, according to the investigation, to declare him a war criminal.

He remained in Australia only a few months; in 1987 a Labor government had set up a commission of inquiry into possible war criminals living in the country, and in 1994 on the advice of friends he went to Canada and stayed there for three years. In 1997 Canada, after a ten-month investigation, expelled him again to Australia, where in the meantime the Labor government had fallen and the commission of inquiry had been disbanded. The relevant research had been entrusted to the Australian Federal Police, but they were not given the financial resources for acting on it. Besides, Australia wasn't particularly zealous about unearthing Nazi criminals; Robert Greenwood, a lawyer who presided over the dissolved commission, had expressed some suspicions regarding the fact that in the fifties more than one Nazi had been employed in the Australian Secret Intelligence Service.

Meanwhile Kalējs got old and sick, and although he suffered from dementia, it wasn't so severe that he was unable to choose the best place to be cared for: a luxurious retreat for elderly Latvians in Great Britain, where he was admitted in 1999.

But Scotland Yard—how about this—had in its files a minor investigation of Kalējs that included a video recording of statements made in 1993 by Harijs Svīķeris, a British citizen. In the meantime, Svīķeris had managed to die in his own bed, but from the videotape he continued to declare in a senile voice that of course he knew his military academy schoolmate Kalējs, they had fought together, upstanding soldiers in Arājs's battalions, on the Russian front. Well, yes, he had to admit, Arājs's commando had been a flying squad of mass executioners. Yes, he recalled having seen Mr. Kalējs at Rumbula. But he himself, why was he at Rumbula? Well, he had stammered—it took five months for the British investigators to persuade him to talk—well, he was at Rumbula because Mr. Kalējs was there.

The British engaged in a delicate dance: to expel or not to expel Kalējs to Australia again? Try him in Great Britain? It was 2000. In all the evidence gathered by the various commissions of inquiry it turned out that there was no one (any longer) who had actually witnessed him "pulling the trigger." There was, obviously, some testimony about the fact that he had overseen the concentration camp of Salaspils, but that he had committed atrocities there was more hearsay, Jack Straw, the British Home Secretary, stated, than certain fact. The paths taken by the old Latvian to enter Great Britain would be investigated, but to ask to arrest and try him was absurd.

Yet pressured by the press and by the fear, shared by others, that Britain's complicity in helping hide Nazi criminals would be scrutinized, Straw suddenly decided, in early January of 2000, to send Mr. Kalējs back to Australia. Besides, he could count on Australia: there was no risk of trials or expulsions, the Australians would keep him; the Latvian community in Melbourne would coddle him. Major Kārlis Ozols, an old comrade in arms of Kalējs in Arājs's squad, was a member of that community. The Australian prime minister, John Howard, said that Australia couldn't take away Mr. Kalējs's citizenship by making retroactive a law passed in 1997 that denied the right of naturalization to immigrants guilty of war crimes. Mr. Kalējs had been in the country as early as 1950.

Tiny Latvia, solicited to intervene and ask for extradition of the now "criminal"—in January of 2000 journalists all over Europe were following the "Kalējs case"—first tried to imitate its larger predecessors. It invoked its own history as a victim of the USSR: Latvian officers like Konrāds Kalējs had fought against the Soviet dragon; they were not German collaborators but defenders of the homeland.

Rudite Abolina, the attorney general of Latvia, declared that the country's investigators, after making contact, in the course of three months, with 250 potential witnesses regarding Kalējs's activities during the war, hadn't traced any "valid" proof against him. A case so serious required, certainly, "concrete evidence."

Dzintra Subrovska, spokesperson for the attorney general, explained that "the people"—among whom, I note, were seven key witnesses identified by the Wiesenthal Center in Jerusalem—"interviewed, in some cases twice, recounted nothing new."

The prosecutor who was the head of the section for war crimes, Janis Osis, had revealed to reporters from the *International Herald Tribune* that the investigators had found only "secondary witnesses who told what they had heard, not what they had seen."

So far Latvia resisted, writhing painfully in the net of a past that the West can't, at first sight, untangle and accept. The arguments of the Latvian judges were also sustained by the president: the Latvians would continue the trial only on condition that new evidence was presented.

Suddenly, however, there was a general show of zeal: the hot potato had finally been handed to Kalējs's homeland, which was just. A good seven countries sent suitcases of solid evidence. First among them the United States, then Canada, Great Britain, Israel, Germany, and Australia, then Russia, which released seven hundred pages of formerly secret KGB records. Included was a photo of the handsome young

Konrāds Kalējs in a black uniform that to my inexpert eye looks like that of the SS.

In the spring of 2000 the lawyer Janis Maizitis became attorney general of Latvia, replacing Abolina; the latter had already declared that she hadn't realized the importance of the material of the charge. Meanwhile, in Australia, Prime Minister Howard also changed his tune, and in September of 2000 he said on the radio in Melbourne, "We've worked hard with the Latvian authorities to resolve the question of extradition."

The relevant treaty was nearly ratified, but meanwhile the Latvian attorney general resolved to make the charge of genocide against Kalējs official. The matter of extradition had to be preceded by an arrest warrant issued by a judge of the district court. At first the judge refused to sign it. He had seven days to decide. Evidently, in the end he gave in. The formal charge of the Latvian attorney general reads, "With these actions he [Kalējs] caused the administration of the camp [of Salaspils] to create conditions of life for the imprisoned Jews such as to lead them to complete or partial [sic] destruction."

In May of 2001 Australia held, by law, a brief, two-week trial to deliberate on the request from Latvia, and finally allowed the transfer of the old man to his native country. Commenting on the case, Leonards Pavils, the spokesman for the Latvian Ministry of Justice, said, "It's an excellent result for us; we counted on it."

The fact that the accused is so old and ill is the only aspect of the case that doesn't embarrass the Latvian judges:

Alfons Noviks, former head of the NKVD of the Latvian Soviet Socialist Republic, died in prison, in 1996 after being sentenced at the age of eighty-eight for helping organize the deportation of more than sixty thousand people to Siberia.

This is the story of Kalējs. I recounted it to make it clear that no one wanted to try him. Latvia—this had been happening for centuries—had to submit to stronger powers. It may be that, if Kalējs doesn't die before appearing in a courtroom in a wheelchair, there could finally be the open discussion about the slaughters perpetrated by the Nazis (with Latvian cooperation) that the president wishes for. Yet it seems likely to me that some nationalistic resentment might first spread throughout the country because of the blackmail: Latvia has to enter the European Union with a clean "criminal record," but was forced into it.

Nonetheless, maybe it would have been better for the Australian citizen Konrāds Kalējs to be tried in great Australia, if it hadn't had its own skeletons in the closet. What can the Latvian trial add to the suitcases of evidence already recorded? Certainly not the whispers of the people of Liepaja, not the mouthfuls of bread of the Baptist peasants, not the depositions of the five thousand merciful: they, too, are now dead.

(In any case the question was resolved by the providential death of Kalējs in early November 2001. He had appeared two weeks earlier on a stretcher in the federal court of Melbourne, where his appeal was discussed. In reporting his death, an Australian journalist resorted for the last time to the adjective *frail.*)

The ***** Latvian Jews, commemorated in history books and by the flag of mourning that the Latvian republic flies on July 4 (the date that marks the burning of Riga's synagogues in 1941 by the Aizsargi), were in actuality buried and incinerated forever by the events that followed. The fourteen thousand Jews now living in Riga are Russians who arrived later. Apart from the commemoration, we may wonder what the population today truly remembers about the massacre.

More than the recent attack on the Peitavas synagogue in Riga, which destroyed its old entrance, more than the black "SS" smeared on the plaque commemorating the slaughters in Liepaja, more than the publication of anti-Semitic texts ("But Were There Really Six Million?," edited by the publisher Leonards Inkins, photographed in the gala uniform of the Aizsargi), what seems to me symbolic of this loss of memory, and also of a certain undissipated political and moral embarrassment, is the march of "SS veterans." Precisely the one discussed in the interview I quoted with President Vike-Freiberga, who shows up in polls as the most popular personality in Latvia.

In 1998 a short-sighted law passed by parliament established March 16 as the day celebrating the "Latvian soldier." The date commemorated the battle on the Velikaja River in 1943, in which, in a unique situation, the two Latvian divisions of the SS, the 15th and the 19th, fought together against the Soviet Army. Members of the SS Latvian Legion divisions are portrayed on a rare green stamp of the German military post of the time, in the combat uniform of Hitler's SS, and in another uniform, on a blue stamp, wearing the helmet with the death's-head and the runic *S* on the collar; maybe, not unlike their German comrades, they had their blood type tattooed on their armpit. But, says Ezergailis, defending them with drawn sword, these battalions were formed in the fall of 1943, two years after the slaughters of 1941, and these men were soldiers, not murderers of Jews. (Anyway, there were very few left to murder.) Hitler wanted to call them "volunteers" to avoid violating the Hague Convention. But they were not, the historian states, either volunteers or criminals or genuine SS. Above all they weren't even allowed to go to the brothels of their German colleagues, or the shops reserved for them, nor were they enrolled in the National Socialist Party.

United States immigration law was interpreted similarly, and after the war allowed them to enter, as did the Canadian court that absolved one of them of the charge of war crimes, since he hadn't concealed the fact that he was a Latvian veteran of that corps when he asked to be accepted as a refugee by Canada. They were SS, but not to their core, it seems. They disgust us just the same, and, no doubt, in the Russian villages where, according to the universal custom of war, they burned houses and raped girls, no one distinguished them from the others.

The general at the head of the Latvian Army marched with the SS veterans on March 16, 1998, to the Freedom Monument; at the monument there was a scuffle with Russian and Latvian veterans of the Soviet Army, and in Europe it provoked a certain emotion. The general was forced to resign and, less than two years later, the ceremony of March 16 was abolished and replaced by one on November 11, Armistice Day of 1918, which marked the origin of the Latvian republic. But the controversy is still debated in Latvia today. More than a hundred thousand soldiers fought with the Germans. Around half died. In Berlin in April of 1945, eighty men from the 15th division desperately defended Hitler's chancellery. They were well aware of what awaited them if they fell into the hands of the Russians.

Latvia is a tiny country, barely more than a fifth the size of Italy. Before the Second World War it had a million and a half inhabitants; after the war the Soviet Union flooded it with Russians. The families of a hundred thousand fighters make up a substantial number of them, a number that counts. There are bonds of blood and here, yes, of memory. How many members of those divisions are the grandfathers of today's youths?

In turn, how many of the parents of those fighters had in early May of 1915 seen forty thousand Jews passing through the station in Riga, expelled from Courland on the order of the Grand Duke Nikolai Nikolayevich, uncle of the tsar and commander in chief of the Russian Army? They were suspected of collusion with the enemy, in this case the Kaiser's army. German in language and culture, they were all, stated the ukase, including old people and children, undoubtedly (if secretly) on the German side. They were crammed with their belongings into cattle cars and transported to the provinces in the middle of the empire. In Riga they had been welcomed and nourished by members of the Jewish community before the distrustful eyes of the inhabitants. Not all forty thousand returned—some stayed in Russia, some emigrated—but a significant number did and among them was the family of my father's uncles, to be killed twenty-five years later by the Nazis as collaborators with the "Bolsheviks," that is, spies of the Russians this time.

The Jews were suspect, by definition. The young republic granted them, it's true, freedom of religion, schools, nurseries, hospitals, synagogues, cemeteries, but it was seven years before they were made full citizens by a government of the left. They were industrialists and bankers, dentists and doctors, merchants and artisans, but in 1925, out of a total of 5,291 government employees, only 21 were Jewish; a single Jewish policeman in Riga, out of 4,316 police in the country, not a single Jew in the courts, 2 in the post office, 33 on the railroads. In Libau Dr. Glinternik was one of the few army officers, and Jasha Foss one of three sailors in the Latvian Navy. They were one-seventh of the population but only 0.4 percent were employed in the government. There were few mixed marriages and no cases of conversion to Christianity. The Jews had all the rights of their fellow citizens, and did the usual military service, but they hadn't yet formed with them those bonds of blood and memory that come only by degrees over the centuries.

And if necessary the Jews could always be loaded onto cattle cars and shipped off, according to what the master of the moment ordered.

Andrew Ezergailis has tried in his book—and it's understandable—to narrow the degree of his compatriots' responsibility whenever an opportune occasion presents itself. We've read how he defended the fighters of the Latvian Legion by defining the limits of their actions. He discusses the dates when a battalion of the Latvian police would have taken part in slaughters, although he doesn't deny that, in at least three places, the police were directly involved. He reports, accurately, that Latvian radio, on Tuesday, July 1, 1941, didn't broadcast the national anthem but, instead, an anthem from the time of Ulmanis, and, equally accurate, points out that the Latvian Legion had pastors, unlike the legions of the German SS. But after presenting the most complete and exhaustive picture possible, he can't in fact explain the reasons for what then happened in Latvia, what caused the apathy of the population: Might it have been greed for money, he wonders, or general insanity?

In the appendix of his book we find some excerpts from the reports of the Riga police. This force, made up of volunteers until January 1942, was later transformed into *Schutzmannschaften*, battalions of auxiliary police, who were entrusted with various duties and sometimes, unfortunately, "actions." We have the reports of their activities, preserved in the Latvian State Archives. Almost all of them—those from the end of October to around mid-December of '41—are missing, the ghettoization and the massacres. Someone took them and, we can assume, destroyed them. It's certainly not a random fact; however you look at it, it's an implicit accusation, whoever it was who removed them.

Ezergailis gives us the likely numbers of police who participated in the days of Rumbula. But does it really interest us to know that they weren't many, that they themselves didn't shoot? We saw them beating, dragging by the hair, driving with whips and rifle butts a terrorized crowd; we saw them shoving into the snow old people unable to walk, "if necessary" killing a young mother with a child in her arms. Furtively, unknown to the Germans, picking up a ring on the ground, carrying off a fur coat.

We know names and surnames of some of them: those who presented stamped applications to take from the ghetto the furniture and clothing of the murdered Jews, emphasizing their merits for the services rendered in the days of Rumbula. In Rumbula, November 30 and December 8 of 1941, they were not insane; they were drunk and greedy for loot, and were above all obedient to the master of the moment. The period when they had been allowed to be free citizens was too short; they hadn't had time to be convinced of it deep down.

On those two days, no longer described in any report, in an orgy of violence they let go of the double life they had been forced into by the necessity of appearing professional.

In the first months of the German occupation, in fact, Ezergailis writes, they were as "professional" as possible; they tried, for example, to control the numerous recruits, young unruly soldiers coming from the disbanded Latvian Army.

He states: They arrested and disarmed two policemen caught raping Aleksandra Tihomirova, a Jew, threatening her with a weapon. And so they arrested a certain Karlis Kapsis for stealing a bag from a Jewish woman who was working on Avota Iela filling a ditch. In the 2nd Precinct they arrested three policemen and an ex-policeman who, unauthorized, had "searched" (quotes mine) an apartment.

Some policemen, therefore, even protected the Jews, and, Ezergailis states, many of the police continued to work as professionals in the city, if not impeded or disturbed by the occupier. But, I would say, this was only one of the two lives that the police all led in the months preceding the great slaughters of the winter of 1941.

The other life, which was regularly transcribed in the reports, concerned activities not expected before but performed now with the same professionalism: registration of Jews, sequestration of radios, control of the "yellow stars"; offenders, according to orders, were handed over to police headquarters. Fining shop owners who sold under the counter to Jewish customers, arresting Jews found shopping in unauthorized stores. Arresting those (Jews, should we be surprised?) who at the sight of Soviet planes in the sky over Riga had shown "excessive glee." How had the policeman been able to find out? Had a zealous neighbor informed on them? If your police monitor a certain group of citizens and punish them in a particular way, you collaborate, right?

The 2nd Precinct reports that on July 7, 1941, following German directives, seventy Jews were assembled and handed over to the Germans to be assigned to "social labor."

The 6th Precinct reports on July 8 that it has a hundred Jews available to perform social labor and that the 2nd Precinct has sent thirty-five more, evicted from their apartments and settled temporarily on Jezus Baznicas Iela.

July 12, 1941, a report from the 2nd Precinct notes that the Germans have requisitioned seventy apartments and that fifty Jews have been evicted from their homes.

(The date and place struck me; they match Lidija Blechman's disappearance from her home.)

The 9th Precinct reports that during the night of July 22 inspections were carried out in the Jewish hospitals on Ludzas Iela 25 and Latgale Iela 24, where three Jews were arrested.

July 23, 1941, the 3rd Precinct states that two Jewish women, Rohle and Hanna Resman, residing on Skolas Iela 9, gassed themselves.

The chief of the 6th Precinct complained on July 9 that police from other districts are carrying out searches inside the boundaries of the 6th, causing disorder and damage.

July 18, 1941, the 2nd Precinct reports that three auxiliary police and a former auxiliary policeman have been arrested for carrying out unauthorized searches.

On July 22, we read in a report from the 1st Precinct, the body of a dead Jew was pulled out of the Daugava and sent to the morgue.

And so on and on we see the second life of the Riga police unfolding. In the reports, the Jews pass smoothly, without disruptions, from an existence as citizens to an existence as the specially monitored, of whom police with lesser scruples begin to take advantage, "searching," that is, their apartments. Having been *ebreji* they again become *žīdi.* And gradually, day by day, the police themselves are transformed, yielding to old and not always conscious biases, to the ease of looting. If the police set this example, should we be surprised that the citizens in turn become greedy and indifferent? Because it wasn't insanity; besides greed, it was simply and only indifference again.

And yet it's not greed and indifference that I would hold against my homeland. I realize that in fact there is little the Latvians could have done for their Jewish fellow citizens under the German occupation. Following a "fundamental order," whose author it wasn't even necessary to name, the Germans, sooner or later—maybe a little later—would have killed them even without Latvian help. But that terrible zeal to obey, that brutality, how to forget that? And the complicit denial afterward? Of course, what court today would condemn a Latvian "only" for that? Nonetheless, it is precisely that denial that has consumed the memory no differently from the pyres that consumed the bodies.

What else can I say? My book is almost finished, I have handed over to it the life and death of my father and his family. As I've already said, I don't think anything remains of them, and certainly not blood descendants through us, so few, severed from their story by a sharp cut that won't heal. To repeat their gestures and their prayers, to find again their customs, sufferings, joys, words, songs, to continue them, in short, there would have to be some minimal trace of them in the place where they lived, in the heart of those who now live there, in the stories that the grandparents tell the grandchildren. Now, in Latvia, there is only a void, the grandparents are silent, often not even a cemetery remains. The majority of the Latvian Jews hoped that their race and their faith would continue in the land where their forebears were born and had spent their lives, and where they themselves were born: for the ***** killed here, very few could have emptied the sand from their shoes to carry it to Israel or elsewhere. They no longer exist except in our sorrow.

But, from across the world, after very long years, a last, unexpected greeting from my family reached me.

At the end of the report compiled by the Latvian Archives on the history of the Gersonis was a mention of the fact that a certain Ethel Kaplan, in the United States, had in 1997 asked for the genealogical chart of the Gersonis. This woman, granddaughter of the Jankel who was my great-grandfather, was the daughter of the younger daughter born from his second marriage, to the sister of the wife who had died prematurely. Accompanied by his second family, Jankel Gersoni, so they wrote from the archives, had, already an old man, emigrated to the United States. They sent me her address in case I was interested in getting in touch with her.

At first I wasn't interested; Ethel Kaplan, cousin, therefore, of my father (let's simplify the complicated relationship), must be very old, if not dead by now. Her mother, stepsister and cousin of Grandfather Maurice, was five years older than my father, fifteen years older than my mother—how old could her daughter be who was still alive? And what could she know of the Gersonis remaining in Latvia?

After two months I made up my mind, and one day, unexpectedly, I wrote a letter to the address I had been given; I didn't think any more about it until, to my great surprise, an answer arrived. Cousin Ethel was eighty, but she was completely lucid, self-possessed—I spoke to her on the phone and we managed to understand each other very well—and moved. She promised to send me any documents and photographs she could find. In a letter she told me about herself, at my request: her mother was thirty-eight when she was born, the youngest of four children; she had been a nurse during the war in Germany and France, and had met her husband, Ed Kaplan, after the war; he, too, had fought in Europe. Both had received the expected scholarship for veterans and had got their degrees. They had had a son and a daughter; now retired, they lived in Newton, Massachusetts. Her family was large, and they'd had so many great evenings, she and the Gersoni cousins, singing together!

In the package carefully put together by my cousin the engineer Ed Kaplan, which reached me three weeks later, came the family photographs on stiff and thick cream-colored cardboard that I had looked for in vain in the attic in Torre Pellice. My father at twenty, very handsome, with a curl on his forehead; and at fifteen, long face, tall and thin, head shaved, in a severe student jacket, standing next to his father, seated, elegant and slim, his expression energetic and intense. The photographer had retouched the eyes, to make them blacker and more striking. Uncle Simon Joseph, grandfather's younger brother, bore an astonishing resemblance to him; slim, elegant, with a mustache, he was in the same pose, leaning on a fake balustrade, proud of the meek, closely cropped boy, in the same student jacket, next to him, my father's cousin—was he that Joseph Gersoni, also born in 1886 and found on the list of those killed in Libau? Finally Aunt Betty, a young bride, small and a little stocky, as she had remained in my memory, her round face, with features so similar to my sister's more delicate ones. In a strange joke of memory I first recognized next to her unlikable Uncle Talrose, just as I remembered him.

From a photograph of a framed portrait, the patriarch Jankel stared out at me, austere and sad, with a beautiful white beard; Jacob, Ethel called him, and told me how Beile, about to die, had made her husband promise to marry her sister Yetta so that her children would have as their stepmother a loving aunt. Jacob had been a fur merchant (from him, then, Grandfather Maurice had inherited his career!) and was accustomed to traveling throughout Russia dealing in furs that were later used, in part, to line the gloves he made. Thus he was listed as a tailor on the long document of disembarkation in the port of Boston in 1906, a photocopy of which accompanied the photographs. Following regulations, the document listed his measurements and those of his wife and daughter, Ethel's mother. My great-grandfather was tall, five feet eleven inches, with a robust and healthy complexion; he had black eyes and grizzled hair. And he had the *i* at the end of his surname! But, what a surprise, I see from the extensive genealogical table made by the engineer cousin that Jankel's descendants all changed it to *y*, and some of his great-grandchildren Gersony live in the United States today.

I put the photos on a shelf, the great-grandfather in the middle, and only after a while I happened to notice that on the back of the photocopy of the immigration document there was a note from Ethel: after several years—Ethel didn't know how many—Jacob, who wasn't happy in America, had resolved to return to "Russia." He had left his second wife and three children and embarked alone, taking a hundred and eighty dollars, which at the time was a good sum. Ethel writes that she doesn't know the reasons for this departure, and that her grandfather died in Russia in 1912.

The Russia of my cousin Ethel and of the ship's document was, naturally, Latvia. Here, I think in what today is Liepaja, is perhaps the grave of my great-grandfather, who wanted to re-enter the family circle of Jewish Libau, of his son Simon, his grandchildren, to be buried there beside his family, his brother Abram who had died almost twenty years earlier, his young wife Beile. Latvia was his homeland and, contradicting the old Yiddish song "*Ess firt kejn weg zurick*" ("No road leads back"), he found the way home.

The Jewish cemetery of Libau is intact even if uncared for; what could I tell him if one day I found a bench there to sit on and converse with him?

Probably none of his Gersoni descendants are left in Latvia. I could, however, tell him one more thing.

At the end of my research news reached me from the archives that my cousin Benno, who I thought had perished with the rest of the family in Riga, had instead been deported to Siberia, on June 15, 1941, with his wife and daughter Gabriela, ten months old, along with the five thousand "capitalist" Jews who, as I said before, had been relatively lucky. It seems to me very likely that the acquisition a year earlier of Grandfather's factory had attracted the attention of those who compiled the list of deportees. He was also among the few thousand survivors, freed in 1956. While I learned this about Benno, who was interned after being separated from his family in far eastern Siberia, in Magadan, a place sadly known for Stalin's gulags—again we're talking here about millions of dead—the fate of his daughter Gabriela was reported to me by Vladimirs Talroze, the son of Saul, who also sought refuge in Russia, not deported but among those who had managed to cross the border before the Germans arrived. Gabriela now lives in Israel.

And finally I would tell my great-grandfather about the Friday morning when we left the hotel and set out in the car to look for Rumbula.

It was drizzling on the road to Salaspils. We went the wrong way twice. There were no signs. At a certain point I said to Pietro that, in my opinion, we should keep more to the right, and we followed, in fairly steady traffic, a road in a distant outlying suburb. Pietro, as usual, drove a little too fast; a policeman driving past looked at us with threatening eyes. Pietro slowed down. We turned onto a wide gray street, rainy, nameless, woods on the left interrupted by a few factories, on the other side very occasional houses. I felt suddenly tired and besides, I was sure we would never find the place.

"Let's go back to the center," I said to Pietro. "We won't find anything."

"No," he said, "I still want to look in that direction."

So we turned and kept driving outside the city; after a few meters, we passed a factory on the left, and suddenly Pietro said, "Look, there!"

I saw on the edge of a patch of trees a stone memorial, I think, covered with flowers. I didn't have time to wonder what it was because a moment later, high up on the right, I saw an enormous sign, "Rumbula," the station sign, and just at the same moment, on the other side of the street, a black stone with the Star of David carved, very noticeably, into the top corner on the left.

Here is my family, my father, Irene, and Levin and Beile and Frume and Juddel and Abraham and Isaac. Here is my family.

While Pietro turned the car to cross over to the edge of the woods, I retraced backward in my mind the sudden and instantaneous path that had led me from life to death, kneeling beside Gianni, my husband, who one morning, at dawn, I had found in the doorway of his room, lying rigid on the floor. I touched his wrist of icy marble and said to myself: it's not possible, it's not possible.

Now, on the contrary, what became true and present in that Star of David that marked the place where they had killed him wasn't my father's death, it was his life. I found him alive.

Getting out of the car, I stood, weeping, before the black stone placed on another black stone. On top of this, some pebbles. Pietro stood silently behind me. I didn't read the writing; I dried my eyes and prayed. So, praying, I asked forgiveness in German, our language, from my father, my Papi, for what they had done to him and for leaving that morning in December, never to return.

MARINA JARRE (1925–2016) was born in Riga to a Latvian Jewish father and an Italian Protestant mother. She spent her childhood in Latvia until 1935, when her parents separated and she moved to Italy to live with her maternal grandparents, among devout, French-speaking Protestants in a community southwest of Turin. Jarre wrote over a dozen novels, short story collections, and nonfiction works, including her celebrated autobiography, *Distant Fathers*.

ANN GOLDSTEIN has translated *The Neapolitan Novels* and other works by Elena Ferrante, as well as writings by Primo Levi, Giacomo Leopardi, Pier Paolo Pasolini, and Anna Maria Ortese. She is a former editor at *The New Yorker*.

Distant Fathers
by Marina Jarre

This singular autobiography unfurls from the author's native Latvia during the 1920s and '30s and expands southward to the Italian countryside. In distinctive writing as poetic as it is precise, Marina Jarre depicts an exceptionally multinational and complicated family. This memoir probes questions of time, language, womanhood, belonging and estrangement, while asking what homeland can be for those who have none, or many more than one.

Neapolitan Chronicles
by Anna Maria Ortese

A classic of European literature, this superb collection of fiction and reportage is set in Italy's most vibrant and turbulent metropolis—Naples—in the immediate aftermath of World War Two. These writings helped inspire Elena Ferrante's best-selling novels and she has expressed deep admiration for Ortese.

Untraceable
by Sergei Lebedev

An extraordinary Russian novel about poisons of all kinds: physical, moral and political. Professor Kalitin is a ruthless, narcissistic chemist who has developed an untraceable lethal poison called Neophyte while working in a secret city on an island in the Russian far east. When the Soviet Union collapses, he defects to the West in a riveting tale through which Lebedev probes the ethical responsibilities of scientists providing modern tyrants with ever newer instruments of retribution and control.

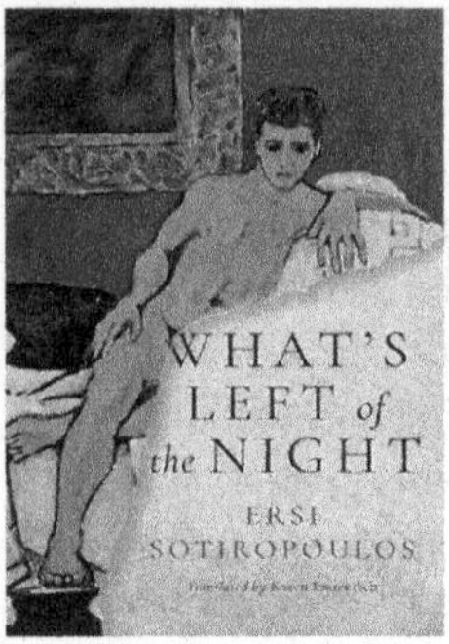

What's Left of the Night
by Ersi Sotiropoulos

Constantine Cavafy arrives in Paris in 1897 on a trip that will deeply shape his future and push him toward his poetic inclination. With this lyrical novel, tinged with an hallucinatory eroticism that unfolds over three unforgettable days, celebrated Greek author Ersi Sotiropoulos depicts Cavafy in the midst of a journey of self-discovery across a continent on the brink of massive change. A stunning portrait of a budding author—before he became C.P. Cavafy, one of the 20th century's greatest poets—that illuminates the complex relationship of art, life, and the erotic desires that trigger creativity.

The 6:41 to Paris
by Jean-Philippe Blondel

Cécile, a stylish 47-year-old, has spent the weekend visiting her parents outside Paris. By Monday morning, she's exhausted. These trips back home are stressful and she settles into a train compartment with an empty seat beside her. But it's soon occupied by a man she recognizes as Philippe Leduc, with whom she had a passionate affair that ended in her brutal humiliation 30 years ago. In the fraught hour and a half that ensues, Cécile and Philippe hurtle towards the French capital in a psychological thriller about the pain and promise of past romance.

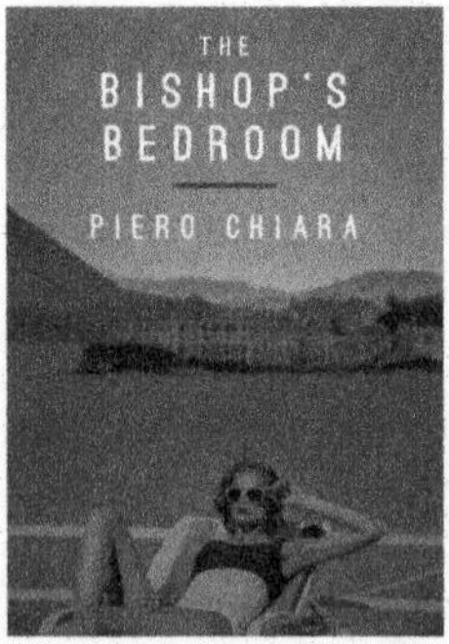

The Bishop's Bedroom
by Piero Chiara

World War Two has just come to an end and there's a yearning for renewal. A man in his thirties is sailing on Lake Maggiore in northern Italy, hoping to put off the inevitable return to work. Dropping anchor in a small, fashionable port, he meets the enigmatic owner of a nearby villa. The two form an uneasy bond, recognizing in each other a shared taste for idling and erotic adventure. A sultry, stylish psychological thriller executed with supreme literary finesse.

The Eye
by Philippe Costamagna

It's a rare and secret profession, comprising a few dozen people around the world equipped with a mysterious mixture of knowledge and innate sensibility. Summoned to Swiss bank vaults, Fifth Avenue apartments, and Tokyo storerooms, they are entrusted by collectors, dealers, and museums to decide if a coveted picture is real or fake and to determine if it was painted by Leonardo da Vinci or Raphael. *The Eye* lifts the veil on the rarified world of connoisseurs devoted to the authentication and discovery of Old Master artworks.

The Animal Gazer
by Edgardo Franzosini

A hypnotic novel inspired by the strange and fascinating life of sculptor Rembrandt Bugatti, brother of the fabled automaker. Bugatti obsessively observes and sculpts the baboons, giraffes, and panthers in European zoos, finding empathy with their plight and identifying with their life in captivity. Rembrandt Bugatti's work, now being rediscovered, is displayed in major art museums around the world and routinely fetches large sums at auction. Edgardo Franzosini recreates the young artist's life with intense lyricism, passion, and sensitivity.

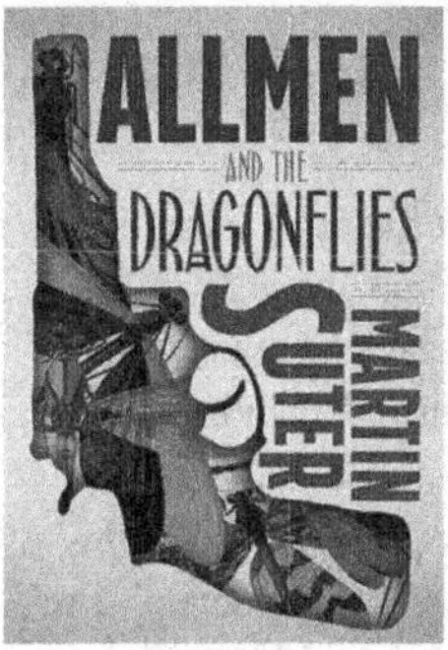

Allmen and the Dragonflies
by Martin Suter

Johann Friedrich von Allmen has exhausted his family fortune by living in Old World grandeur despite present-day financial constraints. Forced to downscale, Allmen inhabits the garden house of his former Zurich estate, attended by his Guatemalan butler, Carlos. This is the first of a series of humorous, fast-paced detective novels devoted to a memorable gentleman thief. A thrilling art heist escapade infused with European high culture and luxury that doesn't shy away from the darker side of human nature.

The Madeleine Project
by Clara Beaudoux

A young woman moves into a Paris apartment and discovers a storage room filled with the belongings of the previous owner, a certain Madeleine who died in her late nineties, and whose treasured possessions nobody seems to want. In an audacious act of journalism driven by personal curiosity and humane tenderness, Clara Beaudoux embarks on *The Madeleine Project*, documenting what she finds on Twitter with text and photographs, introducing the world to an unsung 20th century figure.

Adua
by Igiaba Scego

Adua, an immigrant from Somalia to Italy, has lived in Rome for nearly forty years. She came seeking freedom from a strict father and an oppressive regime, but her dreams of film stardom ended in shame. Now that the civil war in Somalia is over, her homeland calls her. She must decide whether to return and reclaim her inheritance, but also how to take charge of her own story and build a future.

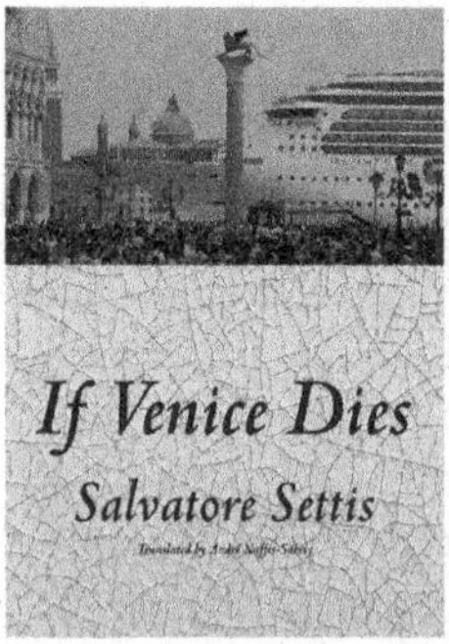

If Venice Dies
by Salvatore Settis

Internationally renowned art historian Salvatore Settis ignites a new debate about the Pearl of the Adriatic and cultural patrimony at large. In this fiery blend of history and cultural analysis, Settis argues that "hit-and-run" visitors are turning Venice and other landmark urban settings into shopping malls and theme parks. This is a passionate plea to secure the soul of Venice, written with consummate authority, wide-ranging erudition and élan.

The Madonna of Notre Dame

by Alexis Ragougneau

Fifty thousand people jam into Notre Dame Cathedral to celebrate the Feast of the Assumption. The next morning, a beautiful young woman clothed in white kneels at prayer in a cathedral side chapel. But when someone accidentally bumps against her, her body collapses. She has been murdered. This thrilling novel illuminates shadowy corners of the world's most famous cathedral, shedding light on good and evil with suspense, compassion and wry humor.

The Last Weynfeldt

by Martin Suter

Adrian Weynfeldt is an art expert in an international auction house, a bachelor in his mid-fifties living in a grand Zurich apartment filled with costly paintings and antiques. Always correct and well-mannered, he's given up on love until one night—entirely out of character for him—Weynfeldt decides to take home a ravishing but unaccountable young woman and gets embroiled in an art forgery scheme that threatens his buttoned up existence. This refined page-turner moves behind elegant bourgeois facades into darker recesses of the heart.

Moving the Palace

by Charif Majdalani

A young Lebanese adventurer explores the wilds of Africa, encountering an eccentric English colonel in Sudan and enlisting in his service. In this lush chronicle of far-flung adventure, the military recruit crosses paths with a compatriot who has dismantled a sumptuous palace and is transporting it across the continent on a camel caravan. This is a captivating modern-day Odyssey in the tradition of Bruce Chatwin and Paul Theroux.